The Shattered Dream

Margaret Sloan

The Shattered Dream:

A Southern Bride at the Turn of the Century

The Day Book of Margaret Sloan

edited by Harold Woodell

University of South Carolina Press

Women's Diaries and Letters of the Nineteenth-Century South

Carol Bleser and Elizabeth Fox-Genovese
Series Editors

A WOMAN DOCTOR'S CIVIL WAR:
Esther Hill Hawks' Diary
edited by Gerald Schwartz

A REBEL CAME HOME:
The Diary and Letters of Floride Clemson, 1863–1866
edited by Ernest McPherson Lander, Jr.,
and Charles M. McGee, Jr.

THE SHATTERED DREAM:
A Southern Bride at the Turn of the Century
edited by Harold Woodell

Copyright © 1991 University of South Carolina

Published in Columbia, South Carolina, by the
University of South Carolina Press

Manufactured in the United States of America

Library of Congress Cataloging-in-Publication Data

Sloan, Margaret, 1874–1960.
    The shattered dream : a southern bride at the turn of the century
/ the day book of Margaret Sloan ; edited by Harold Woodell.
        p. cm. — (Women's diaries and letters of the nineteenth-
century South)
    Includes bibliographical references.
    ISBN 0–87249–712–7 (alk. paper)
    1. Sloan, Margaret, 1874–1960—Diaries. 2. Sloan, Margaret,
1874–1960—Marriage. 3. Women—Southern States—Diaries. 4. Women—
Southern States—History—19th century. 5. Southern States—Social
life and customs—1865– I. Woodell, Harold, 1941–   II. Title.
III. Series.
CT275.S52345A3   1990
975'.04'092—dc20
[B]   90–39953
                                                                  CIP

To

LINDA LELAND REAGAN,

Margaret's granddaughter

Contents

Series Editor's Introduction

The Shattered Dream: A Southern Bride at the Turn of the Century is the third volume in an on-going series of women's diaries and letters of the nineteenth-century South. In this series being published by the University of South Carolina Press will be a number of never before published diaries, some collections of unpublished correspondence, and a few published diaries that are being reprinted—a potpourri of nineteenth-century women's writings.

The Women's Diaries and Letters of the Nineteenth-Century South Series enables women to speak for themselves providing readers with a rarely opened window into Southern society before, during, and after the American Civil War. The significance of these letters and journals lies not only in the personal revelations and the writing talents of these women authors but also in the range and versatility of their contents. Taken together these publications will tell us much about the heyday and the fall of the Cotton Kingdom, the mature years of the "peculiar institution," the war years, and the adjustment of the South to a new social order following the defeat of the Confederacy. Through these writings the reader will also be presented with firsthand accounts of everyday life and social events, courtships and marriages, family life and travels, religion and education, and the life and death matters which made up the ordinary and extraordinary world of the nineteenth-century South.

Margaret Sloan, attractive, intelligent, and very well-read, wrote in her day book on February 25, 1900, that "we will launch our barque on untried waters, to sail together to a new land, amid the well wishes and good-byes of loved ones we will leave." The grand adventure described by the twenty-six-year-old Chattanooga, Tennessee, belle is her marriage to Willard Carridan Leland, "of the New York Lelands," on June 27, 1900. Willard, described by Margaret as fine-looking and charming, had swept her off her feet, and the day book is a record of two years of Margaret's life beginning with her account of Willard seeking her parents' consent for their marriage.

Margaret, a typical late-nineteenth-century, middle-class, Southern woman, considered marriage to be the centerpiece of her life. Her wedding day she described as a bright happy dream. "I went," she wrote, "without *fear trusting fully* to his keeping my *life*." Their marriage began in the front upstairs room of a boardinghouse in Asheville, North Carolina. From that bedroom, a week following their weeding, she confided to her day book, "How different today to last Wednesday. . . . Then I was awfully excited, today I am *alone* with no excitement at all." But life in the boardinghouse was not all dull—for on another occasion, Margaret wrote, "Willard is so nice about not being mad because the young men make it pleasant for me during his absence, he knows I love him . . . but he is away, I don't like to be *alone*."

The marriage was a wretched one. Margaret, homesick and despondent, had entrusted, as she wrote, her entire life to Willard Leland, who she came to feel had betrayed her by his coolness, his elusiveness, his detachment, and his eye for other women. As they moved from boardinghouse to boardinghouse, from Asheville to Batavia and Buffalo, New York, Margaret carried along her day book and confided in it her innermost thoughts. Three months after their wedding, she pronounced her marriage to her aloof Northern husband as "the *bitterest disappointment of my life*."

Her dream shattered, Margaret cried aloud, "why are men who are so ardent before marriage, later, so cold and insensitive to their wives at the time they should care *most*, when she has

Series Editor's Introduction

lost all that is dear to her for love of him." The final installments of the day book record the couple's continuing marital discord and disputes, their separation, Margaret's return home to Chattanooga, and finally her decision, warily arrived at, to go back to Willard. The articulate keeper of this day book had come to sense that there was no way out of her dilemma—no chance for either a career or economic independence. Out of her feelings of helplessness and her sense of possible social disgrace, Margaret returned to this deeply flawed marriage and closed her book forever.

Professor Harold Woodell effectively edits the account of the plight of this Southern woman caught in the web of a cultural stereotype.

Carol Bleser

Acknowledgments

The Shattered Dream is the result of the encouragement and work of many people. Skip and Cindy Still discovered the diary and passed it along to me. Professor Carol K. Bleser of the Department of History at Clemson University recognized its worth and recommended it to the University of South Carolina Press. Clemson University provided financial support through a Provost Research Grant.

Most of the information for the Chattanooga area came from Clara Swann and the Local History and Genealogy Department in the Chattanooga-Hamilton County Bicentennial Library. The events relating to Douglas, Arizona, were provided by Cindy Hayostek of the Cochise Genealogical Society. And, Dr. Richard Saunders of the Department of History at Clemson generously assisted with the research involving the Rochester-Buffalo portions of the diary.

I am thankful for the encouragement I received from the Department of English at Clemson University and for the assistance of three graduate students: Stephen Davis, Ruth Anne Glasgow, and especially Julie Ellington whose work on transcribing, typing, and indexing was outstanding.

For helping me tame a computer, a scanner, and a word processor, special thanks go to Barry Davis, manager of the Lan-

Acknowledgments

guage Laboratory in the Department of Languages, and to
Carol Ryan of the Publications and Graphics Department at
Clemson University.

The Shattered Dream

Introduction

At the turn of the century in the American South, a beautiful young woman and a handsome soldier fell in love and shortly thereafter decided to marry. Each was the answer to the other's dream. The woman, Margaret Sloan, believed she had found her Prince Charming in Willard Leland, a blue-eyed Northerner with blond hair who stood nearly six feet tall. Willard, too, could be proud of his catch—a real southern belle schooled in the proper graces in favor among the white middle class in the nineteenth-century South. Margaret was a master of polite conversation, she played the piano and sang very well, she was an excellent seamstress, she attended church regularly, and, above all, this sociable young lady was accomplished in the ways to charm a gentleman's heart.

The daughter of a physician, Margaret met Willard while he was recuperating from typhoid fever at the Epsworth League Hospital in Chattanooga, Tennessee. A native of New York, Willard had been learning the skills of the machinist's trade with a company in Knoxville when he volunteered to serve with the United States Army during the Spanish-American War (1898–1899). After enlisting, he was sent to Chattanooga which became the primary training center for some forty thousand American men who responded to the call to action. Here

1

Willard soon became Sergeant Leland, but like so many of his companions, he became ill due to the woeful conditions at the camp and never saw combat. Before he fully recovered, the war was over, and he was mustered out on January 31, 1899, at Anniston, Alabama. After returning to Knoxville to complete his apprenticeship, he and Margaret continued their romance by correspondence and a few visits until they married in June of 1900. The marriage of this young couple might have been a dream come true, but unlike the characters in a fairy tale, Margaret and Willard did not live happily ever after. The reasons for this are many and are all carefully delineated in Margaret's day book.

When Margaret Sloan of Chattanooga, Tennessee, decided to marry Willard Leland of Batavia, New York, on June 27, 1900, she was prepared to begin the greatest adventure of her life. Nothing before or after could equal the grandeur and high drama of that day in late June when Margaret and her "dear boy" would exchange sacred matrimonial vows and become husband and wife. Once the June date was firmly fixed, Margaret, now twenty-six years of age and a year older than Willard, could anticipate the excitement of a formal church wedding and the joys of the first twelve months of a blissful union during which she would be a "bride"—admired by friends, adored by family, and worshiped by an attentive husband. Her expectation of an ideal marriage was nothing less than a dream of perfection.

If Margaret's hope for fulfillment in marriage was extravagant, it was at the same time a noble desire shared by many, if not most, middle- to- upper-class white women of her time and place. And in the nineteenth-century South at least, their dream of the perfect union was closely linked to yet another vision of excellence, that of the splendid young woman who represented all that was good, virtuous, and holy in southern life—the southern belle.[1]

At least fifty years before Margaret was born, the image of the belle began to appear dramatically in the antebellum writings of southern poets, lyricists, and novelists. Initially, it was a literary convention for a poet such as Edward Coote Pinkney,

---

[1] See Anne Firor Scott's *The Southern Lady: From Pedestal to Politics, 1830–1930.*

who declares in "A Health," a verse tribute to an unspecified woman, "I fill this cup to one made up of loveliness alone, / A woman, of her gentle sex the seeming paragon; / To whom the better elements and kindly stars have given / A form so fair, that, like the air, 'tis less of earth than heaven." The apotheosis of woman continued in both southern literature and life until her position on the pedestal was secure as seen in the most memorable of southern lyrics about woman, Edgar Allan Poe's "To Helen" which begins, "Helen, thy beauty is to me / Like those Nicean barks of yore" and concludes "Lo! in yon brilliant window-niche / How statue-like I see thee stand, / The agate lamp within thy hand! / Ah, Psyche, from the regions which / Are Holy Land!" In the works of such writers as Poe and his many followers, the southern woman was an unchanging entity who held out the promise of purity of soul in an ideal realm even if it were not available in the real world. Furthermore, the image of the southern belle became a staple of hundreds of plantation romances such as John Pendleton Kennedy's *Swallow Barn* (1832) and even Margaret Mitchell's *Gone With the Wind* (1936) that renders effectively in fiction two radically different versions of the belle—the ideal Melanie and the realistic Scarlett.

Today the literary belle imaged in story and song is viewed in relationship to the real southern woman who adapted the image to fit her needs. For example, in an article on the impact of the Civil War on a southern marriage, Carol K. Bleser and Frederick M. Heath noted that authentic belles were pursued by men "who expected them to be pretty, unmarried, affluent, charming, fashionable, and flirtatious."[2] Denied power in the economic and political realms, the real southern belle compensated for these limitations by developing in the social sphere her "womanly" charms to exert some control over the men around her: "Playing this dependent and ornamental role not only trained women to manipulate men, important in a patriarchal society, but also had immediate practical compensations because an accomplished player could hope to marry a man of wealth and social position."[3] The goal, then, of the southern

---

[2]Bleser and Heath, 197.
[3]Bleser and Heath, 197.

belle was marriage, and her success or failure as a woman was judged by how well the marriage worked. Even if a marriage turned out to be a miserable failure, it was preferable to being single and unattached. Thus, while the myth of the belle may now be viewed as socially debilitating and politically insidious, as W. J. Cash regarded it in *The Mind of the South,* there can be no doubt that it was a potent one that fulfilled the demands of a people who had endured the trauma of a Civil War and the stress of Reconstruction.

Born in 1874, Margaret Sloan grew up in a southern town that had experienced the war firsthand and, during her youth, was beginning to develop a deep pride in its heritage—this in spite of the final battles of Lookout Mountain and Chickamauga. But Chattanooga in many ways was a dream, too—a "Mountain City" surrounded by high vistas, divided by a large river, and crisscrossed by several important railroads. The attractiveness of the place even led many Union soldiers to return to the area they had once known as hostile territory to pursue their professions, to set up businesses, to marry the local women, and to become active leaders in civic and social affairs. By the time Margaret entered womanhood, Chattanooga was well on its way to prospering in the New South, but it was also not likely to forget its past anytime soon. The Chattanooga National Cemetery, established by a Union general in 1863, was by 1900 a source of great civic pride, and at the same time, a few blocks away, the city had established a Confederate Cemetery for southern soldiers who had been buried in other grave sites throughout the area. The battle locations were quickly becoming tourist attractions and proudly displayed to visiting dignitaries such as Prince Henry of Prussia who toured the city in 1902.

The older southern way of life was also available to Margaret in her home (her father had served in the war), in her church (Protestant fundamentalist), and in the arts. The novels she read, popular best-sellers of her day, were mainly sentimental, domestic romances and pious religious narratives. The many stage plays she saw at the Chattanooga Opera House, some based on these same novels, were frequently romantic musicals or melodramas designed with the prerequisite "happy ending." Additionally, she attended presentations sponsored by the Lyceum Bureau that featured speakers such as former Con-

federate General John B. Gordon, then Commander-in-Chief of
the United Confederate Veterans, whose lecture on "The First
Days of the Confederacy" was received with wild applause.

Thus, it should not be surprising that by the time Margaret
accepted Willard Leland's hand in marriage, she had imprinted
in the deep core of her being the myth of the southern belle. In
effect, she had been handed a cultural role that said: "Be the
perfect woman and you will be rewarded with a perfect marriage to your Beau Ideal. Judge yourself and others by the yard-
stick of a loving, reciprocal marriage. Make adjustments when
conflicts arise, but do nothing to disturb the enduring dream,
for if you do, you will pay a terrible penalty." To read Margaret's
story is to read about a real human being who lived out the
dreams of a true believer, but who finally came to pay the emo-
tional costs that such allegiance demanded.

As noted earlier, no southern woman as fully attuned to her
culture as Margaret was would dare take marriage lightly.
Essentially, it was a career for which a woman trained as dili-
gently as a minister for the pulpit or a lawyer for the court-
room. And no one could have been more earnest than Margaret
in designing the perfect wedding and that first year of bridal
bliss. She attended the weddings of friends and strangers and
studied them carefully to learn the fine points of the wedding
drama. Ever sensitive to fashion in clothing, she became an accomplished seamstress in order to create lovely dresses and delicate accessories to delight her husband. And she spent so much
time shopping that the announcement of her engagement upset
the salesmen at the local department stores who would miss
her lively and charming presence. She even retold the events of
her own wedding ceremony three different times in her diary.
Yet, in spite of all this hard work and dedication to an ideal,
Margaret discovered with deep sadness that she was no more
able to control the vicissitudes of that first year of marriage
than she could halt the rains that fell on June 27, 1900.

Margaret began 1900 with the certain knowledge that this
would be a unique and triumphant year, one that would de-
mand special attention in the way of commemoration. And what
better way to capture permanently both the details and the significance of this most wonderful of times than in the pages of a
diary? For Margaret, a diary was the ideal form to capture the
significant occurrences that transpired over a long period of

5

time—weeks, months, perhaps even years. Along the way, she recorded much that was casual and random, even trivial, but her compulsion to chronicle what was, in her mind, the great event was similar to that of many far greater diarists.

Therefore, on January 1, 1900, Margaret opened a new, three-hundred-page ledger of the type known as a "day book" and began to record in pen and ink the great adventure in her life. All of the training, the practice, the false starts with other men were behind her; now she was ready for the live performance with the handsome man of her choice.

Margaret began her first entry in a deceptively casual manner: "Nothing unusual has happened today in fact I have been occupied with the very ordinary things that take up the time of house keepers." But, before the page was finished, she recorded that Willard had won her parents' consent to their "early marriage" and exclaimed, "What plans, dreams, and hopes we have for this year!" She continued with the belief that she and Willard would be happy a year later and that "our love will grow stronger and each become dearer to the other as each year fades, and another is born." Before she completed the day book and turned it over to a sister for safekeeping, Margaret filled 298 pages with two years, seven months, and twenty-one days of her life. Finally she closed her diary with a plaintive farewell on August 21, 1902, with the words, "Good night, and good bye my old confident"—thereby ending the magnificent venture in a way she never would have thought possible on "New Years Day!" 1900.

The fourth of six children, Margaret was born in Calhoun, Tennessee, on May 15, 1874, to Dr. Rudolphus and Mrs. Margaret Sloan. The other children were Francis (b. 1867), William (b. 1870), Gertrude (b. 1872), Clarence (b. 1877), and Carrie (b. 1881). Margaret's mother, Margaret Spring Sloan (1842–1927), lived in Dalton, Georgia, until she moved with her parents to Tennessee, where she met and married Dr. Sloan after the Civil War. She was a caring housewife and mother who attended unassumingly to the domestic duties of the Sloan household and, to judge from Margaret's diary, a woman who loved her husband and children and who was loved in return.

Dr. Rudolphus Sloan (1830–1912) came from Norfolk, Virginia, where at the age of twenty he worked as a lay minister in the Methodist Conference until failing health led him to move

6

to Nashville. Here he entered the University of Nashville as a medical student and left four years later as a licensed physician. After practicing medicine for a short time in Nashville, he moved to Pikeville and practiced there until the war broke out.

Although he volunteered as a private, Dr. Sloan served throughout the war as a surgeon on detached service in the Confederate Army. In addition to his work as a war doctor, he achieved recognition by advising General Braxton Bragg as to the likely movements of the Union Army in the Tennessee mountains before the battles of Lookout Mountain and Chickamauga, thereby contributing to the South's success in these early clashes in the Civil War.

After the war Dr. Sloan settled in Calhoun where he most likely would have lived for the rest of his life except for an unusual incident that occurred in 1885. While traveling from Nashville to Calhoun, he was seriously hurt when a locomotive engine exploded in the Chattanooga train yards. As a result of this injury, from which he never fully recovered, he brought a damage suit against the Nashville, Chattanooga, & St. Louis Railway, and in an effort to oversee the prosecution of the case, he moved his family to Chattanooga. The case was settled in his favor, and he opened a medical practice which he eventually augmented with a pharmacy business operated from his home.

While it may appear from these few facts that the Sloans could have been quite well-to-do, the truth is that the family, although comfortably middle class, never moved with ease among the first families of Chattanooga. Dr. Sloan, for example, was an acknowledged leader in the city's Democratic party, but he never ran for public office, and although he was an active physician, he never became a member of his regional doctors' association. The Sloans only occasionally came into close contact with the upper echelon of society, a fact Margaret points out in her day book.

By the time Margaret started her day book, her father was almost seventy years old, and her parents had started to take in boarders. Clearly, the family was undergoing a slow but discernible decline as the father's health worsened with advancing age. At times Margaret reflected upon the family's eroding fortunes, a condition not alleviated by her brothers—William, a salesman, and Clarence, who was unable to find and hold a steady job—or her sisters—Carrie, the baby of the family who had no luck with her suitors, and Gertie, whose marriage was falling apart. An eternal loser, Clarence was fated to die tragically in 1913 when he suffered a "shock to pelvis from crushing injury" in a copper smelter in Douglas, Arizona. On a happier note, Carrie eventually became a schoolteacher, married, and had two children, and Gertrude ultimately enjoyed a second marriage.

Overall, the image of the Sloan family was a positive one. Throughout most of the day book, the parents' love for their children, the children's respect for their mother and father, and the brothers' and sisters' concern for one another are genuine and pervasive. Likewise, this dependable, supportive southern family has its counterpart in the northern family of Willard Leland, and although Willard's maternal grandmother Thomson was cast in the role of the wicked stepmother by Margaret, the Leland-Thomson family displayed a similar loving consideration for one another. In fact, both the Sloans and the Lelands were testimony to the strength and importance of the family in America at the turn of the century. Sadly, though, the older, stable family also stands as an ironic backdrop to the unsuccessful attempt by Margaret and Willard to create an enduring one of their own.

While her adventure-narrative at times resembles a work of fiction, Margaret's story is a real one that began with the Sloan-Leland marriage in Tennessee. The wedding itself was highly successful and made quite an impression on the townspeople. The newspaper accounts of the announcement and the wedding that Margaret so carefully sewed into the diary manuscript coincide with her own accounts of the nuptials. However, these same newspaper clippings also contain information that can only be labeled as fanciful exaggerations designed to affirm Margaret's status as a belle. Willard's potential upper-crust status ("Mr. Leland will manage extensive interests and estates for his grandfather") and the bridal trip which was to last two months cannot be taken seriously.

In fact Willard's maternal grandfather Thomson was a farmer of moderate means. So, too, was Willard's father, Mr. Leland, who was also a regional representative in the Batavia-Attica area for the Buckeye Buggy Company located in Watertown, New York. Willard was a machinist who worked for a railroad company in Asheville, North Carolina, when he and Margaret were married, and throughout their marriage he remained a machinist by trade. Margaret clearly knew these facts and knew that they were going directly to Asheville after the wedding so that Willard could go to work. Although Margaret did at times complain in the day book about the state of their finances, she never once blamed Willard for pretending to be the heir to some large estate.

The happy couple moved to Asheville, North Carolina, where they lived in a boardinghouse and Willard worked for a railroad (a fact almost never mentioned in the day book), and then they moved to New York. In Batavia and Buffalo, the couple resided in more boardinghouses, where tensions over Willard's flirtations caused deep rifts in their relationship. In what appears to be an almost trivial matter in passing, the fact that Margaret and Willard lived in boardinghouses turned out to have a serious impact on their marriage. Now a rarity on the American scene, boardinghouses, private homes converted into rental property that provided meals along with lodging, were a significant form of housing in America throughout the nineteenth century and during the first half of the twentieth.[4]

At their best, boardinghouses served well the demands of immigrants who came to large American cities. Also, young men and women moving from the country to the city and others who were just starting their careers found boardinghouses congenial with their ready-made substitutions for family life, represented best by the common dinner table, or "board," at which the lodgers took their meals. By and large, boardinghouse lodgers were single, unattached men and women who needed a home for food preparation, laundering, social amusement, and recreation. At their worst, however, boardinghouses meant a lack of privacy and the potential for sexual encounters between the young men and women living in such close proximity. While there was a wide range of boardinghouses regarding the era's standards of respectability, even the boardinghouse keepers who were concerned about such matters had little or no control over the relations between the sexes.

At first, it appears that Margaret and Willard could not have made a happier choice in housing, yet the boardinghouse proved to be an unfavorable environment for the newly married

---

[4]See *Urban Housing,* eds. William L. C. Wheaton, Grace Milgram, and Margy Ellin Meyerson.

couple. While living in their fourth boardinghouse, for instance, Willard had what appears to be an affair with a woman named, curiously enough, "Miss Belle." The flirtation developed with "the little fool," as Margaret called her, blatantly pursuing Willard, who obviously enjoyed her attention. Margaret endured many "utterly wretched" hours, but in the end left the boarding-house reconciled with Willard.

Next, the couple moved into the Attica home of Willard's grandparents—for the second time in their short marriage—where Margaret's struggle for her husband's attention ended in defeat with his grandmother banishing Margaret from the home. Forced to retreat to her father's house in Tennessee, Margaret became increasingly frustrated by her alternatives: one, return to Willard, who apparently does not want her back; two, stay with her parents and suffer their reduced circumstances and humiliation from the townspeople; three, leave Willard for another man; or four, move to New York City and open a millinery.

All of this uncertainty led to such an agitated state of mind that Margaret finally realized she needed to seek professional help—which she did in the form of spiritualism, a pseudo-science that was enjoying widespread popularity in the South at the time Margaret was writing her day book. Chattanooga, for instance, had been the site of a national convention of mediums in 1885 when the "First Spiritualist Society" held its annual meeting on Lookout Mountain. Though recognized by the general population as cranks and charlatans, most spiritualists tried to convince the public that they were not witches or wizards but caring professionals whose Christian practices were divinely inspired—a notion not too hard to accept by those who still had fond memories of Emersonian transcendentalism and the concept of the Oversoul.

With increasing desperation, Margaret consulted three mediums: Dr. Rock ("The Hindoo Seer"), Mrs. Dr. Hall, and Professor Prescott. The first one she conferred with, the "Hindoo," was clearly a fraud who fed Margaret a line about Willard's infidelity and then skipped town before she could press him for details. The second one, Mrs. Dr. Hall, reaffirmed her doubts with messages that sound suspiciously like reruns of Dr. Rock's act.

The third one Margaret visited turned out to be, interestingly enough, a fairly good amateur psychologist. Director of the Southern Sanitarium and Magnetic Institute, Professor Prescott may indeed have cured his patients with "MAGNETISM" and he may have pretended to contact Willard through the ether. But finally it was the professor who helped Margaret resolve her difficulties with Willard. Through his shrewd observation and genuine concern over her well-being, the professor pointed the way for Margaret to return to Willard and join him in a small town in the midwest; thus, the day book ended with Margaret's resolve to begin life anew.

All in all, the day book presents a touchingly sad story. When Margaret the southern belle was placed on the pedestal and made to perform in the role of the ideal woman, she was inevitably limited in the process. Margaret's search for perfection may have gone awry, yet there can be little doubt that she learned much about herself and her culture as her dreams became tempered with the reality of human fraility. That she continued writing in her day book on an almost daily basis as she approached despair over her growing uncertainty about Willard is sufficient proof of her developing personality. The day book evokes anger, sorrow, and pride—anger that she could give in to jealousy, sorrow that she was trapped in a cultural pattern over which she had little control, and pride that she finally began to achieve some understanding of her predicament.

About the Text

In order to maintain the quality and tone of the original, the printed version of *The Shattered Dream: The Day Book of Margaret Sloan* is as close to the handwritten diary as reasonably possible. Margaret's cursive style is quite readable; therefore, only three words or phrases are identified as problematic with a question mark in brackets [?]. Annotations also appear in the text within brackets. For the sake of appearance, the first line of each daily entry has been indented to show the start of a new paragraph. Margaret only rarely indented the first line, but the subsequent indentions within a paragraph are hers. The superimposed chapter divisions are linked to changes in Margaret and Willard's marriage. Specific biographical facts about Margaret and her family have been placed in the Introduction and Afterword.

Introduction

Margaret's prose style is plain and conversational, well representative of a young person of her education and station in life. The most obviously distinguishing characteristic of this chatty, informal style is the presence of comma splices and fused clauses. Occasionally in the editing a comma has been added to a lengthy unit to prevent either a misreading or to resolve an ambiguity.

In almost all cases, the idiosyncratic spelling, grammar, punctuation, and the crossed-out words appear as Margaret wrote them in the original. Misspellings that might cause undue puzzlement and a few words that she only at times carelessly misspelled have been silently emended ("ceratinly" to "certainly," "finist" to "finest," "innisent" to "innocent," etc.), but habitual misspellings, ("didint," "greive," "seperate," etc.) have been retained. Occasional omissions have likewise been corrected ("Willard and went riding" becomes "Willard and I went riding").

The Day Book of

Margaret
Sloan

Margaret, Dr. Sloan, Gertie (seated left to right) Clarence and William (or reverse, standing); photograph described in diary on August 31, 1900

Ray and Willard Leland

Margaret and Gertie in an automobile called a "Schacht"
(sold by Gertie's second husband, Mr. Hay); courtesy of Linda Reagan

CHAPTER ONE

The Wedding

Journal for 1900

New Years Day!

Nothing unusual has happened today in fact I have been occupied with the very ordinary things that take up the time of house keepers.

Have helped cook, clean up, served, read a letter from Willard, wrote and sung and laughed.

Gladys spent Christmas with us and we have romped so much today.

Clarence took she and Carrie to the mattinee this afternoon, but it is so cold and snowing some, that I felt I would enjoy staying home more.

Willard and I had hoped to spend today together, but he worked and of course I couldn't enjoy things so well when he was away.

The 23rd of Dec. he came down and asked my parents consent to our early marriage and gained both, and now we seem dearer than ever to each other, and we welcomed this new year, and we feel that this will be the happiest year we ever spent, and the beginning of a new life to both.

What plans, dreams, and hopes we have for this year!

We believe that next New Year will find us happy with each other, and that our love will grow stronger and each become dearer to the other as each year fades, and another is born.

I wont write any resolutions, but I hope to do more for others, have a better control of my temper, speak less against people, be more generous, more appreciative, and live more as I feel I should this year than I did last.

15

The Wedding

Willard wrote me Wednesday and Sunday since he left both beautiful letters, full of love for me, telling how he needs me and wishes ever for my presence, and ere many days have flown, I will be there to welcome him when the day is over.

Wednesday Jan. 3.—1900.

This afternoon Gertie and I went to town and came home had supper, and went to hear Col. Copeland in his famous lecture, "Seeing the Elephant," [one of several lectures sponsored by the Lyceum Bureau Margaret attended at the Chattanooga Opera House] and it was decidedly the finest one I ever had the pleasure of listening to. Sis gave me this rare treat, and I appreciate it so much. Every body was there and Mr. Brewer came to us, and took us to get hot chocolate, and Mr. Jacoway came in there, and we had a jolly evening.

They brought us home and I entered into the spirit of the evening and lay aside serious thoughts, decided I was seeing life as the six blind men saw the elephant, I had been fragmentizing life and living on a fragment, and so I determined to enjoy each day as it came and I certainly enjoyed the evening. Willard wants me to enjoy every thing.

Friday Jan 5. 1900.

Little Gladys left us this afternoon as Uncle Dave telephoned for her to come and we certainly miss her wonderfully.

I took her to the Cemetary [the Chattanooga National Cemetery, established in 1863, within walking distance of the Sloan home] this morning, and saw her off this aft. Mr. Berger kindly took us in his buggy or we would have missed the train.

These days are spent by me in thinking of Willard and planning my trousseau, but it seems to me I am going to have to change some of my many "wants" unless I get to getting some of those things very soon.

I have material for four hankerchiefs now, all will be pretty, and I want one dozen any way.

Sunday Jan 7 1900.

This has been a perfectly beautiful day and Gertie and I went to Centenary [Centenary Methodist Church] this morning, and Annie and Mary spent the afternoon with us, and told us

16

Stevens was not dead, as we had heard, but was coming to Chattanooga next week to live, and she is happy. I think she is getting ready to marry him too, she seems so happy.

Monday Jan. 8.—1900.

This is an ideal spring day, and the fire is out, the windows open, and pleasant.

Had a letter from Willard this morning and he is dwelling on the events of June too, thinks it cant come too soon to suit him, he wants me with him!

Friday Jan. 12.—1900.

This afternoon is very pretty and we appreciate the blue sky and sunshine since having gloomy rainy weather the past three days.

We were so disappointed in not getting to see the Watkins-Elder wedding at Centenary Wednesday aft. at six.

It must have been beautiful, all in white, and so many attendents.

We thought we might gain some points that would be of value to us some time but it rained all day.

I have made three pretty handkerchiefs during this rainy weather, and read "David Harum" by James Noyes W. Scott [*David Harum* (1898) by Edward N. Westcott]. I like it fine. Think there is a lot of good in his rude sketches, and certainly like David *fine!*

There are so many good things to read if only I felt I had time, but I know I should sew instead.

Sunday Jan. 14. 1900.

Very little of interest happens these days, we sew and keep the household machinery running, and write and read our spare moments.

Gertie read us Opie Reids, "Wives of the Prophet" [*The Wives of the Prophet* (1894) by Opie Read] and it made such an impression on us we all dreamed of it that night.

Then I have read, "When knight hood was in flower," [*When Knighthood Was in Flower* (1898) by Edwin Caskoden] and enjoyed it so much. Have commenced "Richard Feveral" [*The Ordeal of Richard Feveral* (1859) by George Meredith] now.

The Wedding

Wednesday Jan. 24th. 1900

Miller [a department store, Miller Bros. Co., est. 1889] had had a wonderful sale for over a week, called the "Mill end sale," and I have invested in laces and imbroderies, and ribbons, and only wished I could have gotten some of those elegant silks selling so cheap.

I am anxious to begin working on white goods, but I want to finish the winter dresses first.

Had a nice letter from Willard on Monday. Tonight Pa, Gertie, Carrie and I went to hear Miss Ida Benfrey lecture on "La Miserables," [*Les Miserables* (1863) by Victor-Marie Hugo; lecture also included readings from Mary Wilkins and George Eliot] and she impersonated eight characters perfectly, then closed the evenings entertainment with a half hour of comedy.

It is jolly to go to this lecture course [the Lyceum lectures at the Opera House] for there is so much style, and every body is in such good spirits and the cream of the population attends.

Friday Jan. 26 1900.

Pa hasint been well since the lecture and will have to be careful.

Mrs. Allin came in and spent the afternoon.

Smallpox is raging in different parts of the city, and I am going to stay home awhile.

Jan. 28 Sunday.—1900.

Will Stine and Annie came out this afternoon, and he certainly is a handsome corpse! We told him of how grieved we were when we heard he was dead.

He was en-route to New Orleans and San Francisco.

We are staying home closely, afraid of small pox, and leading a very, very uneventful life.

Sunday Feb. 4.—1900.

Mr Rankin, Mr Scott, and Farrel were coming down today, but we have been having bad weather and they want to see the sights when they came, so have postponed their visit until Spring weather sets in, and so I was glad for today is rainy and bad and we wouldn't have enjoyed it much. He sent me a box of Kerns candy today. I received a letter from Mrs Thomson

[Willard's maternal grandmother] with a half tone engraving of Mr. C. J. Thomson. Also sent me a little material for hoi tan work [Honiton lace, made in Devonshire, England].

Wednesday Feb. 7.—1900.

Gertie and I went to town today, the first time I have been out of the house in so long and the fresh air was so delightful I feel so much better.

We ordered a [sewing] machine and I got some white goods and laces and ribbons to make the remainder of my lingerie, and must sew faithfully this month.

Sunday Feb. 11. 1900

They sent us a handsome improved drop head Singer [sewing machine] Thursday, and while I haven't had much time to work on it, yet I have run over a hundred yards of tucks, and I only wish it was *ours.* I am enthusiastic over pretty lingerie now, as the time is so fast approaching.

Two weeks from last night until Willard finishes his "time," [his apprenticeship as a machinist] and then he will feel so independent.

He thinks we will go North as soon as we are married and of course I want as pretty clothes as I possibly can get, for all depends on first appearance.

Oh! how I know we will enjoy that trip together, and how excited I get when I realize how *near* the time is.

I believe I am going to have some pretty clothes now.

My boy intended coming to see me the latter part of the month, but I dont know whether he will or not, it depends on where he goes to work.

I am awfully anxious to see him. This is a gloomy rainy day, it seems we have so many bad Sundays lately.

Sunday Feb. 25.—1900.

Well this is a perfectly beautiful day but those who have been out say it is very cold. We had intended if this afternoon was pretty to call on Mrs. Arnold, as we have been wanting to see her some time and she is busy all week.

I have been sewing hard on lingerie for nearly all of Feb. and haven't gone any place hardly to town, and I think when I have completed these I will have dainty sweet clothes for a girl in my circumstances.

I take pains to make everything as pretty as possible, and then Ma is kindly helping me get those materials necessary.

Experience is a fine teacher, and had I known *how* to make pretty things when I began as much as I did now, I would have had a lot prettier ones, for I have wasted so much. After I finish these I could begin another trousseau and make a handsome one, but I shall be contented with mine.

I find pleasure in fashioning these dainty things, and knowing Willard will admire them, and love me in them.

Pa, Ma, Gertie, Carrie attended the lecture given by Chas. K. Underhill last week, and I am going to take Willard to hear Max O'Rell [Paul Blouet, a French comedian who pretended he was an Irishman] if he is here the 2nd. of March.

Friday evening Mrs Hultz entertained in honor of Rev. Aikman and daughter, and they insisted on my going and I did dress in my best and for an evening I was apparently "one of the Park-placeites," [Park Place, an exclusive subdivision] but I dont enjoy mingling with them, and will be *glad* when my home will be in a nice place, among congenial people.

Nice refreshments were served and some music and recitations interspersed with conversation formed the evening entertainment. I liked Miss Aikman very well.

We have had such changeable weather warm and Spring like, then windy and cold, and yesterday it snowed nearly all day, but didn't lay on the ground.

If we dont have snow soon we wont have any this winter to amount to any thing.

Yesterday was the long talked of and expected day of the *"24 of Feb. 1900!"*

Willard has completed his four years apprenticeship at last.

He has remained firm, worked hard and steadily, amid temptations and *at last,* the time has been served and he can accept any position he is offered and if he ever needs a trade to fall back on he has one, a *good one now!*

I feel proud of my boy, for it required pluck and determination to overcome the difficulties that lay in his way so long.

Last February when he wrote that one year from the 24th. his time would be up, it seemed to us both, that it was almost an interminable time, yet it has been lived and reminds me how near that day is, when we will launch our barque on untried waters, to sail together to a new land, amid the well wishes and good byes of loved ones we will leave.

While it seems sad to think of it in that light yet to think that our dreams would never be realized would be sadder still, and some times my heart leaps for joy when I realize that the seperation will soon be ended and I will have my boy with me every Sunday then.

Only a little time now to wait.

Tuesday Feb. 27.—1900.

This afternoon Gertie took me to the mattinee to see James Young in "Lord Byron," [a play written by Rida Louise Johnson] this afternoon, and it was splendid, he is a fine actor, and certainly the grandest lover I ever saw on the stage.

In act *3rd.* that love scene in Greece is simply superb!

They are staying at his castle in Greece situated on a river or lake, and the moon light is beautiful on the water, and he throws a cloak over him and comes out to sit on the steps and dream, for as he said that was a place made for love, and could eat of the lotus tree and love and dream forever.

And Thursa [Thyrza], the Italian girl he loves and who loves him, comes to him, and they have the most natural conversation, then when she tells him how madly she loves him he is skeptical, but at last he is over come by love for her, and her passions and tells her they *will* love and be happy, life was made for love, and then commences that ideal love scene, in which he is *grand!*

I enjoyed it so very much, and would have hated to miss it.

After the performance we were at Millers shopping and Mrs Eummons and Dora and the girls commenced teasing me about going to marry soon, and they certainly gave it to me hot and heavy.

Friday March 2nd. 1900.

Wednesday Gertie and I cleaned up entire house and baked a coconut cake, and yesterday we were busy all day for we entertained Pa's friends at 6 o'clock dinner.

The Wedding

Dr Monk, Judge Estell, and Capt. Donaldson, and for once we made Ma act hostess in the parlor, and we girls served, and did the honors in the dining room and kitchen.

Every thing passed off pleasantly, and the dinner was a success I think.

We had for our menu the following:—Oyster soup, roast beef, baked potatoes, gravy, peas, tomatoes, rice, chicken salad, chow-chow, sweet pickles, cranberry sauce, celery, crackers, butter, pear preserves, biscuit, light bread, coffee, cream, boiled custard, coconut cake.

Every thing was well cooked, served nicely, and without haste, or flurry, and the table looked *beautiful!*

The evening was spent happily by all in merry conversation, music and laughter. Carrie and I dyked out [variant of "diked out"; to dress in fine clothes] after supper and I forgot how tired I was when I listened to the jokes exchanged by our father and his guests, and we all like them so very much, and I think so much of Judge Estelle.

Pa was so pleased with his family, and it did him good to think we would entertain *his* friends so nicely for him.

It was a very enjoyable dinner.

This morning I dont feel the liveliest in the world though, and tonight Max O'Rell, too at opera house.

Clarence left this morning at four o'clock for a trip up the Southern road, and was too busy last night to come home, and he missed all of the festivities.

Heard from Willard Monday and he didn't know where he would go, or when he could come down, and I am awfully home sick to see him, and yet if he goes any distance I wont see him any more after this time till he comes to claim me for his own.

Monday March 12.—1900.

Very little of special interest happens in my life at this time, and I am failing to write many things that I would if I had more time for pleasure, making this the poorest Journal I ever pretended to keep, but while there is nothing startling to relate, yet I am very well contented making up my lingerie and dreaming of the time I am to wear them for the admiration of the dearest boy living, and I know he will appreciate their beauty, for he is interested in dainty pretty things and is lovely about any thing I do or make for my self, compliments me, calls me his smart little girl.

Yesterday morning about nine o'clock I was dressing to go to church with Clarence and the bell rang and he went to the door and said, "Hello Willie," and opened the folding doors and I knew that *my boy had come!* I put on my new dress and he sprang to meet me as I entered the parlor and expressed admiration and love and thus commenced a happy day, one that comes as a bright spot in my very quite life, and which is I hope a fore taste of what all the days are to be later on.

We went to Centenary and Lloyd was watching all who left the church and I was heartily glad he saw us, for I am never ashamed of my boy, he is fine looking and carefully dressed.

We came home to a nice dinner and spent the afternoon and evening discussing our plans and as there are several points to be decided this month that will affect our plans we decided to wait for developments before putting things in motion for the wedding, but we will have to move up after April 15th. for the time will be here before we are ready if we wait.

If they go West we will marry very quietly at home, if not we will have a white wedding at Centenary.

He went down on the Rapid transit and I walked around to the side steps with him and the moon light was making everything beautiful, and he took me in his arms and said, "Remember darling I love you devotedly, and am coming for you soon, and we will be so happy." Then he left me standing alone watching his tall form disappear, and wishing he did not have to leave me at all.

Wednesday March 14.—1900.

Today was Millers opening and Gertie and I attended of course for they could not have a successful one without us, and it certainly was *grand.*

Saffers orchestra discoursed sweet music while the array of silks, crepe de chines, trimmings, laces, ribbons etc, etc, etc, was dazzling, and the display of their summer goods the prettiest Chattanooga has ever had, and it was decidedly the swellest opening ever attempted here.

The Wedding

Mrs Alt and Mannie came out this aft. and she took Gertie and I to town in the buggy and we had lots of fun, the ride did us good and I feel better for having laid my sewing aside for awhile.

I got a pretty silk green parasol. We bowed to Mr Burk who seemed so delighted to see us.

Wednesday March 21.—1900.

Gertie went to see Louie Morrison in "Faust" [Lewis Morrison, owner of the acting company, played Mephisto in *Faust*] this afternoon, and I stayed home to sew, and Pearl came, then Mannie and I didn't accomplish much sewing.

Had a letter from Mrs Thomson and she told me not to wear my self out sewing, for Mrs Leland made clothes to last twenty years, she had many of them yet, and for me not to make a lace 'kerchief, as she would send me one for the occasion, that belonged to Willards mother, of real lace.

She hoped we would do well if we went home to live, and that Mr Leland wanted us to go to Waterbury to live.

We went to Highland Park to hear Rev. Frank Jackson of Knoxville, and he is *good,* he came in on the same car with us and we like him fine.

Frank, Gertie, and I walked out before dark, and as we walked by the National Cemetary, some one was playing taps, and all the bugle pieces that we heard so often during the army, and it made me sad to think of those days, but more thankful when I realized how happily all seemed going to end, after the grief, heart aches and tears of those dark times. [U.S. troops trained at Chicamauga for the Spanish-American War (1898). Typhoid fever and other diseases killed more men in camp than died in combat. Although Willard became a sergeant in the Third Tennessee Infantry Regiment, he contracted a "dreadful fever" and never saw action.]

Only fourteen weeks at most till we will be united, and happily I think!

We passed the little cottage where five years ago we used to have so many good times, Gerties home, and to me, I rejoiced that I did not have to relive those five years, while she would love to recall them again.

24

Thursday March 22.—1900.

Gertie and I went to Mrs Alts to dinner, called on Mrs Chester, Mrs Underhill, Anne, saw Mrs Mull, Mrs Pryatt, Mrs Ham and Ella, Mrs Arnold and Manny who said lovely things to us, and we felt better for having taken a "day off." Mr Hightower, Mr Anderson, Mr Burk, and Mr Brewer make shopping pleasant. Heard from Willard, he had ordered his wedding suit, and wants us to marry the first of June, says he has gotten to the place where he dont want to do without me *one day longer* than he can help, he needs me and loves me so!

Sunday March 25.—1900.

Had letter from Aunt Lula, Gensie, Paul and cousin Jack, Willard and Mrs Thomson last week, and when will I get all my letters written?

Cousin Jack is witty and I feel sure I like *him fine.*

He wants me to visit them, will meet me in Nashville and promises me a good time in Linden.

Gwine wants me to visit her too, and if only I could make both at the same time it would be fine.

Sunday April 8—1900.

How rapidly time passes, it hardly seems possible that one week of April is gone when there is so much to do before June.

I am worrying over the uncertainty of my plans, I want a church wedding, but cant tell yet whether I can or not.

I am sewing steadily so I will have time to rest awhile before hand. Willard wants it the earliest possible and dont care when, where, or how the ceremony occurs just so he gets me.

Willard is in Asheville working, thinks I may get to live in Asheville a month or so yet.

It seems so strange that as large as this world is those two [Willard and May Bowers, see entry for July 30, 1900] should both be in the same place.

Mrs Alt spent the day Wednesday with us and took Ma to church in the buggy in the afternoon.

Fannie dont want me to marry, says she hates to think of me marrying at all.

25

The Wedding

Clarence is still out of a job, but I keep hoping he will get something soon.

I made three waists [blouses] last week.

Easter Sunday.—April 15. 1900.

I did not go any where today as I am tired and then I had nothing new to wear. I made Irene Rule a dress from Thursday afternoon until last night.

Wednesday. April 18. 1900.

Well we have had a jolly time today and I sew so steadily that I feel I have to take one afternoon a week to run around in.

We started out right after dinner to go the dog show, but the rapid transit was so late that we didn't get to go in, so I went to get my silk dress and Mr Nash said I looked nice, then we went to Millers and Mr Anderson as usual took on over me copiously, asked if I was going to marry as he heard I was, said, "don't tell me you are" and when I said I hadn't told him, he said "but if it has to be told me tell me," and I said "It doesn't have to be told," and he feels satisfied that I am not going to marry now.

I threw Mr Brush off the track in very much the same manner.

Mr Anderson says there is no one in the world he thinks more of than me, and is so lovely to me when I go in there that I find it a pleasure to trade with him.

Mrs Dodds and Clara came in while we were talking with Mr Anderson, and we all went to the 2nd Presbyterian to the Russell-Peak wedding at 4:30 and she looked prettier than I ever saw her, though she wore a foulard [scarf] very plainly made.

The church was beautifully decorated. We took cream at Brukofzers [a drugstore], went to Mrs Underhills for supper and while she went to no trouble at all, she had a splendid supper, and we all did enjoy it so much.

Kate Mack came in too, and we all attended the Tonsand-Mall wedding at the Stone Church at 7:30, and she was as pretty a bride as I have seen in a long while, attired in white organdie trimmed in white satin ribbon, with veil and orange blossoms.

26

May Bradford as maid of honor was very pretty in white dress, decollete [low neckline] and carrying pink roses.

We went to prayer meeting afterwards.

Sunday April.—22.—1900.

Well such a crowd of disappointed girls as we are today, for after we were dressed ready to receive the three young fellows from Harriman [a town north of Chattanooga] this morning a telegram came from Farrel saying they could not come, he would explain by letter.

We have planned all week for a glorious day, and this is an *ideal* Sunday for driving, and as I have been writing so many traps and buggies have passed and it adds to my disappointment.

Gertie helped me finish my skirt last night, and it is *beautiful!*

I commenced it Thursday, and Mrs Barnes came that afternoon and I had to loose that time from sewing and as it is stitched and so much work it took hard work to finish it last night.

Have only three more dresses to make and my work will be done, then I will rest and get some flesh. Received a sweet letter from Willard Friday, he says he wishes he could come to claim me for his bride next week. Says he wants me for his queen, that he loves me so devotedly his happiness will be *complete* with me.

Oh! I do so hope we will be happy and that there never will come one regret into either life for having taken that step that we so soon will take now. Only two months, now that seperates us.

This is a perfectly glorious day and how I would love to have my boy with me this afternoon.

Mr and Mrs Eummons and Mr and Mrs Ward are living in Cincinnati now.

Tuesday April 23.—1900. [Mon. 23 or Tues. 24]

Last night we went to hear the "Catherine Ridgeway Concert," and it was fine.

The evening was so enjoyable, being taken up with violincello selections by Miss Adams, vocal selections by a fine tenor singer, piano selections by Mr Bush and many splendid pieces

beautifully rendered by Miss Ridgeway. She is a fine elocution-
ist and gave us all kinds of selections showing off to advantage
her ability.

We came home at eleven oclock. Carrie, Clarence and I
went to the closing exercises of medical college [Chattanooga
Medical College] tonight and it was attractive. Dr. Monk [minis-
ter at Centenary Methodist Church] made a fine address.

Thursday April. 26.—1900.

Carrie and I went to Mrs Wheelers last night and we had a
very pleasant time.

This afternoon Gertie and I are invited to a reception at
Mrs E. G. Richmonds this afternoon.

What a perfectly delightful home we went to this afternoon!
It is the richest home in Chattanooga and there fore I wont attempt a description. The parlors halls and dining room was decorated with palms and lillies.

Neopolitan cream, layer cake, lady fingers and bon bons
were served. Mrs. Richmond was regal in black silk with applique over dress, and as sweet and gracious as she was beautiful!

Many elegant ladies were there, 250 were invited. We enjoyed it very much indeed.

Saturday April 28. 1900.

Last night Clarence, Carrie, Gertie and I went to hear J. D.
Stafford lecture on "Macbeth," [Lyceum lecture] and he was fine
indeed.

I am awfully tired, we have cleaned and baked today, and I
wouldn't go any place tonight for pay, I must rest. Received a
telegram from Farrel this morning saying he and his friend will
be here tomorrow sure, so I want to look my very best.

Just had a card from Willard this week, he had been out
with a wrecking crew for several days, and he was too worn out
to write—poor boy, so I wrote him today.

Sunday April 29.—1900.

Well the boys have come and gone, and it seems like a
dream, *so short.*

Mr Rankin is tall, slender, and rather good looking, and I
like him fine, we have had more fun today.

They both looked nice, wore their Easter suits, and straw hats. Farrel, poor boy, sat close to me and said so much to me in an undertone, even while I was supposed to be listening to the general conversation, and I always feel so sorry for him, he loves me so devotedly, and has no encouragement at all, and it seems too bad such love should be wasted!

When I told him I was to marry in June he looked like I had stabbed him, and in a husky voice he said, "who is he Madge?" And while he said very little I read the anguish in his eyes, and wished I could have consoled him but I was powerless!

His love has remained true and fervent for *ten years!*

He always admired me so in every aspect, my hair, eyes, form, etc, etc, and he has said often that the brightest things of this World should belong to me, he never saw any thing lovely without feeling it should be mine.

He is so generous, good and true, and I so hope he may be happier than he ever has been yet.

We waved to them as the train passed awhile ago.

Will came to see Pa too this afternoon.

Monday April 30.—1900.

Well I went to town early this morning to secure good seats for the Coronation exercises [part of the Chattanooga Spring Festival], and if it had been conducted fairly I could have gotten good seats, but the choice ones had been secured by favorites of committee, before the general public had been allowed to select.

Any way I hope we can see the stage and he will enjoy it all.

Will Hudiburg is at deaths door, may be dead now as his death is expected hourly.

Thursday May 3.—1900.

Today is Nats birthday! Poor Nattie, I heard from him through Dr Carter, the other day, and that he was loosing his mind, and the fate that he had dreaded so long had over taken him, his health gone and unable to follow his profession, his magnificent art studio had been closed, contents sacrificed, and he had been taken to his sisters for the rest of his life, and that would kill him, if he had no other sorrows to prey on his mind.

How I do pray he may yet have a bright reward in the other life for his generosity, and noble life, for he has been so unhappy here!

Yesterday I received letters from Mrs Thomson and Willard.

He is rejoicing that only eight weeks seperate us, then we will be together, and I am worrying about how I can carry out my plans in that length of time.

He said the foreman told him he would put him on day work in a day or so, and I am so rejoiced that he will, for then we will have our Sundays and evenings together, and it will be so much more pleasant for us both.

Mrs Thomson says she is planning what she can do to make me happy when we go North.

Cousin Jack says he dont want me to marry, for then he couldn't have much of my time, as I would have to pet "hubby."

Sunday May 6th. 1900.

I very seldom find time to pen my experiences or thoughts in this journal now a days, and should I write my thoughts— they would be *varied,* I want to see Willard, be with him all the time, for so long I have wished for him every time I go out any place, and of course, I will have him in a few weeks but then I find I enter this new life with fear and trembling too.

I have stayed *home* so long, been with them in pleasures as well as disappointments till now it seems hard to realize that I am going to leave them, and it will *never* be the same any more after I go.

Well Gertie and I sewed all last week so that we need not have to miss any of the festival this week on account of having sewing to do.

Tuesday May 8. 1900.

Gertie had not heard whether Miss Mayme Lambright and her friend would accept her invitation to come for one day or not, and we were all dressed starting to the flower parade, when the postman brought her letter saying they would come on early train (theu ev,) and knowing they were intown among strangers, we determined to find them as soon as possible, but it seemed an *awful* undertaking in that crowd, and we looked until most time for the parade to pass, when Mr Wilcox kindly

30

let us have a nice window filled with wicker rockers, where we were so comfortable and had a splendid view of the flower parade.

It was more beautiful than usual, and as soon as it was over we joined the mad rush, and renewed our search for the girls.

Gertie went into Lovemans [a department store, D. B. Loveman Co.], and I walked to Voights corner [Voight Bros. drugstore], spied a girl that I took for her, and when I asked if she was Miss Lambright, she said, "Yes, are you Mrs Hobbs sister?" After I was introduced to Miss Cook, Mr Johnson, and Mr Daily, we had the picnic of watching Mayme and Gertie fall on each others necks, and then commenced the hardest confetti battle of the day standing in front of Lovemans, and unless one wanted to come off worsted they had to fight as hard as possible. I did not mean to joint in it but found I would be forced to in self defence.

We came home, had a most enjoyable lunch, without making fire in the stove, composed of veal loaf, fresh bread, langdon [?] biscuit, sweet pickles, chow chow, peas, tomatoes, radishes, butter, onions, pound cake and strawberries.

We four girls with Messrs Johnson and Daily went to the mountains, and had a very nice time, were on the Point [Point Park on Lookout Mountain above Chattanooga] and watched a storm come over the mts. in the distance, and on up the valley, and pass Lookout follow the river, and disappear beyond the mountains far above Chatt. We came home to supper, and Frank joined us and took us to the street-fair and midway [part of the Spring Festival], where Mr Clay, Mr Smith, (cadets) and Mr Will Headrick, Mr Daily, & Mr Johnson joined us.

We took them to the train at 10 o'clock, and I am *dead tired!*

Thursday May 10.—1900.

Farrel came this morning, and we had a long chat, I told him I was going to wed in June, and after dinner we went to the Cemetary, and to Nixons flower garden, and he ordered me some husideo [?] roses to wear tonight.

I wore my white organdie, and roses and he declared I was a *queen!*

31

The Wedding

On the car we chatted with several cadets, one very handsome fellow, and were sorry when we had to get off.

My! the Coronation exercises were just *glorious!* The sweetest sight of the whole week! That stage filled with arches of flowers belonging to each court, and the many novel ways in which the various maids and knights formed to escort their queen to her throne, was fine!

The unmasking of "Baldur," (Chas. R. Evans) and his gallant manner to his Queen Miss Julia Leech added much to the effectiveness of the scene, and their costumes were more appropriate for the occasion than any before now, one could fancy they were of Royal family. Mary Belle Cope was led to the Queen of Chatt. by the King, and crowned Queen of May, presented with a diamond pendant and taken to a rose-covered throne above all the others in the center of the stage, and an arch of incandescent lights were lighted amid applause.

Only because of her graceful, modest manner in accepting so much honor though as Hill City [a suburb] deserved it.

We came in the dining room after we came home, had a little lunch, and lots of fun. He is going to stay over tomorrow.

Friday May 11. 1900.

Gertie, Farrel, and I went to Lookout this morning and walked all around to the Point hotel, and I found the seats on the hotel veranda the nicest place yet.

When we got to the mountain we were all thirsty so we took lemonade, and it made us all ill, and I didn't enjoy my self much, was too sick coming home to pretend any longer that I was not. We had dinner at 2:30, and had intended going to Midway but after I got gay and couldn't I told him to go any way, so he left at four o'clock.

Saturday May 12.—1900.

Gertie, Carrie, and I went out to East Lake Park to dress parade at 6 o'clock this evening, and Frank came for us.

We met Mr Cornelison, the young man I talked to Thursday evening on the car, and Mr Clay.

Frank took us to Midway, and we saw "Willie Stout," "Wild Man from Phillipines," "Mummy" with five ears. Wild animal show that was *fine*, "Philion" in his wonderful feat of rolling a huge ball up and down a spiral tower with him standing on it, and he was handsome, and fine fire works came from every part of the tower while he walked or danced to music!

We saw the man dive into the little pool of water from a tower 90 feet high.

Carrie and I saw "Lucette" be put to sleep by her Prof. and *fly* actually floated in space, and he made her strike her attitude as if praying while in mid air, then he changed her, put her white draperies in her hands and she made the motion like dancing while floating. Then he fixed her like an angel and she flew like one too.

It was jolly as tonight was confetti night and what a crowd as was there! Before we went to Midway we stopped at Millers and heard Saffers orchestra play, chatted with Hightower and Anderson, who seemed awfully glad to see us.

Wednesday May 16.—1900.

This afternoon we went to town and to the dress makers, had lunch, and then went to see Jessie Jarrauld and Percy Wilson married at Stone Church.

It was a beautiful wedding, she had three brides maids, and was dressed so beautifully in full bridal toilette, and the attendants in full dress.

We went to prayer meeting and the Baptist Church to a concert given by the music club.

Thursday May 17. 1900.

Tonight the general Assembly of Cumberland Church met for the first time, and I hoped that Rev. Wallace would come, but he didn't.

Sunday May 20.—1900.

We went to Cumberland Church this A.M. and I found a lady from Miss. that wanted to go to the Christian Church to hear her old pastor but didnt know the way, so I proffered to show her the way, and I never saw any one appreciate a favor more than she did.

She said if I ever came to Miss. to come to her home, and when she went to leave me she said, "let me kiss that dear sweet face, you have won my heart dear, I want your name, I will never forget you!"

I really didn't think I was doing any thing but my duty, and it came so natural to take her down there, I was surprised at her appreciation.

Gertie told Ma though she never was so surprised than when I did go.

If I have always been careless about little things I must *think* more, and do more for others comfort.

Only five Sundays more till Willard and I will be together! Five weeks from Wednesday until we will be married!

Willard says only a little while until he will take me in his arms every evening when he returns home, and how happy we will be. We have been seperated so much during our courtship, that to be together means much to me.

Sunday May 27.—1900.

One month from today will be our wedding day! And as it is the last one, it will disappear like "mist before the sun."

Had beautiful letters from Lydia, Mayme and Emily, all of whom I had invited to be brides-maids, and they were wild to accept, but it *cost too much!*

I will have only ushers then, and matron.

So many people will be dumb with surprise when the cards appear in a week or so, for they tease me about not marrying, and say they thought Willard and I would be married long ago, and I throw them off.

Thursday I went by the Assembly to tell my friend good bye, Mrs Allin D. Powell, and she came out on the street, met Gertie and talked beautifully to me. Gertie fell in love with her, and if all her good wishes come true I will be happy!

We all went to see Carrie graduate [from high school] for the third time Friday night, and she looked *fine,* and did her part *beautifully.*

She wrote her poem her self, and recited it in her own way, and I was pleased with her in every way.

She fully deserved the large amount of praise she received.

Many compliments have been paid them as a class and individually in the papers.

Friday the girls gave a luncheon to Prof. McLellan, and Prof. McCallin at the Unitarian Church, and notices of that and the exercises, also the pieces in full have been given in the News.

This is a beautiful evening and if this day next month is only as fair, I will not ask for better.

Clarence left for West Tenn. last Sunday and was having a lonely time when he wrote. I am so glad the dear boy is having this chance to visit awhile, and hope they *will make money* soon.

Four more Sundays to spend without my boy! Received the handkerchief from Mrs Thomson today, and it is 25 years old, trimmed with *real* lace, and is pretty indeed.

Farrel says he and the boys want to come next Sunday.

Mr. Anderson and Mr Hightower said they were coming next week.

I have just written Willard 16 pages.

Last Thursday Sis and I went to see Will Hudiburg and he wanted us to sing so we sang hymns to him, and Carlotta said he was happier than he had been in weeks, and wanted us to come back tonight and sing for him, and Gertie and Frank have gone, but I didn't feel that it was justice to my self to go, as I feel so badly, and too there is so much for me to do in the coming days, and I need *all my strength.*

Sunday June 3rd. 1900.

Received a letter from Farrel Friday saying he had decided not to come today in fact it was best for him never to see me again, for to see me and know I so soon belong to another would be more than he could bear!

His letter was certainly pathetic, and yet he tried *so hard* to be brave.

Three more Sundays to be spent away from Willard!

Wednesday June 6.—1900.

All the morning was spent up town with the dress maker, milliner, at the bank and shopping, and tired as we were Gertie and I addressed and stamped 100 invitations, and now I am most dead, guess I wont rest well.

Tonight was the time I had first *thought* we would marry, and it is just a perfectly horrid day, raining so hard.

How we are hoping it will be bright the last week of June!

The Wedding

Thursday June 7.—1900.

All this month it has rained, and it makes us wonder what we would do should it be raining that night, and I tremble to *think* of it even.

If my wedding dress will only be *strictly all right,* and every think is O.K. that night I will be *satisfied.*

Had letter from Willard yesterday afternoon, and he said Mrs Thomson wanted to know what to engrave silver ware, "Madge" or "Marguerite," so I wonder what it is she is going to give us.

Mr Leland said he thought the best thing Willard could do was to marry and get a home of his own.

This wont do for me, I must get to *work.*

Tuesday June 12.—1900.

Well this aft. Gertie and I went to town and we were looking at trunks at Lovemans, and Jacoway and Brewer came up, and Pat and I went to another part of the store, and when I told him I was to be married he was so dumb-founded, and he looked and acted so strangely, that I was amused.

Bernie Loveman came up and was so awfully nice to us, and we had lots of fun. We went to Millers and on the way down Frank handed me the News [*Chattanooga News,* est. 1888], and I read such a nice piece about me I will put it in the Journal, for I will never forget the sensation I had on reading it in cold print the first time. It certainly was a strange experience, and so many congratulated me, and others teased me.

Willard says he has not even thought of being excited and what is more he dont intend to be nervous, but he will, when it comes to him forcibly as it has to me today, that it is not just plans and daydreams, but a *reality,* we are going to stand before people and plight our troth, and as it is in two weeks I think it is time to tremble, and I am. Oh! I do hope that every thing will go off smoothly, and no one will have a reason to ridicule us.

We are so anxious that our wedding will be beautiful! [Margaret had sewn this and the following article into the journal.]

LELAND-SLOAN

The following invitations will be issued this week:
Dr. and Mrs. Rudolphus A. Sloan

request the honour of your pres-
ence at the marriage of
their daughter,
Margaret,
to
Mr. Willard Carridan Leland
Wednesday evening, June twenty-sev-
enth, nineteen hundred,
at eight o'clock,
Centenary Church,
Chattanooga, Tenn.

To the majority of her Chattanooga friends, Miss Sloan's announcement will be a surprise. Her most intimate friends here and elsewhere have known the happy secret, however, for some weeks, and to the fair bride-to-be have come the sweetest expressions from distant friends that the happiness she so truly deserves may be hers in the new ties she will soon form.

Most of her life has been spent in this city, where her womanly charm and attractive beauty have won and held hosts of friends. Aside from personal attractions, Miss Sloan possesses the advantage of fine family connections, being related to some of the best old families of South Carolina and Georgia, through her mother, and her father is descended from distinguished pioneers of the states of Virginia and New York. She has the culture which attends extensive travel and visiting in various portions of the country, and is in every way fitted to adorn the position she will attain through her marriage.

Mr. Leland is the only son and only grand-son of the New York Lelands, one of the most notable families in the financial and social world. He is a young man of superior attainments and education, and entirely unspoiled by the great prospective wealth which is his. He is also closely allied to the California Lelands, who are universally respected in the most influential circles. After their marriage the young couple will reside in Buffalo, where Mr. Leland will have the management of his grand-father's large estate.

The wedding will be free from ostentation, the only attendants being the matron of honor, the bride's sister, Mrs. Frank Hobbs, the best man, Mr. Ed Cureton of Knoxville, and the ushers.

Rev. Alonzo Monk will officiate.

A very informal reception will be given at the home of the bride's parents, on Fairview avenue and Tenth streets.

The Wedding

Mr. and Mrs. Leland will go at once to Asheville, where they will spend three or four weeks. From there they will go to New York, via Savannah and the steamship line, and in New York will meet Mr. Leland's father, who has planned a delightful summer for the young couple. They will take the trip up the Hudson, will visit relatives at Albany and at Attica, a swell home party will be given them during August. Later they will spend some time at the cottage of a relative at Connecticut Beach.

The sincerest good wishes will accompany them as they enter life together and the hope of their friends will be that the entire journey will prove as cloudless and free from care as will the weeks already planned.

Wednesday June 13. 1900.

All the invitations are out this day, all over the country, people are discussing it, and I know it is a surprise.

We went to town this morning and so many jumped me about it.

I saw Mr Anderson and he had a cold miserable look on his face, and he came up and said, "Well I'll say howdy and good bye all at once", and I talked to him some time. He thinks I didn't treat him right not to have told him, he has thrown up his job and is going away.

We saw him just walking the streets, restlessly. I wonder what his reason is for going away.

We found Mrs Pryatt and Pearl here when we came home, also a note from Pat wanting to call tomorrow evening.

Pearl liked to have squeezed me in two, she is so happy that she can come to the reception.

Thursday June. 14.—1900.

We went to see Mrs Wheeler, and she will help us wonderfully, and she is glad I am going to marry Willard.

Had a long talk with Mr Keith, he said he would give any thing to be as happy as I.

Mr. Brewer called tonight, and it seemed funny to have company now, but Willard dont care, and Pat said he didn't know where he was at, he felt so strange, since he knew I was going to marry.

Willard is too sensible to care for me to do any thing I want to, for he has confidence in me, and feels that I wont do any thing, so I could not betray that *trust*.

38

Sunday June. 17.—1900.

The Times did at last give a notice of our wedding this morning much to my surprise.

We had a letter from Clarence yesterday and poor boy, cant come to the wedding, and this causes me so much worry, for I had hoped to see him again.

Had a letter from Farrel and it was lovely, though I feel so badly to think he is taking to so hard.

Willard says the passes have come and he is impatient for the time to come, for he wants me with him.

Mr Wheeler sent me two lillies by Irene this afternoon.

Oh but we were half scared to death last week, when we went for my clothes and could not find the girl, and no one knew her, but she brought them home last night.

Willard said he had to laugh at the write-up, the part about him self but that they didn't half do me justice, he said it didn't half do his little girl justice.

It has rained company this last week, and I look for many more this coming week, but I have so much to do yet, and only a few days in which to do all that must be done.

[*the notice in the* Times]

The following-cards were issued last week:
Dr. and Mrs. Rhudolphus A. Sloan
request the honor of your presence at the
marriage of their daughter
Margaret
to
Mr. Willard Corridan Leland,
Wednesday evening, June twenty-seventh,
nineteen hundred,
at eight o'clock
Centenary Church,
Chattanooga, Tennessee.

Miss Sloan has been the recipient of many felicitations since the cards fluttered through society. Miss Sloan is a very lovely young woman, and the scion of prominent southern families. She is a pretty, talented belle, and she confers her hand upon a splendid young gentleman. Mr. Leland is the only son of Mr. and Mrs.

Leland, of New York, and a kinsman of the well-known California family of the same name. After the marriage he will take his bride to Buffalo, where he has the management of his grand-father's large estate. The attendants at the church will be the bride's sister, Mrs. Hobbs, Mr. E.H. Cureton, of Knoxville, and four ushers. Mrs. Caroline Arnold will preside at the organ. The event is eagerly anticipated by many friends here and in Knoxville.

It has cleared off this aft. and I do hope that the 27th. will be lovely.

Sunday June 24.—1900.

This is my last Sunday at home!

How it has rained all this month and is still coming down just like it never meant to quit again, and I cant think what I will do if it is raining Wednesday evening.

Willard leaves Asheville at 12:20 for Knoxville, and will be here Tuesday morning, and he says he is getting impatient for our marriage to take place, he will be glad to start on his trip to claim me as his darling little wife!

I cant define my feelings, for I am leaving home and loved ones to go with him, and that casts a shadow over the happiness that I experience when I realize that I will *soon see him,* and we wont have to be seperated again, that we really are to be married so soon.

Numbers of congratulations have come the past week, and many callers, and if I am as happy as they all wish me to be, I will indeed be blessed!

Several presents came last week two express packages, and it seemed strange to be receiving wedding gifts.

I wrote to Clarence this morning and tried to cheer him up, and make him feel better about not getting to come home to the wedding. I feel awfully blue over it my self though.

I am nervous over every thing, for fear it wont be managed properly, wont go off all right, and we both are so anxious that it should be *beautiful!*

Oh! the worry we have had over our four dresses! Miss Olliver just botched them up, soiled them, and so much had to be done over after them since we brought them home.

The washer brought my clothes home torn, dinged, and flimsy, after having kept them two weeks, and now I haven't time to get them done properly.

40

I wonder if all brides have this all to contend with?

Mr Leland wrote Willard that he admired "Madge" and wished for us both a life of happiness, and while he couldn't be here the 27th, his whole affections would be centered in Chattanooga and that hence-forth he must not be jealous if part of his fathers love went to a *new found daughter!*

The family will all leave Chatt. for the summer, and Clarence thinks perhaps they will live in Nashville or St. Louis.

Monday June 25.—1900.

Gertrude, Charlie, Mrs Mill and Mrs Wheeler, had been here this afternoon, when Mrs Arnold came, and she said every one was talking about our wedding, there was so much interest in it, and that they all wanted to know when I met him, and where. Said one young man said I was radiantly beautiful since I was engaged. We had supper and came up to light the gas in the parlor, and ran right into Willards arms in the reception hall; I was awfully surprised for I had been looking for him Tues. morning and when Ma came up she found Willards arm around me and Sis, Carrie, and Mrs Arnold were so surprised to find the bridegroom had arrived!

Mrs Arnold played beautifully for me and we practiced at home.

The time draws near, and with *him* I dont care.

Tuesday June 26.—1900.

Willard has been helping me pack my new trunk, and he went to meet Mr Edd Cureton, (his best man,) and we went to practice tonight at Centenary. Mrs Pryatt, Mrs Chester, and Ma, and Pearl, Callie, Gertrude and Carrie, were the spectators.

They all complimented me on being graceful, and said we made a nice looking couple, etc.

We enjoyed it very much indeed.

Thursday June 28.—1900.

"Wednesday June 27th." has passed away! The time that we have been planning and fixing for has come and gone like a bright happy dream!

The first thing I saw on waking was clouds, and occasionally through the day, faint gleams of sun shine would struggle through the clouds, but it rained most of the day, and after I was dressed it thundered and was quite threatening, and I worried my self ill most, wondering how I *could* get to the church and look nice, but when I heard the last carriage drive up, and knew that my Willard had come for me, I ceased to worry, and enjoyed the drive to the church and when we neared the church and heard the music pealing forth, and saw the crowds at windows and doors, I felt I was equal to any thing!

Lloyd Bowers stood by the door and gazed at me, but I didn't move an eye lash, might never have seen him before.

Mrs Arnold struck up the bridal chorus from Lohengrin, the electric lights flashed up, and the march to the altar began.

Maj Charles Evans and Judge Estell, entered from the 8th street, while Judge Garvin, and Mr Harry Chapman entered from McCallie street side, as they crossed over Gertie entered by McCallie entrance, while Pa and I followed, and Willard and Edd came from the South vestibule just as Dr Monk came from the study, and we met at the altar, Pa handing me to him, and taking his place with Ma.

The decorations were beautiful, and I was so at ease I enjoyed it all. We were married with the ring, and after plighting our vows one to the other a thrill of new found happiness entered my heart, as he pronounced us "man and wife in the sight of God."

We knelt together for his blessings and as he assisted us to rise he congratulated us, and Gertie fixed my veil, handed me my flowers and Dr Monk smiled and said "good bye," and I told him "bye bye" and smiled as we turned to leave the altar, and he turned and talked to me all the way out, and we could hear murmers of admiration on each side all the way out the church, and many spoke to me near the rear of the church telling me how lovely I looked etc, and they soon surrounded the carriage, and I *know* no bride ever had nicer things said to her, lovelier wishes made, than I did.

But pleasant as it was our time was so limited that we had to drive away. Mr Brewer said, "I hope you will ever be as happy as you looked tonight." Mrs Mill told Willard that he had won the sweetest girl in Chattanooga, she had known me for years and knew that I was as lovely as sweet as can be, and I couldn't begin to remember all, but after we got to the house all the girls kissed me and said I was beautiful, I was the sweetest bride they ever saw, and Mrs Warner said you was the *grandest* bride I ever saw, you acted your part perfectly, and are so graceful. Gertrude said I said I said [*sic*] "I will," the sweetest she ever heard it. Then they commenced to speak of *my husband,* how nice he was, *handsome,* fine looking, so in love with me, and the time flew, so Willard said we must go change, and I spent that time with Gertie.

We went to the parlor for refreshments and had a jolly time, till time to leave. Ice was white block, with pink heart in center, and we had chocolate, and white cake, bon-bons, and macaroons.

So many sent beautiful flowers to me, and we had them banked in bowls, & vases in parlor, halls, and sitting room, the loveliest bank of pond lillies were on the table in the sitting room.

The gentlemen in full dress, the ladies in reception dresses made a sight not *soon* to be forgotten.

As we drove away from the house, the last time I shall ever be there, it looked gorgeous all ablaze with light, the carriages in front, and many years will pass ere that fades from my memory.

Carlotta came in on train just as the party was taking us to ours, she wished us much happiness.

They all crowded around the train to talk as long as possible, and it made a pretty group, all waving a fare well to us, as the train pulled out.

It made me sad to think that there was no longer a Miss Margaret Sloan, instead of Mrs. Leland.

Mr Edd made me fall in love with my new name very soon though as he says "Mrs Leland" the sweetest I ever heard it.

We got to Knoxville at 1:10 took a carriage for "Flanders," and had a nice room, and it was all so new and Willard left me alone awhile so I feigned sleep when he returned.

He treated me with so much delicacy, and I love him for it. We had breakfast, and I wore my black suit, and as Willard likes it so much, I enjoyed wearing it. Went up to Mr Edds, met Mr Lowry, and all the young men, and they were certainly nice to me.

I bought a black comb, beautiful sun burst pin for stocks [ties worn around the neck], curlers, pins etc. Wrote a note to Mayme, telephoned Pearl and she said they would be down at once, but train time came, and she hadn't.

The Wedding

Mr Edd said a note came for me and he sent it to the hotel, but we had no time to wait, so I think it was from Mayme.

Mr Harry Defenbach took dinner with us, and Mr Cattrell, and Prof. Stein called at the Flanders to see us. Mr Edd gave me a lovely rose when we started, but what he said in parting touched me more than any thing else, I could scarce repress the rising tears.

All day it seemed we were out on a little trip, but I realized that we had indeed begun life in earnest together, and the uncertainty of the future, mingled with a little home sickness, sent a pang to my heart! Willard was so kind and good though, and I felt reassured.

We took a sleeper at Morristown and Willard knew Mr Jones the nice conductor, and he was indeed kind, he fixed chairs on rear of trains so we could enjoy the scenery up that magnificent French Broad river.

I could not describe it if I were to try so I wont attempt it.

We reached Asheville at 6 o'clock and took a car to the place he thought he could get, but she had no vacancies, and we came on to Glen Rock hotel for the night.

I saw a woman astride a horse riding by the car this afternoon.

CHAPTER TWO

$Bliss$

Friday June 29.—1900.

We started out early this morning to find a pleasant place to board, and we saw "The Bonair," [one of many boarding-houses in Asheville for visitors and for victims of tuberculosis, cf. Thomas Wolfe's *Look Homeward, Angel* (1929)] and got off the car, and found her rates high, 56 and 60 dollars per month, so it was so pleasant, I liked the location and all, and we talked it over and she finally let us have a front up stairs room for $40.00 per month, and we are nicely fixed and I think I will be pleased.

Sunday July 1st.—1900.

This our first Sunday of married life we are not together, he went to work this morning.

I have dreaded this time for ever so long, when he would have to leave me and go away for the day. I think the family here, very nice, and the boarders are too. Messrs Bryant stay here, but the handsome one, is *so nice,* he asked to take me to church this morning but for looks sake I went with Mrs McDonald and Miss May to the Methodist church.

Tonight Willard took me to the Baptist church, and I like it fine.

We are very happy together, I hope we will always be so.

Received notice of the wedding in News this aft, and I was surprised at the kind of write up it was, it is entirely different to what I expected, for I didn't think she would dwell on my fairness of face and extremely youthful appearance, and I know that when arrayed in full bridal toilette with veil that I *did* look stately, and as Mrs Warner said twice I was the handsomest bride she had seen, I rather expected the compliments to the bride would be of an entirely different nature. I am sorry I could not see that scene, as every body raved over it so much. The electric light made the church brilliant, and the decorations were handsome, and I know with those fine looking ushers in full dress, and the groom, and best man well dressed with Gertie and I in beautiful gowns, it *was* a lovely scene. The church was crowded and those in the ribbon seats were well dressed, and as I walked down the aisle on Pa's arm I heard murmers on each side, but as Willard and I left the altar together we could hear people complimenting us on every side, and several spoke to me.

[the article in the *News*]

LELAND-SLOAN WEDDING

The Leland-Sloan nuptials at Centenary church last night were attended by a very large audience.

Elaborate decorations of green and white formed three pyramids back of the altar rail. Palms, ferns and begonas were artistically grouped, while the white touch was given by exquisite jasmine. The handsome new decorations and electric lights were very appropriate to the brilliant scene.

The ante-nuptial music, furnished by Mrs. Caroline Arnold, was very lovely. She played selections from Wagner and Schumann and promptly at 8 o'clock the Bridal Chorus from Lohengrin announced the arrival of the hour for the ceremony. The ushers entered in couples, Judge Floyd Estill with Maj. Charles Evans and Mr. Harry E. Chapman with Judge Garvin. They crossed over and took their places facing each other, awaiting the arrival of the remainder of the party.

Mrs. Frank Hobbs, sister of the bride and matron of honor, entered alone, followed by the bride, Miss Margaret Sloan, on the arm of her father, Dr. Rudolphus A. Sloan.

Dr. Monk entered from the study door as the groom, Mr. Willard Carridan Leland, came from the opposite door accompanied by his best man, Mr. Ed Cureton, of Knoxville.

The young lady was given to the man of her choice by her father, and Dr. Monk spoke the words which made them man and wife.

Several of the front seats had been reserved for relatives and special friends, and were closed by ropes of smilax intertwined with rose buds. The bridal party and guests in these seats left the house to the strains of the Mendelssohn wedding march, and were driven to the Sloan residence on Tenth street and Fairview avenue, where a delightful reception was held. It was of the most informal nature, with not a trace of sadness, but only cheer and brightness for the sweet bride to remember as her parting gift from home friends.

The bridal toilet was exquisitely pretty, being of sheerest white organdie over taffeta silk, elegantly fashioned. The gown was en traine, and a tulle veil fell to the hem. Lace and ribbon were combined in trimmings, and rarely beautiful appliqued lace formed the yoke. She carried an arm bouquet of Bride roses and asparagus fern. The costume fully accorded with the sweetly girlish appearance of the fair bride and many charming compliments were heard for her as she passed from the church.

Mrs. Hobbs wore a costume in perfect harmony with her blonde beauty and fairly radiated sunshine at the reception, after sharing the honors with her sister at the church. She wore white silk mousseline elaborately trimmed with silk lace of most delicate texture. A yoke of embroidered chiffon and ribbon trimmings made a notably pretty finish to a handsome gown. She carried Bridesmaid's roses.

Mrs. Sloan was handsomely gowned in black silk with chiffon trimmings; Mrs. Monk wore a becoming costume of black; Mrs. Arnold wore black chiffon, and the other ladies at the reception wore white. They were Misses Carrie Sloan, Pearl Pyott, Gertrude Chester, Hallie Barnes and Mrs. Lon Warner.

The gentlemen were in evening dress, with buttonniers of rosebuds and smilax.

Delicious refreshments were served, after which almost the entire party escorted the young couple to the train, and they left at 10 o'clock for Asheville, N.C.

The bride's going away costume was a stylish white shirt waist and black satin skirt, with daintiest possible accessories, and a becoming turban of black with green and purple trimmings. It was an exceptionally attractive traveling costume.

The presents were very handsome, including elegant cases of silver, many pieces of rare china, cut glass and bric-a-brac.

Mr. Leland, who has won this fair Chattanooga girl, is a young man who impressed all who met him with evidences of true culture and nobility of character. He is very fine-looking, combining dignity of bearing with charming cordialty of manner.

In resigning to him their daughter, Dr. and Mrs. Sloan have no fears for her future happiness, and the young couple have in prospect a sunny future if the fond wishes of their friends will be of any avail.

After a bridal trip, which will extend over two months and include visits to Asheville, New York City and Albany, a trip up the Hudson, a house party at Attica and a stay at the seashore cottage of a relative of the groom, they will reside in Buffalo, where Mr. Leland will manage extensive interests and estates for his grandfather.

The girls all kissed me as I got out of the carriage, and said they wanted to kiss me once more as Miss Margaret, then as they came in home to the reception they all kissed me, and called me "Mrs Leland," and raved over me, said I was so sweet, the *sweetest bride they ever saw!*

Monday July 2nd. 1900.

Mr Bryant is so nice, and he is a great deal of company to me, we sit out on the cool veranda and talk until it seems he is an old friend. He was awfully surprised when he read the notice of our wedding, as he thought we had been married a long time. He told me of his Mothers death, and of his home life, and poor fellow I feel so sorry for him.

Willard took me to Mr Dakes green houses tonight and he was going away, but Mrs Dake invited us in the parlor and we had a very nice chat with her. Asheville is scattered, and has many *beautiful* homes, well kept grounds.

Tuesday July 3.—1900.

Mr Bryant kindly took me up town this morning and helped me shop, and we got to be good friends, he said when I came to dinner that he had spent two hours of lonliness, wished I had staid and talked to him, but I wrote fifteen notes of thanks for gifts received our wedding day.

Miss May played my accompanist at noon, and I sang some of those pieces I cant play my self, I think it will be nice to sing now, and Willard wants me to sing for him.

I got my white parasol mended today. Willard and I sat out in the fine swing chair, and watched the stars twinkling above us, and as the pleasant breezes fanned our cheeks, we talked over our happiness, and I would be happy indeed if I could hear from home.

Wednesday July 4th.—1900.

Have been ill all night and did not go to breakfast, and now I dread to go to dinner.

One week tonight since we married. How different today to last Wednesday. It was cloudy and rainy, and today is clear and bright, then I was awfully excited, today I am *alone,* with no excitement at all.

Willard is doing every thing in his power to make me happy, and he seems afraid he will fail, but I think we will be happy together.

Cant hear from home though, and am uneasy about them, do hope I *can* this afternoon.

Miss May has just been up to see me and brought me a vase of flowers, that was so sweet I thought.

I had hoped that he could get off earlier this afternoon it being a general holiday, but he did not. He brought a letter from Grandma. My foot is getting too sore to wear my shoe, and that will keep me home for awhile I fear.

[notice in the *Times*]

Mr. Ed Cureton who came down from Knoxville yesterday to officiate as best man at the Leland-Sloan wedding, is a very popular young man of that city and met a number of friends and acquaintances here who regretted that he remained so short a time. He returned home last night, going as far as Knoxville with the bridal couple.

Quite a party have come in now teachers on their way to Charleston to attend the Teachers convention, and they are certainly a rough crowd.

Sunday July 8.—1900

This morning I went to church with Mr Hills, and Mrs Williamson, Mrs Dans, and Miss St John of Memphis. After services I introduced my self to Mr Weaver the pastor of Methodist church here, and he said he would call upon me soon.

At dinner I was taken ill and I cant write, I feel too badly.

Bliss

Sunday afternoon Mr McDonald brought my mail to me, and Gertie sent my slippers to me and a note inside, and I got a letter from Gertrude, and a paper from home.

Sis said she wrote to us Saturday a week ago, and I have never heard a word since I left, only her note.

I am wearing my slipper, for my foot is so sore, and I will have to be careful of it. Oh! I suffered all night Sunday night, and feel bad yet, and I was embarrassed the way Mr Rufe Bryant greeted me, he seemed *so pleased* that I was able to be up, said he had been lonely, and every body had missed me while I was ill. Willard is so nice about not being mad because the young men make it pleasant for me during his absence, he knows I love him, prefer his society to any ones, but when he is away I dont like to be *alone*.

Wednesday July 11.—1900.

Two weeks ago tonight since we were married! When Willard came home this evening he brought me Gerties *long lost letter,* and it was *fine!* I certainly would not have lost it for pay for she wrote me so much that was of *intense interest* to me.

The wedding certainly must have been beautiful, from all that has been said by the leading people of the city, and I would not take any thing for it, since it came off so well, and is called *brilliant!*

After all my fears regarding it to feel it was such a success is gratifying. I will write down her letters so that I can remember all that she said of it. She said——

"Every one speaks in the highest praise of the wedding, so many have said it was the prettiest wedding they ever saw, W. G. M. Thomas for one.

Louis & Sara Belle came just as the prayer began, he hated it so that he did not see it *all.*

Mrs Purse & Mrs Burt said it was the tastiest most sensible, yet at the same time the most elegant wedding they ever saw, that all the participants did their part with so much grace, the costumes were in such perfect taste, in fact there was nothing but good breeding and refinement displayed.

Several young men have said that if Pa would lead that youngest daughter of his down the aisle for them as proudly and

50

gracefully for them, as he did you for Willard, that he should *never* want for any thing as long as they had a dollar. One young man just begged to bring about a meeting between he and Carrie, but he said he didn't know her him self."

"We just will not allow our selves to think of the seperation, we plunge right into work to avoid thinking about it. I could have just cried my eyes out Thursday morning when I passed through the rooms, and inhaled the heavy odor of the magnolias, and realized that she for whom all this was done, was *far away,* but I would not allow a tear to fall, went bravely to work to packing the dishes, and singing the wedding march, as it has rung in my head ever since the wedding."

Gertrude & Charley were out the next day, and said their mama had not done a thing but *rave* over "Maggie," the wedding, Mr Leland, etc."

"Ora said Maggie waited a long time but she got a fine man, and had the sweetest wedding she ever saw.

Mr A G Dickey said it was the verdict of all the people at the Southern hotel that it was one of the prettiest weddings ever held in Centenary, so many of the members dont except Irene Elders even, when they say the prettiest.

So many rave over our dresses, and from every source comes nothing but compliments and praise, so we can safely say it was a brilliant wedding.

"Frank said,—*"It was indeed beautiful, I never witnessed a more brilliant wedding, no one could say ought against it!"* "

Clarence wrote home that all day Wed. he thought of *darling Marge,* and to keep from getting too blue, he went with a party to see the high tide.

We have had beautiful evenings ever since the wedding, I was heart sick Thursday it was so pretty, I could not keep saying over and over, "Oh! why could not yesterday be like this?"

But if it had been a pretty night I dont see how we could have gotten in the church. "Mr Huffaker had come home late but as Pa gave him such a nice invitation to come he went *tired* as he was, and as he left the church, he felt he would not *have missed it for any amount of money,* it was the *sweetest, best* wedding he had ever witnessed!"

"Crabtree just raves over it, and regrets *Oh so much,* that he did not act as an attendent *now.*"

She says in closing—

"I hope you will each always fill each others lives, and that the first discord will not arise, may you always be as happy as you were when you rolled away in the carriage from the church Wednesday night."

Affectionately Gertie.

Two letters were handed me at breakfast this morning one from Mother, and one from Grandmother. Ma is over at "Valley Home" [in Bledsoe County near Pikeville, Tenn.] with Grandpa, and I do hope she will rest up and enjoy fully her summer.

Gertrude said she had had strange pains around the region of her heart since rehearsal and asked if I could not send her a *Cure* (ton).

Mr Edd certainly made an impression.

Willard comes home as soon as he can get here after he gets off, in the evenings dresses up, and we enjoy being together so much, some times he says, "Isn't it nice we are together this way, and dont have to seperate?"

He folded me close to his heart and said he had been *just as happy for two weeks, as he had dreamed he would be before we were married,* and says we will *always be sweet hearts, always.*

In the morning he wakes me by taking me in his arms, and kissing me on face, neck, and brow, and it is a happy existence to feel that I am so cherished by the man I have married, for I prize his love far more *now* than before.

Sunday July 15—1900.

I have not written in my Journal since Wednesday for while I am enjoying every day there is nothing startling that I have to record.

Another party of Northern teachers came Wednesday night on their way to Ohio, and Michigan, from the teachers convention in Charleston.

Mr Jerry Tyson of Atlanta is here also, and a funny character too, and he, Miss Daisy Farley, Miss St John, Mr Bryant, Miss Mary Morrison and I have certainly been having a good time.

This morning we went to the Methodist church, and heard the sweetest song, "Heaven will make perfect all imperfect love." The words were *beautiful!*

I found Willard when I came home, and we all had our pictures taken after dinner, and at four o'clock Willard brought a swell turnout [horses and carriage], and took me for a drive, and we both enjoyed it more than any drive we ever took!

We had a rubber tired rig, and a span of horses, and how we did *travel*. We went to Biltmore [Biltmore Estate, built in 1890s by George W. Vanderbilt], way past to the country, then drove by the beautiful Swannanoa river a long distance, and across the mountains, and through valleys, and on Beaucatcher Mt. the view of Asheville is *fine,* reminds me of the view of Chatt. from Valombrosa [Vallambrosa, a picnic area at the base of Signal Mountain]. At times the trees over hung the road so that there was just room for a buggy to pass, and it was so shady, and we could see the clear waters rushing over the rocks, and hear the birds chirping and it was so romantic we kissed as of old when we came to a secluded spot. We ate blackberries, and June apples, rosy and sweet, and enjoyed the fresh air and sweet scenes so much.

This was our first drive since we were married, and we were talking about it this aft. On all our former drives we have been planning for this time always, the time when we were together! We were so happy, and both enjoyed the drive so *very, very much!*

We didn't get home till 8:30, how we enjoyed our freedom, for after we drove so far we could not have been home sooner, and if I had been a young lady they would have made unkind remarks about us, but being married nothing could be said.

We appreciate being together, when we get tired of the crowd at night we can just come to our room, and there are no good byes to be said, he folds me in a long embrace and lulls me to sleep.

Every body was sitting on the veranda when we came home tonight and no one can say he did not treat me as beautifully as any young man could his sweet heart.

Tuesday July 17.—1900.

Mr Jerry Tyson has gone, and it seems like some mischievous, bad boy has gone, but he did not make all the noise, for those of us that are left, have kept the house ringing with music, laughter, and fun making.

I wish Sis was here, she would have a fine chance to be *gay*.

I wrote to Clarence yesterday, rather looked for a letter from Sis and Ma too but nothing came this morning.

Bliss

Three weeks ago tonight we were married and as yet we have had no shadows to come between us, and I sincerely hope we wont have.

Had a letter from Sis this morning and she had lots more to tell of what Mrs Rohr and Mrs Trotter, & others had to say of the wedding, the prettiest, sweetest one ever held in Centenary, the bride was *charming,* the groom *splendid,* he made an impression on every one that saw him, etc, etc.

She dont think she can come to see me and I feel awfully sorry, as I know she is disappointed, and I am too.

Mr Bryant brought me a fine basket of fruit, the nicest peaches I ever saw.

He treats me nicely, and I like him.

Tonight Mr Bryant, Miss Bessie, Willard and I went to Battery Park hotel, and we certainly enjoyed promenading on those verandas, and looking at the visitors from all points of the compass, they were wonderfully and fearfully made, and their manners are very amusing indeed.

It is a beautiful place and it formed a pretty scene to see the gentlemen in full dress, and the ladies in decolette, but some of those swells were gotten up regardless! We sat in the star light and chatted, and had more fun, as we came home, Miss Bessie kept us laughing and Mr Bryant treated us to peaches again.

They had lots to discuss after we came home, so Miss Bessie and I came up and left them talking & laughing.

Thursday July 19.—1900.

Mr Hyott Bryant and Willard & I went to Battery Park hotel tonight, listened to the music and had a good time generally. Miss Bessie had a date with Prof. Barnes.

We have great times here, after we came home we had peaches in my room, and enjoyed it splendidly.

Friday [July] 20.—1900.

Mr Rufe, Willard and I went to Lookout Park tonight to a vaudeville performance and for a change it was *good,* we had some splendid well water and had a jolly time. Mr Bryant treated to cream, and chaperoned us royally.

He is so nice to us, as is his brother too.

54

June–September 1900

Sunday [July] 22—1900.

Miss Bessie and I went to the Central M.E. [Methodist Episcopal] church today, and we had a lovely sermon, Rev. Sharrington of Ohio.

We had planned to go to Biltmore, but it was so dusty, and we are glad we did not.

Willard is late tonight again.

Thursday July 26.—1900.

One month ago tonight we rehearsed for the wedding! Will I *ever forget* the 25th 26th and 27th of June 1900? *Never I know!*

I went to several places this week to see about board, and we went to "Waldheims" last evening and decided to go there, we leave here Saturday, and I rather regret it too, as it has been so pleasant for me and I dont like to change.

All the boarders are sorry we are going to leave soon but they want me to stay till they go too, but the die is cast, I must go now. It is a pleasant place and I hope the people will prove as nice and pleasant as they all have here.

Mr Bryant seems to regret so much that we will leave.

Mrs Patterson told Willard last night that she has fallen in love with me, and didn't see how he could help loving me as he did. They assure me of a good time.

Mrs Beaver, and Miss May are here now and I went driving, with them yesterday and they want to go when I do.

Willard and I are very happy together and are growing nearer to each other day by day. I must write to Ma and not be careless of home folks while we have so much to take up our time with.

Friday July. 27 1900.

One month ago tonight since our sweet wedding, the happiest evening of my life!

I have been sitting by the window looking over the beautiful view, Biltmore gleaming white in the distance, and dreaming of that day one month ago, reliving it all.

We walked up town tonight to see how much I weighed and I weigh 102½ lbs. having gained 2½ lbs in the month I have been married.

This morning Mr Bryant, Bessie Gilland, Mrs Berry, Miss Bessie, Jo St John, May Beaver, and I climbed Beaucatcher Mountain, and not being satisfied with that we crossed to the other side of it, where we found a fine spring, and certainly enjoyed it immensely. But I came home and after dinner I commenced packing my trunks, and so have been on my feet from 3 o'clock this morning till 5 this aft. and I am *awfully tired.*

So that is the way I celebrated, and Willard was late too, so it was very unlike the 27th. of June!

Saturday July—28th. 1900.

I succeeded in moving down this morning and have about gotten straightened up again and I feel that I will enjoy living here, it is lovely!

We went up to the Bonair to get a few of the things I had to leave, and all the people were so glad to see me, and Mr Bryant was so delighted he showed it by shaking hands warmly, and hates to have us leave, it will be lonely.

Sunday July 29th. 1900.

This has been a very happy Sunday. Miss Katherine and I went to the Baptist church this morning and heard a fine sermon, and Mr Bryant came home with me, and Miss Katie had a beau.

Willard was home for dinner, and we were going driving but it rained, so we rested at home, enjoyed being together *so much,* as we have so little time to spend together.

We had a fine dinner and supper, and walked out on the lawn, and sat on the delightful verandas, started to church but it commenced raining again, so we had a pleasant evening at home with Mrs Patterson & Katie. I like them so much.

We have a beautiful room, brussls carpet, white curtains, nice bed room suit, *large* dresser, & mirror, centre table, rockers, and I have fixed it up, until it is beautiful. Then we have a fine dressing room with a bed & washer in there, giving us three windows over looking the grounds.

There are four acres in the lot and the house is large and sits back from the street, with stone walk from the gate to the house, and has a drive way from one side gate to other, up by the door, and bordered on each side by oaks and pines, and the main walk is the same, this with rustic seats and hammocks makes an ideal home, and it is lovely to stroll amid the shadow of the pine.

Monday July—30—1900.

Mr Green, Mrs Bently of Denver, and Miss Howard came this morning to board, and the ladies are swell, and very pretty.

Miss Katherine and I took a glorious drive this afternoon, we had a rubber tired trap with fast horse and, we dressed up, and went through town, and she is so well acquainted out at Vanderbilts place that she showed me so many beautiful drives and lakes, and it is an ideal place.

Seventy five miles of micademized roads [macadamized, a road paved with small, compacted stones], bordered by flowers and shrubs from all over the world, and occasionally at a turn in the road we will drive in dense shade, and the trees and vines are thick while we see a stream at one side and it is certainly romantic. We went quite close to the mansion, it is *grand!*

Built entirely of stone, and is a *castle* of magnificant proportions, and is indeed something to rave over, and I cant find words to express how charmed I was in the entire estate.

We certainly did have a lovely drive, and Katherine told me all about she and "Jack," their case is so similar to ours, and she sees that we have married at last and so takes *heart.*

She is a dear girl and deserves to be happy.

Coming home I met May Bowers face to face, and I have been so happy it was like the serpent in the Garden of Eden, she will destroy my happiness if she can, and she certainly has come for no other reason, that to tell over and over her falsehoods.

I found a letter from Gertie and Clarence, at the Bonair, and all the folks were so glad to see me. Sis has been to Atlanta and had a glorious time, and her letter gave me the blues, for I feel she is being tossed on treacherous waves, and fear her life's happiness will be ship-wrecked.

I came home found Willard sitting by the window, smiling, and glad to see me, I kissed him and he said I looked *sweet as could be,* wanted to know how I enjoyed the drive, and I wished that Gertie was only as fortunate as I am.

Tonight Miss Katherine, Willard & I went up town to see the torch light parade by the Democrats, and Jack was in the band and we saw all the crowd from the house and Miss Bessie said Mr Bryant said that I was the *most charming lady he ever met.*

They all said they missed me so much at the house, and every day they go out some place.

Tuesday July 31.—1900.

We have spent the day, shopping, sleeping and writing, and eating, and have certainly enjoyed fruit and cream today.

Willard came home and asked me if I would like to go to Battery Park [Hotel] to the dance tonight, and I dressed, and with Miss Katherine we went, Jack came up and we had a nice time watching the girls in beautiful dresses, and the ball room is beautiful.

I wrote to Father this afternoon.

Wednesday Aug. 1st. 1900.

Tonight is the musicale and lawn fete given by Miss Katherine.

How rapidly the summer is passing away, I can hardly realize that August has begun, the month that we were to go forth. I am going home soon, but as I have been invited to attend a wedding this month here, I dislike to miss it.

We have arranged the lanterns on the lawn and fixed tables and chairs in cozy nooks, and flowers on the tables and the house is all arranged for the guests, and no doubt they will have a fine time.

Thursday Aug. 2nd. 1900.

Well the garden party and lawn fete and dance was a success!

Willard came home and dressed up, was so handsome, and more like he used to be.

I waited on him at supper, and we fixed the dining room for dancing, and after the guests gathered we sat in the hammock while he smoked his cigar, and we looked at them dancing, and when supper was served he took me, and we sat with Mr Green and Mrs Bentley, and she is a fascinating woman, full of fun and *beautiful!*

58

We retired early and heard them singing some tune but was so surprised when they told me this morning that they danced till 2 o'clock!

There were 24 couples, and it was very nice, the cream was elegant.

Friday Aug. 3.—1900.

Katherine and I went up town this aft. and met Mr Bryant and "Jack," and they went around with us and came home with us. Willard and I went to see how much I weighed after supper and I had on my heavy skirt and weighed 112½ lbs. but I will allow for that and say I weigh 111 lbs. any way.

Just so I am gaining is all I care for.

There was a lawn fete that Jack & Katie wanted us to go to, but we enjoy being with each other more than a crowd, so we came home, and sat in the moon light awhile with Mrs Patterson.

Sunday Aug. - 5.—1900.

Last night Mr Young came to take Katherine for a walk, and he told her I was the sweetest thing he ever saw, I had better watch my husband, for he certainly would do him up, and a lot of such thoughtless talk, but he is a cute boy, and dont mean any harm by his foolishness.

We sang for Mr Hamill and Mr Johnson and Willard to-night, but my boy was sleepy so he retired, and we sang till *late*.

I went to the Baptist church this morning, heard a good sermon, and came home alone, even if I did see Katherine & Jack coming behind. I knew they wanted to be alone, and I would not intrude.

After I waked from my nap Katherine and I went for the mail, and after dinner two young men came in to board, Mr Holland of Augusta Ga, and Mr Ayers of Washington D.C. and in passing their door she said, "I hope I'll get a letter from my true love," and they laughed as long as we could hear.

While at the office she introduced me to Mr John Baird, who sings well and makes girls have nice times, and he said he would come down and sing for me or do any thing I wanted him to.

I got a letter from Pa this afternoon and the day Gertie left he came near dying of cramp colic. Dr Nolen and family and boarders were doing all they could to save his life at 12:30 and she left at 6:12.

Poor father so ill and none of us near him, all away, it hurts me to think of it.

Willard didint get home till late tonight so we did not go to church.

I read him Pa's letter and he was very sorry to hear of his illness, said he wrote a good letter.

Wednesday Aug. 8.—1900.

Monday I was taken ill and Mr Young came down Tuesday and found me not able to be up, so he sent me a dozen and a half white carnations, and his best wishes, and it cheered me up so very much, they are beautiful still.

Katherine said all the boys wanted to know who the young lady was that she chumed with now, and those who know me sent kind messages when she told them I was ill.

Last night our first shadow came to darken our bright path way, and for a while I was intensely sorry I had married him, for I thought he didint love me, and if he should fail to love me life would be ruined, for—I have given up all for him, and life could never be the same again, the old life is gone, and will never return again!

This afternoon he put his arms around me and said, "Darling forgive me for being angry with you last night," and of course I forgave him, after he asked me to, for to apologize for a fault is manly or womanly, and he said he loved me so dearly life without me would be a blank, he loved me more and more as time went by, and I asked him if he would hate to give me up now as much as before we married and he said, *"More, I could not give you up now!"*

Of course the dark clouds that had obscured the sunlight all day, lifted away when we kissed and made up and we have been happy since.

Mr Ayers left for Washington today and he was ill when he left.

Thursday Aug. 9.—1900.

Mr Young came down early this morning and found us in the living room, and we laughed and run on till at last I decided

60

I would learn carams [carroms; a board game developed in 1889, related to pocket billiards, played with wooden rings snapped into play with the forefinger], so we played many games and he stayed for dinner and he, Katherine and I played till time to dress for evening, and I had just taken off my belt and stock [a tie] and ran down to get Katie to mail a card for me, and Mrs Patterson was asleep and she undressed when the bell rang and I answered it and to my embarrassment and surprise there stood Mr *Rufe!*

He wouldint let me dress, made me sit down and talk as he only had a few moments to stay. He acted strangely this afternoon as if he was in trouble, said he might tell me some day what he would not then.

Willard came late and then had to go back tonight and we hated it *so much.*

Katherine is with me tonight, has written to her Jack.

Friday Aug. 10th. 1900.

I waked Willard at ten o'clock and we had a splendid dinner, and were up here teasing each other when Katherine called to me that the carriage was ready. I wore what she likes me to, my pink dress, white hat, white parasol, and Willard and I sat on the back seat and she with the driver, and it was fine to have such a small turnout and have my boy with me too, he enjoyed it so much, and kept looking at me with tenderness in his glance, and I was happy. We drove around Asheville and saw the fine sanitarium at Lookout Park [one of the city's many facilities for the treatment of tuberculosis].

After he came home she took Jack for a drive to Beaumont [Mountain]. We played carams on the cool nice veranda and certainly enjoyed being together, he has been lovely to me all day, after supper he took me in his arms, and told Katherine about our wedding and said he would never have been satisfied if we had married quietly, wouldint take any thing for our *sweet wedding!*

Saturday Aug. 11.—1900.

This morning Willard went to work as usual and came home about nine o'clock and I thought he was fired but he was told to come home and rest as he would have to work tonight,

cease regretting that he failed to see me married, especially since his absence did no good, and he feels blue over the prospect but I do hope he will succeed.

Thursday Aug. 16.—1900.

While in Chatt. I saw Margaret Middleton, Sam Sykes, Ferd Voight, Annie Speck, Mr Anderson, and Mr Corkling that I knew, all glad and surprised to see me.

I came up on the train with Mr Fergusson, Capt. Donaldson, & Judge Pope, and saw Peter Gunter and Rex Kilpatrick at Bridgeport.

The conductor refused to let me off at the crossing, so as Uncle Dave thought I would, he didint go to Lee's to meet me, and I had a *time* getting some one to take me or show me the way to his home, so finally I got Mrs McGarr to take me in her buggy one mile and she asked *20 cents.*

Found them all suffering with sore eyes, and I fear I will have them.

They were delighted to see me.

Friday Aug. 17.—1900.

Victor brought me to Grandpa's this morning and I was awfully glad to see them again, and I received a warm welcome.

Didint find my darling Mother looking as well as I wanted to, but I was glad to see her, Carrie too.

Reeve has taken up with me, and Harry is so sweet and pretty. Aunt Mollie and Carrie have gone to town this afternoon. The place seems changed it is so long since I was here, and I miss Aunt Lula too. So I find I am not contented as I used to be.

Saturday Aug. 18.—1900.

Carrie and I went to town this afternoon and I met Mrs Byerly and Miss Ida, & Mr Charlie Fergusson, Farrel's cousin.

We were disappointed about mail, but Carrie told me all the lovely things said of the wedding, and we enjoyed the drive.

Thursday Aug 23.—1900.

I have been gone ten days and havint heard a word from Willard, no doubt there is one from him at the [post] office, but no one has been there this week, and I am wild to hear.

Since dinner I begged for the buggy, and they let me have it, and I took Ma to town, found letters from Pa, Fannie, Gertie, and my darling. I felt better as soon as I saw the envelope, and he misses me more than he had any idea he would, and wants me with him all the time.

Gertie is coming tonight, but as the creek has to be forded, and it is dangerous after night, we wont see her till morning.

Sunday night the hotel where Pa and Clarence stay was on fire, and Clarence waked Pa by putting his hand on his arm and telling him not to be excited, the house was on fire but they would get out alright and he dressed and took his best suit down stairs, met severel who had started up after him, knowing he was ill, and directly he saw Clarence was not there, and he started up after him, met him coming down steps with his trunk and telescope, having cooly collected all their belongings, and had it burned, the only thing that would have been lost was a tie of Pa's. The fire was checked however. Clarence is a brave, dear boy, and I feel that Pa is in good hands.

Ma and I drove slowly through the country roads, and talked confidentially of many things, and I feel that many times I will wish I could see her to talk in this way after I leave this time.

Friday Aug. 24—1900.

Aunt Mollie, Uncle Will, and children went to spend the day with Mrs Byerly, and Aunt Hallie brought Gertie over, and we were all glad to see her of course.

This afternoon we went down to the creek and climbed over the rocks and cliffs as we used to do in the long ago.

How many memories those familiar scenes recalled, I saw the famile-retreat of mine where I used to go to read "Phils" ardent love letters, and where I would answer them too. It made me sad to see how Ma thought of her happy child hood days as she found the sight of her old play house and many things that carried her back to the time where she knew no heart aches or had no cares.

Sunday Aug. 26.—1900.

We dressed early this morning to see our guests Mr & Mrs Charlie Fergusson, Mr and Mrs De Grieff, Mrs Byerly and Miss

Ida, and they came about eleven, and Miss Ida brought me a letter from Willard that made me glad yet gave me the blues too. He has resigned his position, and we wont live in Asheville any more, and he said for me to meet him in Chatt. the middle or last of this week, and so I will have to leave Ma and all sooner than I want to, and Gertie wont get her visit out, as she insists on going back when I do.

I want to see my darling again, and he says I never will leave him again, he is miserable without me, and says all he wants is to have me with him, and be able to make me perfectly happy, for he loves me better and better as time goes by.

He says my visit away from has taught him as nothing else could, how dear I am to him, and how blank his life would be had he not won me.

The dinner was simply elegant, and served beautifully, and Aunt Mollie certainly deserves credit, few hotels ever set such a dinner no matter what they charge.

Mrs Ferguson invited us to spend the day with her Tuesday.

Aunt Hallie and Uncle Dave came over this afternoon and we are going to spend Tuesday night with them.

Tuesday Aug. 28—1900.

Well this morning Ma, & I, and Gertie & Carrie drove to Pikeville and spent the day with Mrs Ferguson, who entertained us royally.

Mr & Mrs De Grieff were there, and this aft. we had a group made, Ma, Gertie, Carrie and I. Mr Myers argued with Mr Charlie Ferguson that Gertie was better looking than I, but he was loyal to me.

We came on to Uncle Daves tonight, and what a nice supper she did have for us.

Wednesday. Aug.-29.—1900.

This morning Gertie and I drove to town and I got the letter from Willard saying for me to meet him in Knoxville Friday, so we drove home to Grandpa's and I packed my trunk, and Aunt Mollie was so sorry we were going. We didint get to leave till late, and Uncle Will helped us to the creek, and then I forded it, but I was awfully scared, the water came into the

66

buggy most. Grandpa had been spending the day, and by the time we got there, he had to leave, so we didint get to be with him much.

His parting with me was touching, he took me in his arms and said, "God bless you my child, and keep you safe." I felt that I would never see him again, *Grand old man.*

Since supper we all went to the big spring, fine water, and lovely view.

We saw where my Great, great Grandfather is buried. We leave in the morning so I will stay with Ma all I can.

Thursday Aug. 30.—1900. Chatt.

Gertie and I drove in a hurry to Lee station this morning, and then had to wait some time, and I was sorry I hadint stayed longer with Ma and Carrie, for I did hate to say good bye, and not know when I would see them again, or what would happen before we met again, some way I feel that there will be much trouble or sorrow come to us before we meet again, but I must not think of it or I wont be contented while away.

Ma threw herself into my arms and wept bitterly at parting, poor Mother I know she will be sad now that we are gone.

We had company down on the train, and found Pa at the depot, and looking very much better than when I left here before.

Tonight Pa and Clarence took supper with us, and we had a table to our selves, and a very pleasant time, we appreciated Gerties thoughtfulness, in planning this little reunion. They didint stay long, and I was getting ready to retire, when Mrs Miller came to the door and said, "Mrs Lelands brother wants to see her," and I went in and found *Patsy* [William], as innocent and nice as ever, and as handsome.

What he said of our wedding was the *sweetest* I have heard, it made such an impression on him, he said he didint need a picture of it, it was impressed on his brain, and he could close his eyes and see it all over again any time.

He was in the ribbon seats and felt so happy that he was fortunate enough to be so near to that sacred, beautiful place, and he felt that he was in Heaven as we knelt at the altar, for a blessing.

He spoke beautifully of it, said he had feared he would not like my husbands looks but he *did very much,* and he hoped I would be happy.

He took Gertie, Frank and I to get cream, and he left soon.

Mr Harry Bayer was quite nice to me, and he and Gertie have been cutting at each other all the day, and I laughing at them.

Friday Aug. 31.—1900.—Knoxville.

I reached here at 8:40, found Willard at the depot to meet me, and he seemed *so glad,* and I know I was delighted to see him. He has been telling me often since I came how glad he is to see me back, to have me with him again.

We are at the "Arcade hotel," and it seems strange that after three years we should have our wish gratified.

When I was here that memorable summer we came up with Gertie and Frank to see rooms here and every thing was so clean and pretty, Willard and I felt we would be as happy as could be if we only could be married and board here and now we have one of the very rooms we were looking at then, and are together for life! How I hated to tell all of them good bye today, Clarence this noon, and Willie, Gertie and Pa came to the depot with me, and they hated to have me leave as much as I hated to leave them. It was harder for them to see me go this time than when I left the night I was married. Gertie and I went to the photographers (Mudge's) at ten o'clock this morning, and we got through at 12 o'clock, and then Will, Pa, and Clarence joined us and we had a group made, which I hope will be *good,* for we cant tell when we will all be together again.

We saw Ethel Allin, on the way to the train, and she said my wedding was the prettiest she ever saw, and that I was as high headed as ever, lots of other "opinions" that she airs freely always.

Sam Barden Russell shook hands and he asked who the fortunate man was and extended his heartiest wishes for my best happiness in my new life.

Mr Taylor, (Alta Sheltons ex beau), came up on the train with me to Knoxville.

Saturday Sept. 1st. 1900.

We leave in the morning at one oclock for Washington, Mr Edd Cureton ate supper with us, and was nice in his farewell remarks to us, as he always is.

We walked out after supper, saw Mr & Mrs Querry, Prof & Mrs Garratt, and (black) Tom Davis, and Edd Goetz. *Never see Goodie* any more.

We fear today has been unlucky for us, of course we hope not.

Monday Sept. 3—1900.— Washington

We had written to friends at Asheville to meet us and when I went to bed Saturday night when we left Knoxville I told Willard to be sure to wake me in time to dress for Asheville, and I kept waking him to see if it was time to dress, but when I did wake, I found it awfully light, and on investigation found we were this side of Asheville, coming down the mountain like something possessed, and I felt so sorry I had missed them. Willard held me up in his arms, and we watched the fine scenery from the sleeper window. We got to Salisbury [North Carolina] at 9:42—and had a long hot journey, but we took another sleeper from there on to Washington.

We ate breakfast in cafe car, and dinner in dining car, supper here.

We got here at 8:10 last night and came right to the National hotel, the largest in Wash. and on Pennsylvania Ave. *the* avenue of the city, so wide and the moon was shining so the white buildings on either side of the Ave. looked lovely.

I took sick last night at 12 o'clock and have been in my room all day, only since supper we walked around some, and I think it *beautiful!*

Tuesday Sept. 4.—1900.

This morning we went to the Southern R.R. offices, found Mr Raymond Ayre, who tried to get off to show us around, but couldint, as he was off yesterday, but he said he would call for us tonight, so we went to the Navy yard, had a guide that took us through, and I found it quite interesting, saw three guns that are to be used on the "Maine," two on the "Oregon". Saw the place where the models for ships are tested before they are built, also the old building where ships were made during the Civil War.

Mr Ayre called at eight o'clock, took us to meet his Mother, whom we found very nice indeed, then he and Miss Brewer and

Willard and I went to "Glen Echo" and "Cabin Johns" [in Maryland], the two prettiest resorts I ever saw, both beautiful, yet *unlike*. A stone wall surrounds Glen Echo, and there is a pavilion, theatre, lake with a bridge to the centre where stands a summer house where the band plays, and there are thousands of electric lights in artistic designs in every direction, making it *fairy land*. There is a lane down hill, with cliffs, and rustic bridges over streams, and nooks of all kinds all lighted, and I raved over it all the time.

We went to the boat house, and Willard rowed us up the canal, and the moon was bright, and it was ideal for this little trip, we all sang as we floated along and the way was *too short*.

"Cabin Johns" is gorgeous too, elegant hotel pavilion, merry-go-round, and Scenic rail way, and we certainly had a fine time on that. Miss Brewer screamed until I hurt my self laughing nearly.

It is lots of fun, and the bridge over from grounds to waiting station is a beauty, it is long and brilliantly lighted.

I got my feet wet, by my skirt being wet in the boat and I feel chilly.

Willard has gone for something now for me to take to counter act the cold.

Wednesday Sept. 5.—1900.

This morning we went to the "White" house, only saw one room (east), it has many velvet parlor pieces, three immense chandiliers, fine carpet, and mirrors from ceiling to floor, gilt framed, with more than life sized pictures in oil of Washington, Jefferson, etc, between them.

The grounds are beautiful, trees, flowers, fountains, and drive ways, the park back of mansion is very much prettier than in front, and the conservatory is *lovely*. At the east entrance there is a basin of pond lillies all shades, and over the iron fence and gate there are vines like cover Grandpa's porch.

There are so many parks, we have seen all well kept, and all the Government buildings are immense, handsome ones, imposing entrances, and pretty grounds, especially the State, War, and Navy department. Executive Ave is beautiful.

This afternoon we went down the Potomac river to Mt Vernon and Marshall Hall, on the steamer, saw old fort Washington, weather stained and over grown with ivy, very picturesque indeed.

The barracks are on the river side too nice quarters. We saw the church where Washington worshiped in Alexander, and as we came in sight of Mt Vernon, his birth place and tomb, the bell tolled till we landed, and it was quite impressive. Marshall Hall is beautiful, everything there to make a complete resort, yet it was deserted today most.

We got back at 6:12 had supper and Mr Raymond Ayre, Mr Edwin Ayre, and Misses Price of Philadelphia, & Brewer of Washington came for us and we went to the Capitol and the Congressional Library the most superb sight I ever saw, and I *cant* think of attempting to describe it for I never could, one must see to appreciate. It is built of white marble with a polish like glass, and different scenes sillouhetted on the ceiling and in niches in the walls, all illuminated with electric lights, and it is *gloriously beautiful!*

It cost 6 1/2 million dollars to build it, and took ten years to build, from 1889 to 1899.

I feel that I have seen the finest building to be seen in America, and that with the Capitol and grounds, with marble court around it wide enough for a company of men to walk abreast, with entrances wide enough for a regiment to walk and never break ranks in ascending the steps, is enough to pay any one for going, rather coming to Washington. Besides all the other sights.

I like Miss Mary Brewer so much, she is a pretty stylish girl, and was lovely to me, she kissed me good bye, and hoped I would not be ill from getting my feet wet last evening.

We leave in the morning on a Niagara excursion at eight o'clock, and I will retire.

Friday Sept. 7.—1900.

We left Washington yesterday morning at 8 o'clock, reached Baltimore at 9:15 where a bridal couple came on and sat right across from us, and they furnished amusement for those back of them all the way. Quite a nice young man was sitting in front of me, and in the afternoon he began to talk to us, and continued till we all got off at Buffalo, he was going to his old home too. We walked around a little at Williamsport Pa where we stopped

for dinner, and it is quite pretty. By the time we got to Rochester I didint want to get off and stay with the Geers, neither did
I want to go to the Falls, all I wanted was to get here where I
could *rest,* so we came to Buffalo, and caught the midnight
train, and got here at 1 o'clock [the Thomson home near Attica,
N.Y.]. They had been looking for us severel days, as some mail
had come for me Tuesday, but not at that hour, and when
Grandma opened the door, she said, "Why Willard Leland, I'm
so glad to see you," and she hugged and kissed him, then me,
and directly here come Grandpa, and he danced for joy at seeing
Willard, and seemed delighted to see me too. I have been ill all
day, took breakfast in bed, but got up to dinner and severel have
called, Aunt Laura, and Eva came as soon as they heard we
were here, and I like them, especially Aunt Eva, who looks
young and is so cordial and vivacious. She had a lovely grey coat
suit, and white hat.

CHAPTER THREE

Shadows

Saturday Sept. 8.—1900.

Mrs Skinner and Mrs Putnam called this aft. and when Willard entered the room and shook hands with them I felt proud of him, he was so easy, and treated them so cordially.

Mrs Farnsworth came from Lockport for a visit. She is a cousin of Grandpa's, and strange too their fathers were named *Spring* [also the maiden name of Margaret's mother].

I got the proofs of pictures taken in my wedding dress, and they are *good* I think.

Sunday Sept. 9th. 1900.

Willard and I went to church with them this morning, and after services held a regular reception, met every one that was worth knowing, they were all glad to see Willard and to see me it seemed.

Tuesday Sept. 11.—1900.

Grandparents, Mrs Farnsworth, Willard and I were invited to dinner this evening at Aunt Eva's and she had a nice spread, and I felt like eating the first time since I came.

We enjoyed the evening very much indeed, and I like Aunt Eva, better than ever, she said, "let me kiss that sweet cheek," and she showed so plainly that she liked me, and I have fallen in love with her.

Shadows

Yesterday morning Willard and I got out in the back yard and the sun was warm, and we got to eating grapes and throwing hulls at each other and I chased him all over the garden, yard and orchard, and havint had such a romp in years, rather enjoyed being rough for this once, had an appetite for dinner too.

This morning we picked hopps, and this aft. we went driving, went to the Gulf and way out through the country, saw Stevens beautiful country home, and lots of sugar groves, and we came into the main road leading to Attica way south of here, and that gave us a *long* nice ride, got home at six o'clock.

Willard picked up a half bushel of butternuts from trees by the road side, and we enjoyed the drive *fine,* but I always do.

Sunday Sept. 16—1900.

We went to the Presbyterian church this morning and to the Baptist tonight, met severel new ones but I cant remember names.

We went to dinner with Aunt Eva & Laura, Willard went for the mail, Aunt Laura stayed to Sunday school, and Aunt Eva, came home with me, and how kind she was to me, she got magazines, papers and books for me to read while she was getting dinner, and set an easy chair for me, put a foot stool under my feet, a pillow in the back of chair, and gave me a shawl for fear I would be cool.

I told her she was kind and she said "Why shouldint I be, when I have such a sweet niece? I think Willard a fortunate boy to have won such a bride!"

When an Auntie will say that, it is proof sufficient that she likes one, and I do think so much of her. She prepared a very nice dinner and we did full justice too.

I have been quite blue severel days last week, only broke down and cried once though and Grand Ma was so kind to me, she put her arms around me and tried to cheer me up, and I tried to keep Willard from knowing it but he found it out when he came home. It is cold as December here today, and so gloomy, bleak as mid winter. I heard from Fannie, Ma, & Gertie last week and felt better for hearing of course. They hated to have me leave this time more than before.

September–December 1900

Willard went to Batavia this morning at 8 o'clock and I am going at ten this A.M. Had a letter from Pa last night and he is rejoiced to *think* that I am happy and that Willard is so good to me, and loves me so well. Well I want them to think it for nothing can help me now and they need not be unhappy because I am.

Monday Sept. 24. — 1900.

It was a fine thing that we went to the fair Wednesday for it was an ideal day, and the rest of the time was *awful!*

Willard and Mr Decot met me at the train and Mr and Mrs Thomas went with me from Attica, so we stayed together all day.

We went to Hotel Richmond and waited till they were "treated" and returned it, then they returned with a carriage for us and we drove to the fair grounds, and it was fairly good, the display was small but very creditable I guess.

Dont come up to Southern displays though. We got dinner in the dining hall, after the awfullest struggling through an immense crowd, and had a very good dinner, then we went to the grand stand, secured fine seats and enjoyed the races *fine.*

That was the only enjoyable part of the day, and they gave vaudeville between races that was welcome, as it filled up the gap, amused us, any thing to keep from *thinking.* We left at 5:30 went to Hotel expecting to find some one to meet us, and Willard ushered me into the waiting room and I sat there in darkness for two hours, and after looking in vain for him to return he came *at last,* and said he had been right at the hotel all the time.

We went to Arthurs and they had only gotten home from the grounds, and soon as supper was over he took us in his fine trap to Uncle Henrys and they had all retired but Aunt Julia got up and showed us to our room, and next morning it was raining and did all day so that I couldint get out any where, and oh! dear such a *visit* we had there, only saw the ladies at meal times and as they passed through the room, and when I went into the kitchen to think I would help them, things were in such confusion and so many clattering around I would go crazy, so I stayed out, and was *glad* when Friday afternoon Willard said we were going else where.

One of the boys took us to Uncle Johns and we found Aunt Nell waiting to see us, and she met us talking and she was talking the last I saw of her when we left Sunday aft. But while she talked of family troubles, and at times I was weary of it, yet *that* was a relief to the other places.

The drive way has maples a mile each way, on either side of the home, and the lot is surrounded by spruce pines, and there are lots of trees and shrubs in the yard and the walk down to the well is beautiful so quiet and shady.

Willard and Arthur drove to town Sat. and Sunday we four went to the Baptist church, a very pretty church, and I met her sister Mrs Potter of Batavia.

After dinner Arthur drove us over to Fred Fago's and his wife Grace treated us nicely and I like them better than any of the name. Warren and Jessie came in awhile and she was awfully sorry she didint get to be with me more at Uncle Henrys, and regretted that she wasint keeping house so she could have us with her awhile. Gave us a cordial invitation to visit her as we passed through going South.

We drove in Monday afternoon and up to the Blind Institute, and the grounds are *beautiful*. We called on Mrs Gardner an old school mate of Willards on Washington Ave, did some shopping took the 7 o'clock train and came home unexpectedly.

I must make a waist tomorrow, we have a new machine.

Thursday Sept. 27.—1900.

Three months ago today we were married! Willard left early this morning for Buffalo and Grand-pa, Grand-ma, and I go to Rochester at 8 o'clock this morning, and he will be there tonight.

Wednesday Oct. 3—1900.

We got to Rochester at 10 o'clock, and Maurice Geer was there to meet us, and he said at once, "Where is the other one?" and when we reached their home on Brown St Mrs Geer said, "Where is Willard?"

He came down on the Empire state [on the New York Central Railroad] at 2:15 but didint come home till Maurice did, they went out on the oil car for a ride and stayed till late.

Feeling naturally home sick, and among strangers I wanted him to come home so much, and when at last he *did* come he seemed so distant, and didint retire till after he thought me asleep, and so that day that we had been married *three months,*

76

we were not together one bit, and he seemed to care so little for me that I tossed and felt that my heart was *breaking,* and I know full well that had I dreamed that so soon Willard would not *care* whether I was happy or not and when I pleaded with him to be more kind, to me, he turned a deaf ear, and was even more inconsiderate, had I only known that this would be the state of affairs before three months were up, the good people of Chatt. would never have had the Leland-Sloan wedding to discuss. Little did I think this possible and I pray God to help me to bear this the *bitterest disappointment of my life!*

If he dont ever mean to make me any more happy than now *my life is ruined.*

Grandpa and Grandma came home and we stayed from Friday till Tues. after they left.

Friday morning we all went up town and I enjoyed seeing Sibley Linsley & Curr large establishment [a department store], and that was the only place I did get to go.

I took sick Sunday morning, and had a hard nervous chill late in the evening and they gave me whiskey and seem to have a lot of fun over it.

I like them both very much indeed, am sorry I was too *miserable* to be natural.

When we came home we found lots of mail, I have letters from Fannie, Gertie, Ma, Katherine P., visiting cards came and an invitation to the Rock Band concert Saturday evening at the Baptist church.

Aunt Lula is engaged and says he is far superior to Barney Thomson, and I dont know whether they will marry out there or he will come to Tenn. for her, and I am quite anxious to hear too.

I only hope she will be happy, better a thousand times to remain single if she wont be. The big Masonic fair commenced Monday and I am sorry Ma and Carrie cant be there, for Gertie will have a big time and could make Carrie have too. I would give much to be there *my self!* Aunt Eva and Miss Manning called this evening and Mrs J. R. Bailey this aft.

Thursday—. *Oct. 4.—1900.*

This morning Grand pa and Grand ma drove to Batavia to see Uncle Henry and Uncle John, and we have been "keeping house alone", and it seems odd too.

Shadows

The first day I ever kept house for Willard, was not in our own home.

He seems more like him self today and yesterday, but I fear that *never again* will the same sweet joy that was ours so short a time return.

I could cry my eyes out in longing for that happiness, but it would not gain it for me, and to greive as I am only injures my health, and so I must try to be brave.

Since supper we walked to town, and the moon was beautiful, and I hoped that it would reawaken in his breast some remembrances of happy days gone by, and it may have for he seemed more attentive and broached the subject him self of our changed relations, and he thinks *I* am changed too. That is just what I have been fighting against all this time, I know that *coldness* and *neglect* from him will turn my love to hate, because I loved and trusted him so fully, believed that he would always love me above all else and think of my happiness first, and if he *did* this, then *I* would live for his pleasure, exert my self to make him happy, and he gave me every reason to expect lovely treatment at his hands, and when he is so different and I ask him to be more considerate, and he pays no attention to my pleading, when it reverses my nature, brings out the worst that is in me, and I feel resentful, and love dies within my heart.

Oh! if we both can only be as we were at first and stay constant and live up to the vows that we made at the altar in the presence of all those witnesses, and God him self! It is a solemn, awful thing, to allow any thing to come between us to cause us to waver in our purpose to be *true till death do us part!*

He goes to Buffalo in the morning at seven o'clock and then I will be alone till they return, and I dont fancy it in the least either.

Sunday Oct. 7.—1900.

Friday afternoon while Willard was in Buffalo Grandma and I called, paid nine [visits] that I owed.

Willard came home on the 7 o'clock train and we went down to Miss Kathie Eastmans an old school mate of Willards, and after we retired that night and he had told me he was going to Buffalo Sunday to commence work, I felt so blue and unhappy,

78

yet had come to the conclusion that he did not care whether I was happy or not, and though I felt so miserable I didint feel that I need tell him and expect sympathy, so as he told me good bye, wanted to sleep, I could control my self no longer, and I began to weep, and that of course brought on a long controversy, and it seems a shame to think that we who loved each other so devotedly, went through so much for each others sake before marriage, should *so soon* have had such thoughts, but thank Heaven we loved each other too well to commit such a sin, and allow little misunderstandings to come between us, and at last we found we loved each other, and meant to be happy yet. He said, "I love you as well as I ever did, you are as precious to me as ever," and then feeling that he did, all my tender feelings for him returned, and I slept in his arms happier than I had been for many days.

Yesterday he was more like him self and we romped and teased all day. I helped him pack his grip, and get ready, but how I hated to have him leave me. I put off the sorrow for today though, and last night we all went to the Baptist church to hear the famous Rock Band concert, which was very good.

I thought my boy looked handsomer than he has in some time, and I was happier I know.

I wore my white hat, and pink dress, and it was moon-light and warm, we walked home in it and I hope he loved me as I did him. I went with him to the train this morning at 10:25, and *never hated* to see any one leave as badly in my life before!

Afterwards we went to church and I felt so blue I could hardly keep from crying.

This afternoon I went over to Aunt Eva's and felt better as soon as I saw her, and we were having a nice chat while Aunt Laura was getting supper, when Grandpa came over for me with rubbers, parasol, mackintosh, and after it began to rain in aft. I intended to stay all night, but when he came for me so well prepared my good excuse was gone, so I came home. The only reason I wanted to stay was that they had prepared supper for me, and seemed to want me to stay, and they cant have me just any time.

Oh! how will I stand to have Willard away all that time? He dont intend coming home for two weeks yet, and it seems a long time since morning.

Shadows

Well Mrs Farnsworth left this morning and I will have to stay up stairs all alone tonight the first time yet, and yet I wont mind it like I would have Sunday night.

I had a letter from Willard this morning and would have been awfully disappointed if I hadint. He says he misses me, and when he goes home in the evenings he finds no one to meet him, and gets so lonely he dont know what to do. I am glad he misses me. Glad that I am necessary to his happiness, but sorry that he is lonely, for I want him to be happy.

Had another letter from Gertie, and they are uneasy about us, having failed to hear for over three weeks, but they have heard by now. Carrie has been with her since the Fair begun, and is having a glorious time. Gertie says she is popular and does as well as an old society belle could.

If Willard was with me and as sweet and lovely as when we were sweet hearts I would not feel this regret that all my good times as a young lady are over *forever!*

While in Asheville I did not care if I could not have other company, or that life was so changed for me, and if we only will fill each others lives, and live up to our *promises one to the other,* I wont regret it now.

His absence is hard to bear, it seems that I am alone, with no one to love me, or want to make me happy, a state I was never in before, for I have had love wasted on me by as fine men as ever lived on Earth!

Farrel and Mr Rankin were at Chattanooga last Sunday, and the first thing he said was "How is Margaret"? and he said to feel that I was happy, was all that kept him able to bear it, and when people taunted him about losing interest in Chatt. he told them he felt it an *"honor* to be even jilted by such a girl."

The girls are having such grand times, and Gertie is popular as Chairman of committee.

I trust she will get the prize for most popular one, a cut glass salad dish.

We called on Dr Young this aft. and rubbered [looked] around the city awhile.

Yesterday afternoon we went to the Cemetary to see Willards Mothers grave, and I did feel so tenderly for him as I stood above her mound, and thought of my boy having lost his Mother so young, and I want to make up to him all he lost in her.

How thankful I am my darling Mother is living, how I pray both she and Pa may be spared to us many years.

Mrs Loomis, Mrs Smith, and Mrs Lee, called while we were away.

Today was opening day at all the millenary shops, and cloak stores. We went down, but I had a spell with my heart before I started that makes me feel badly.

Willard has been gone a week in the morning and how I do *hope* he will come home tonight. I wont give him up till after the nine o'clock train comes tonight.

Sunday Oct. 14.—1900.

Willard *did* come last night, and how I did enjoy his visit, even though it was so fleeting. After the train came I sat with my watch and timed it, and after he had had time to come and didint, I then looked for him on the nine o'clock train but we took Mrs Baccus to the train and was disappointed again, so I sat up till after ten o'clock when Grandpa returned from the political meeting without a letter or him either and I retired with a heavy heart.

At 2 o'clock I heard him try my door and say, "Let me in hon," and I was so glad he came, but felt hurt that he preferred going to the theatre instead of being with me. He seemed happy to be with me after he *did* come, called me "precious," and petted me, and I stilled the sickening doubts that arose at once in my heart, for they are enemies to *love and peace.*

We went to church and I wore my new hat, Willard liked it, and that made me like it better, he said it reminded him of Gertie. After dinner he asked me if I wanted to take a drive and I *did* of course, so we went to "Chestnut knoll," and the day was *perfect,* and we enjoyed the ride so much, were happier than we have been in some time. He has promised if I die up here to take me to "Forest Hill" [cemetery where Margaret's parents would eventually be buried] in Chatt. to bury and I am glad I mentioned it when I did for we none of us know what will happen any moment, and I want to be laid to rest in the dear old Southland.

We drove all afternoon and he was so much more like he used to be that I took fresh hope that all would yet be well when we get to our selves and can be closely associated together, and how earnestly I do trust we may live for each other, and keep our vows always.

I took him to the train at 6:35 and did hate to have him leave so much, I went to the B.Y.P.U. [Baptist Young People's Union] and church too, they came to come home with me.

Monday Oct. 22—1900.

Mrs Hall came at 1:30 and took me driving and we drove till 5 o'clock, went everywhere, and all over town, and the afternoon was fine, of course I enjoyed the drive of yesterday with my sweet heart far more, but appreciated this very much.

She says we will go again when it is nice.

Had been wanting to go to Post office when Aunt Eva called for me, and we went up town and always enjoy being together.

I went home with her and she gave me a basket of grapes, and came home with me, she is so sweet to me I love her.

Heard from Cousin Ethie, they are all coming up next Sunday.

Tuesday Oct. 23.—1900.

Grandma and I went calling this afternoon, returned Mrs Smiths, Mrs Dorrance, Mrs Barrons and Mrs Loomis' calls, and it was so perfectly beautiful that I wore my blue silk. Oh! yes we returned the brides call to Mrs Folles.

Thursday Oct. 25—1900.

Aunt Laura went to Rochester today and Aunt Eva wants me to stay with her till her return, and tonight we went to prayer meeting and as I hadint heard from my boy this week we came by home afterwards and sure enough there was a letter for me from him, disappointingly short, but he said as the Geers were coming he would be up as usual Saturday evening, and I will think that is the reason he didint write more.

But by the same mail I heard from Ethie and they have postponed their visit till two weeks, so I have written Willard a card telling him they wont be here and I feel that he wont come now.

It is just as well they will wait two weeks for neither of us feel well this week.

Friday Oct. 26.—1900.

We got up this morning intending to be real smart and make a dress or waist and we went to get it but could find nothing nice enough, so I wrote to Buffalo for samples—and then having no work to do I suggested a drive, and she gladly assented, so we got Grandmas buggy and had an elegant drive to Alexander and the hills, wheat fields and autumnal tints make a beautiful picture, and we are *close friends,* this new Aunt of mine she read me a letter from her old lover and we talked of many things.

Came home at five o'clock, went to depot to meet Aunt Laura at 7 o'clock and had a fine supper when we all got home and it is raining so I cant go home tonight.

Mrs Ed. Skinner, Mrs Norton, Mrs Stone, and Miss May Barrons called while we were out dining so Grandma told us when we took the horse back.

Had a letter from Gertie, she was ahead in the contest for most popular chairman in the Masonic Fair, and Mrs Riddells husband gave $20.00 worth of votes the second night for her, so she got it, a silk velvet couch, only valued at $40.00.

Carrie is having a glorious time, going to theatre and having so many fellows, and I *know* how awfully happy a girl can be when she has so many admirers, and feels all the time that she is *loved dearly.*

Well I had all the attentions and love that any girl could care for, and it is not intended that any of us should have nothing but pleasure, I'll try to be satisfied.

Sunday Oct. 28.—1900.

Four months ago last night we were married, and a happier couple never stood at an altar and plighted their troth!

Only one "27" of these four have we been together, the 27*th.* of July in Asheville at the Bonair, we spent that Anniversary with each other, and I know that neither of us dreamed of being separated this way before we were married, for we used to feel that when we were married we would be together, talked of the cruel separation and were happy in the thought of being with each other after marriage.

The 27*th*. of Aug. I was at Grandpas with Ma, Carrie, and Gertie, yet was sorry that I had to be away from my husband *that day*. The 27*th*. of Sept. Willard went to Buffalo, we to Rochester, he was with Maurice till after I had retired some time.

The 27*th*. of Oct. he was in Depew [a town adjacent to Buffalo, N.Y.], I at Aunt Eva's ill. Yesterday was just about such a day as our wedding day, rainy, dark, cloudy and *blue*. Today is like *his day* the following one, *bright*, beautiful, and a promise to him of *happiness*.

Well I want him to be happy.

Aunt Eva is a fine nurse, and just treats me lovely, and she has helped me to pass this day that I dreaded because Willard would not be home, and I find that time will pass whether we are happy or not.

I have finished, "The Phantom Future," [*The Phantom Future* (1888) by Hugh S. Scott] and together we have read, "The Gates Ajar" [*Gates Ajar* (1868) by E. S. P. Ward] today. We had boiled chestnuts, and a cozy chat this afternoon, and I am feeling better so will go home tonight.

Monday Oct. 29.—1900.

This is another beautiful day, too pretty to stay in doors. I must write to Gertie today.

Grandma and I are both sick and not able to do much.

Another week to begin without having seen the man that I left all those that were dear to me for, and a weary one it will be since I am away from all that is dear to me.

Though treated very kindly by all here, I cant avoid being lonely, and unhappy.

Since supper Grandpa brought me a letter from my boy written Friday evening, as soon as he got my card, and he felt hurt that I did not write a letter said he thought his sweet heart might spare her husband more time, write him a letter, so that he might have something to cheer him while he was working that I might have all the comforts of life.

Said he *did love me,* wanted to be with me all he possibly could, and he thinks he is having the worst of it, works all day, eats supper and spends his evenings alone in the hotel office with no one he cares to associate with, while I am in a good home with those that love me.

He said, "Darling I want to provide for you in the best possible way, want you to have all you want this winter no matter what it costs, or how much I go without."

I shall not allow him to do that, for I love him too dearly for that.

Midnight, have finished a letter to him 12 pages of Southern railway paper, and I think he will feel differently about it when he gets it Tuesday on his return from work, bless his heart I hope it will cheer him.

Tuesday Oct. 30.—1900.

I got Willards letter off this morning and hope it will cheer him up tonight.

It has rained all day, and has been a gloomy, dark day, and if I had failed to get his letter last night I would have been blue, but it helped me wonderfully.

I want to hear from him soon, see how he liked my letter, if it helped him, do hope he will come back Saturday night.

Thursday Nov. 1st.—1900.

Grandpa went to town and brought me a letter from Willard, it was loving, but he misconstrued my meaning in one sentence and felt very unhappy over it, seeing how he would feel if he took it that way, I wrote him a long, *sweet,* letter, and have taken it to mail my self, in order that he get it Friday on his return from work.

I have been to prayer meeting with Aunt Eva and took supper with her too, I do enjoy going over there.

Saturday Nov. 3rd. 1900.

Am very busy over the plan of altaring a waist, have walked to Aunt Eva's twice, to town and am certainly tired.

Although Willard has not said he would come tonight, I am looking for him, and should he fail to come I would be very much disappointed.

I came home from Aunt Eva's, dressed, and arranged my hair, and am looking for my sweet-heart, just the same as I did this time last year, and I will sing and play till he comes as of yore.

Shadows

Well after the 7:20 train passed last night, I listened to every foot step, at last I heard him at the dining room door, and I rushed out to meet him and he caught me in his arms and how happy we both were to be together again for it has been as long since we saw each other as it was when I went home this summer. We have exchanged two loving letters this week and were happy last night and today.

He kissed and caressed me called me his "darling little baby," his precious little darling, and I asked him if he was happy and he said, "Yes, Pet, why shouldint I be with such a sweet little girl as you?"

While he was asleep he kept me folded in his arms, and he kissed me over and over, I could not sleep, but he did, like a child, but I was pleased to have him pet me even in sleep.

In one letter he said, "If I only had you with me these lonely evenings I would ask for nothing else, for I love you dearer than ever," again—"Darling I want to provide for you in the very best possible style, I certainly want you to have every thing this winter that you want."

Now all these things make me love him oh! so much, and we are both planning to have a fine time this winter in Buffalo, and I am anxious to go. We went to church this morning and I wore my blue silk and collarette, and was warm enough. This afternoon we went to Aunt Evas and they did exert themselves to entertain us.

Tonight I took Willard to the train, and it is a *glorious* night, the moon light is fine and the bare trees surrounding each house forms pictures, so varied, yet very attractive, and we enjoyed the walk to the train, it was only marred by the thought that soon we would be seperated for another week, but able to be brave at the thought of being together so soon again.

He says, "We were perfectly happy while in Asheville and I dont see any reason why we should not be in Buffalo," and I hope we will be too. I think we will be.

If we had been in Buffalo today he said we would have gone to Cleveland, could have gone for $1.00 round trip, and I regret that we missed it.

And after our happy little visit together I am *alone* and he is too, poor dear, he says it is like jail to him, he has the worst of it, has *no one* he cares for at all.

September–December 1900

Monday Nov. 5.—1900.

Had a letter from Ma this afternoon, and Gertie tonight. Carrie is still having a good time, is wearing Mr Morfords diamond ring and they like each other fine, and Mr Shoemaker does too, he is going to room with them this winter.

I hope the child will have a good time. And poor dear Sis, the girl that has done so much for every one else, is unhappy and at times nearly wild, had a spell when she wrote this letter to me, and I do wish I could do something to help her, wish I could make her happy.

I think Ma can go home soon, and I hope they will get a house in town and they can all have gay times this winter. Aunt Lula is coming home, is there by now I guess, has fallen out with her fellow.

I had intended attending the Monday Club [a literary discussion group] tonight with Aunt Eva but it commenced to blow and looked so threatening, that although I was ready when she called for me I didnit go.

Tuesday Nov. 6—1900.—"Election Day."

Last night I retired feeling awfully lonely and some one waked me by trying the door and I was awfully scared, and he said, "It is Willard", so I opened the door, and was awfully glad that I was *home* instead of spending the night out as I meant to. Was awfully glad to have him with me. This morning we went to get my black skirt and found it had been in the express office nearly a month sent to C. H. Leonard.

It has drawn up till I shall only be able to use it for a walking skirt.

Grandma is cleaning house so he helped me all day, wiped and put away the dishes for me both meals and swept the floors, and then we felt sleepy so we went to our room and took a nice nap that both enjoyed.

I started to take him to the train but when he found it was sprinkling he told me not to go.

Wednesday Nov. 7.—1900.

I was sewing over at Aunt Evas today when the paper came saying that McKinley [William McKinley (1843–1901), twenty-fifth president of the U.S.] was reelected by startling majority, and so as it *had* to be that way I am *glad it is over!*

Friday Nov. 9.—1900.

Have been over to Aunt Eva's till tonight and have finished my bias waist, and begun my skirt, but as Mrs Geer is coming tonight I had to lay aside my sewing for awhile. Last night Mr Childs came for me to go to choir practice, and Grandpa saw that he was so anxious to have me, he went over to Aunt Evas for me, and so I went, and tomorrow night we practice again.

The table looks real nice and every thing is ready for our guests.

Had a letter from Mrs E. M. Kilpatrick, and it did me good, she is married and Katie is home, and she wished I was there, she did miss me so much after I left, and they so often talk of us, and she thinks Willard is a noble man. Said very few were invited to the wedding, but if I had been there I would have been there. It gave me the blues for I do love Asheville and fear I will *never* like the North half as well.

Had a letter from Willard and some one has stolen his watch, chain, derby, and coat.

Monday Nov. 12.—1900.

Saturday night at 7 o'clock Maurice came and we were all at supper when Willard came, and he and Maurice went to get him a derby, and Ethie and I to practice.

Sunday we were the last to get to church and I went on to the front to sing. Willard wore his dress shirt and did look so handsome. I was real proud of him, with blue tie, cut away coat all black suit he was nice looking.

While singing I didint dare to look at him or Maurice either for they tease me so much about my being "funny" after they gave me whiskey.

We had dinner at three o'clock and then the boys wanted to make butter scotch, and they did, but before it was made Mr & Mrs Hall called for Willard and I, and they stayed quite awhile, so that this left us very little time to all be together. It came time to say good bye to Willard so soon, and we went to church, and I sang again, but this was my last Sunday here.

They left this morning at 8:15 for home, and Aunt Eva sent for me to come over prepared to spend the night and go to the Monday Club with them, so I will go and do all the sewing I can for this week is short and I go Saturday. The first snow we had was Thursday night Nov. *8th*.

Wednesday Nov. 14.—1900.

My! what a snow storm we have had this aft. and it is still coming down, and I was up at the North window and to see the large apple trees in the orchard covered with snow, all the ground white, and the trees by the house, are loaded with it and the branches lap forming an arch far more beautiful than marble.

Monday evening we went to the club at Miss Belle Barretts, and had a very nice time. Miss Madge Seymour, Mr Wring, Aunt Eva and I were together most. He is very nice, and there is to be a japanese tea at Presbyterian church Friday evening and we will go if it doesint storm. There were so many young people and the readers all did well, it was very enjoyable. King Richard *3rd.* is their study.

I was presented to quite a number, and after we got home we had cake and crackers, and it was after twelve before I went to sleep.

Last night Grandma and I went to Miss Athertons to the Authors Club [a literary discussion group], and I like the play, "Macbeth" better than the others study, but there are not as many members and the dont read as well as the other. Mrs Norton and Mrs James Dourance both were especially nice to me.

Every body seems sorry that I am going away, they want me in so many things.

Had a letter from Willard this morning, he is uneasy about me, wants me with him, and that I will be soon now.

Tonight we were going to the social at Baptist church, but it was too awfully bad, and I did mean to call this afternoon but such a snow storm came up we couldint.

Tomorrow half the month is gone and how soon Christmas will be here, and I havint any thing made yet.

Friday Nov. 16—1900.

We heard yesterday that Elmar Fargo is dead, and Grandma is awfully grieved over it, she wants to go to the funerel but Grandpa is ill and she may have to miss it. Aunt Eva wanted to take me to the Japanese tea tonight, but I have sewed all day and feel so tired, so she stayed with us awhile tonight.

Had a letter from Gertie and Pa is ill, has a cold settled on his lungs, and I am worried over that, then Ma isint home and so much else that keeps me blue.

Sunday Nov. 18.—1900.

Yesterday morning I packed three trunks, cleaned my room nicely, and after dinner, Aunt Eva came over and I was to go to supper with her in case they went to the funerel and they didint so she seemed disappointed. She cried and kissed me over and over in telling me good bye.

She has been so kind and good to me and I will miss her up here.

Grandma took me to the train, and when they called out Lancaster I felt like Willard would be there, and sure enough he was, he got on and I soon found that he had taken a bad cold, and he said he had been almost dead all week.

We came right to our boarding place, "Waldemar", and the parlors, hall, and dinning hall are *beautiful,* but our room is so *small,* that when the folding bed is down there is hardly room to turn in, and the bed is *awful,* but I may get used to it after awhile.

This morning Willard and I walked out a great deal, down Main and over on the west side, Delaware Ave, and since dinner we went to see Formine Blauvelt & wife, and they invited us out Wednesday evening. It rained hard as we came home, but we enjoyed walking out there, seeing all the sights. Since supper we have been in the parlors, met the boarders, listened to songs and instrumental selections from Prof. Healey and Miss Whitman.

Mr McHarrn mesmerized severel and had them amuse us.

There are severel pleasant people here. It rained too hard to go to church.

Wednesday Nov. 21.—1900.

Monday and Tuesday were rainy, dreary days and I never felt as lonely and as "caged" in my life, dull in doors, too awful to get out, and nothing to interest one. I turned to "Beautys Daughters," by the Duchess [*Beauty's Daughters* (1880) by Margaret Argles] for amusement, and I have read the Nov. "Ladies Home Journel" through. I wish I had some good books to read here.

If Farrel only knew this what nice reading I would have!

Monday evening we were invited to a concert, and this evening we were, but Sunday we promised to go see Formine Blauvelt & wife.

My, such a gale as has been blowing all day, and I could hardly stand, couldint if Willard hadint held me and we only had a little distance each way to walk from the cars. They were all dressed up and we had three games of pedro [a card game derived from auction pitch], Willard and Mrs Blauvelt winning best two out of 3.

Mrs Blauvelt is quite pretty and had on a beautiful waist. They seem to love each other very devotedly, something I admire so much when I see it.

We were treated to some splendid pop corn, and indeed had a very pleasant time.

The men at the N.Y. Central [railroad] struck this morning.

Thursday Nov. 22.—1900.

This morning I went up town and got a pair of heavy extension sole shoes [high heel shoes], a thing I never intended wearing but maybe, I will get accustomed to them in time.

Also one of those little round camels hair stitched felt hats, and a beautiful blue military waist and I have dressed up in my short skirt, felt hat, military waist and high shoes, and I think I look like another girl and Willard says I look like a kid this way, and I rather like it as it does away with that matronly look.

The young man that waited on me to shoes, was very nice indeed, and he took me for a young lady and in fact all my bundles came marked "Miss Leland".

Oh! there are so many beautiful things I do want so much up town, and to think of how happy I could make my loved ones, if I only had money enough to get some of these beauties.

Had a letter from Gertie and they are going to take a house on McCallie Ave, opposite the school house, and Frank and Gertie, Mr & Mrs Shoemaker, (the match Gertie is said to have made,) are to board with them.

Clarence is in Birmingham at work, and I will be awfully glad if they do get to a pleasant home, where they can be happy again, and I will be happier to think of them at *home* together.

Pa is very delicate like a baby Sis says. She said when she read that Howard Coontz was dead she thought how fortunate I was to have my soldier boy alive and happy with him, while Bernie had only spent four happy weeks with her husband and now he is dead in a foreign land, and had been severel weeks before she knew it. Ah! yes I am very fortunate indeed. Poor child will never get over it! This might have been Willards fate too had he gone.

Carrie has gone to Jasper for severel weeks to visit Lillie who is going to Huntsville after Christmas with Ras who is in business there now.

Havint heard from Ma in *so long.*

Friday Nov. 23.—1900.

Willard has been going morning, afternoon, and he even must go out *tonight,* and as I am *tired to death* of this place through the day, I *must* have some excitement in the evening, and so I was "one of the girls," tonight. I chatted Mr Farrel, and Mr Kelly Michly, and he played for me and I sang some for them, and spent a very *lively* evening.

When Willard came in he said the men had won every thing they asked for.

Saturday, Nov. 24.—1900.

After dinner I bathed and put on my dressing saque and was taking life easy when Louise brought A. W. Leland's card up, said he was waiting for me in the parlor, and when I went down he said, *"My daughter,"* and folded me in his arms and kissed me twice, seemed awfully glad to see me, and we had a delightful visit, then he went up town and I told Willard that a young man had called and I asked him to supper, and he seemed moody and I couldint get him to hurry at all, but *at last* he was ready and I led him into the back parlor, where he found not the impudent young man, but *his Father,* who embraced him and they kissed each other, and Willard was all smiles at sup-

92

per. I was glad to see them so pleased with each other it having been 25 months since they parted here in Buffalo, Willard an invalid going to rejoin his regiment after a months sick leave [in Anniston, Alabama, where he was mustered out on January 31, 1899], and of course they didint know what the exposure and camp life would do for him in that weak state, so to see him well and strong looking, must have made a Fathers heart happy.

Willard went to the train with him, and it is snowing hard.

Sunday Nov. 25.—1900.

Still snowing and too awfully sloppy for us to get out. This morning Willard stayed up in our rooms with me and teased a good deal, and then took a nap, since dinner we sat in the parlor till almost supper, and as soon as supper was over I came up stairs, and Willard went in the parlor, it is most eight and he is still down there.

Pity people couldint always be sweet-hearts.

Monday Nov. 26.—1900.

Five months ago tonight we rehearsed for our wedding, and how happy we thought we were going to be, and we planned and dreamed of the time we would be together all the time! But we see very little of each that is not among a lot of entire strangers, no sweet confidential chats in our own room, no evenings of reading together, and being *alone* together, like I thought it would be.

It is snowing awfully hard, has been all day, and every tree and house is white, and still it is coming down like it had only begun to fall.

I have been talking to Mr Farrel, both Mr Healey's, and Mr Bissle since dinner.

Willard was more lively tonight than usual and nearly all the boarders had engagements, so Mrs Turner, and Mrs Healey were with us in the parlor, and I sang severel pieces and Mr McCaphery came down specially to listen. Said he heard a new voice in the parlor, and came down to enjoy it.

Willard said he would wash my face in snow and I managed to get a handful and I rubbed his face with it, but he made me pay for that, he held me and put it up my nose and my face feels *raw*. But still it was fun, chasing him around.

Tuesday Nov. 27.—1900.

Five months ago today since we married!

When I waked I found the sun shining so brightly, and after breakfast I walked to town and way up Main, and saw some elegant sleighs and fine horses, and many of the windows are beautiful, arranged with the dining table filled with china cut glass, and *beautiful things*.

I walked till I got cold and came home. Mr Farrel and I both wanted to read, "In the palace of the King," [*In the Palace of the King* (1900) by Francis Marion Crawford] and I came up after dinner and read till Miss Healey came about 4:30, then Willard took me for a nice ~~eard~~ walk up Main and of course I enjoyed it far more than this morning, as we admired things together.

He went to Lodge [Benevolent and Protective Order of Elks] at 8 o'clock, and I have finished the book since he left.

It is 12:15 and he is just coming!

Wednesday Nov. 28.—1900.

Willard thought he might be home today and we would go to Attica at 5 o'clock, but he didint come, I am ready to go when he comes, oh! how I wish I was going home to see my loved ones. Gertie is going to have Pa take dinner with her tomorrow.

Friday Nov. 30.—1900.

We went down on the 9 o'clock train Wednesday evening and Edith Eastman came and spoke to us on the train, and she and Willard had not seen each other in years, and they used to play together when children.

Father met us at the train with umbrellas, and mackintosh, and seemed happy to have us come. He came over early Thanksgiving morning and I had been sick all night and had breakfast in bed, and by *will* power I got up and dressed and stayed up all day. Was awfully glad to see my Aunties, and Aunt Eva wanted me all to her self for a cozy chat and I promised to spend the day with her today, but it snowed and was too bad for me to go out feeling as misirable as I did, so I didint get to see her alone at all.

We had a very nice dinner and lots of fun, Father offered his arm to me, and Willard followed with Aunt Eva, and Grandpa with Aunt Laura, and Father paid lots of attention to me, that seemed to please Aunt Eva.

We dined at ~~five~~ two o'clock and they left at five, then we went to see Edith Eastman & I got worse and retired early and Grandma and Willard went to see Miss Miller at Grace Johnsons, and stayed till after ten, and I was *alone* suffering awfully, but I cant believe Willard thought how heartless it was for him to leave me so or that he would have gone if I had asked him to stay with me, but I felt hurt to think he would go away. Father came after they left, and waited till late for him, but left before they returned.

Willard went to Batavia on the eight o'clock train, and Father came over morning, afternoon and evening to see if he came back, looked for him at eleven, 2, and 6:20, and he came at 6:20 and we left, at 7:20. He said he could get a position with the Harvester Works [Johnson Harvester Works, largely owned by the E. G. Richards family of Chattanooga] at $2.25 for two weeks, then get 2.50 with a chance of foremans position at $3.00 per day. We are going the 15*th.* of Dec. and I do hate the idea so much.

Do wish we could stay here during the hollidays, hear the grand music, but then Willard says he wouldint stay here any way, he would go home, so if we had to go to that old dead town, it dont matter much.

Heard from Ma & Aunt Lula today, the letter was at the office so I got it while there. Poor Aunt Lula is so unhappy!

How well I remember last Thanksgiving. Aunt Lula and I went to C.P. [Central Presbyterian] church, Mrs Arnold took supper with us, and the first trouble with the Halls occured.

I knew Willard and I would be married this time, so I sat and dreamed of it all, wondered where we would be, and while I have been very happy part of these two days I cant get over his leaving me alone when ill. I know he would have denied that he ever would do so, had I asked him if he would, before we married, this hurts me awfully.

Every body at the house seemed glad to see us back.

Shadows

Saturday Dec. 1st. 1900.

Willard took me up to the Chippewa market tonight and it certainly is a *sight* worth seeing, such an immense affair!

Everything nice any one would care for was there. We saw the lightening artist in the window of J. N. Adams store painting beautiful oil paintings while we watched, and it is *wonderful.* We walked down to the harbor, saw some large boats, lots of tugs, and Willard said we couldint be down there if we were not married. We had a very nice time.

Sunday Dec. 2nd. 1900.

This morning I went to Grace Methodist church and they greeted me cordially, introduced me to the pastor, and if I stayed here I would have no trouble getting acquainted there if I wished to.

Willard and Mr King went to the Lehigh Valley engine works, and Mr Farrel came home with me, and we teased Willard about it, told him I went to church, had company too.

He took me to Lake Front this afternoon and I saw the Erie Canal, Niagra river, and Lake Erie. Front Ave is pretty, and the park and boulevard is fine, and I know in summer it is perfectly ideal there, the view is *grand,* can see Canada plainly.

We went around the west side on cars, and I have a very good idea of Buffalo now I think, it is quite pretty, some elegant homes, nearly all good sized substantial ones.

We intended going to church tonight but we were both so tired we stayed home. Miss Margaret Whitman and I sang some together and some solos and had quite a musicale. Willard and Miss Johnson flirted openly, and Mr Farrel and I kept up with them. Had lots of fun, and the evening passed very pleasantly indeed. Christmas is nearly here and nothing made.

Monday Dec. 3.—1900.

This is a beautiful day, and I wrote to Ma and Gertie and took the letters up and mailed them, went all up and down Main St., looked through the principal stores, and I find very few things that I could send to Chatt. and am in despair as to what to send Lila & Willie.

Willard & Miss Nellie Whitman, and Mr Farrel and I played pedro till eleven tonight, and Mr Farrel & I beat them, but it was the most exciting game out!

Saturday Dec. 8.—1900.

Each evening has been spent in reading or listening to music, or joking every body in the crowd, some times we have very good times.

This afternoon Mr Healey, Miss Margaret and I went to a concert at some music hall, and it was *fine.* Miss Lapey one of the finest singers in Buffalo was the soloist, and the Prof. played numbers of lovely pieces on the aeolian [a musical device that prolongs vibrations of sound by forcing air over the piano strings] attached to square grand and the pipe organ, among them Lohengrins *glorious wedding march,* and I closed my eyes and saw again that beautifully lighted church, the crowd, and seemed to feel my self leaning on Fathers arm going slowly down to the altar where my big handsome bridegroom was advancing to meet me, feeling I was giving my life into the keeping of a man that adored me, and would do all in his power to keep sorrow from entering my heart!

How beautiful the dream, but I awake suddenly, the music has ceased,—I am in Buffalo, among strangers, far from *home* the *dream is o'er!*

After the concert Miss Whitman made some calls and we came back together, and Main St was crowded, people doing Christmas shopping and the windows are lovely, we watched it all as we came home. He treated to hot chocolate and there we watched the constant stream of passers by and I wondered how many of those restless beings were *happy?*

Tonight Willard took me to the public library and Miss Nellie Whitman was nice to show us around, and it is a nice one. We strolled around sight seeing some time.

Sunday Dec. 9.—1900

This morning I brought Willards breakfast to him and let him sleep, so we didint go to church, and every body complained of it being so cold that we sat in the parlor and enjoyed the music etc. till late then we walked around a few blocks and oh my, but I nearly froze. I ached when I got in.

Shadows

Tonight we went to the Delaware Ave Methodist church and while it was cold going over, I dont regret going at all, for the music was fine, quartette of artists, sang two anthems, and had a bass solo, "Trust in God and He will give you heavenly Peace." And the sermon was *masterful.* I would enjoy hearing him twice each Sunday, and regret that I have to leave. He paid a high tribute to Gen. Rob. E. Lee, and won me on the spot, his broadness.

We had a nice walk home, it was cold but the wind didint bother us, and he talked all the way, and I think we did well to go to church tonight, he enjoyed the singing and sermon too.

Monday Dec. 10.—1990.

Mrs Whitman is such an interesting talker and we have had some nice chats together.

Tonight we have been talking, she told me of a girl that married an ardent lover and how cold and heartless he became in less than a year and wrecked her life!

Why are men that way, dont care for her after they are married, just the time they should care *most,* when she has *lost all that is dear to her for love of him.*

Thursday Dec. 13.—1900.

Last night Mrs Turner, Misses Nellie and Margaret Whitman, and Willard and I went to the Star theatre to see Viola Allen in "In the palace of the King," and without a doubt it was the *finest play I ever saw.* Willard was as much carried away with it as I was, he has raved over it ever since.

She is a perfect actress and has a wonderful support, every one takes their parts fine, and it is exciting, and thrilling *all* the way through, every move they make is of interest and it is one grand "climax" all the time.

"Dona Dolores De Mendoza" is before us all the evening and she is certainly *superb.*

She loses Don John of Austria's brother to King Phillip of Spain, and he comes home a conquering hero, the idol of all *Spain,* and he loves Dolores, and she him, but her father knows it is against the Kings wishes so he opposes it, tells her she must not recognize Don John when he comes before the throng who are singing his praises, and yet she and her sister Inez are in the balcony when he walks into view the idol of all, and as he

98

passes beneath where she stands she throws a white rose which he stoops and picks up and kisses and that calls attention to her, and her father who is Capt. of the guards sees it too, and is enraged with her.

After they all leave he slips back to her and they are *glorious* in that meeting, she says she finds him the *same,* and it is as natural their joy at the reunion as can be. The Princess Eleoli loves him too and wants to make him King, but she determines to rid him of Dolores, and she tells her Father when he has her locked up until he can send her to a convent, to trust her to her care, she will keep her safe so he calls her and gives her over to the Princess, but she fears her, and when she goes to throw a veil on she puts her mantle & veil on Inez, and since the door is ordered opened to the Princess she is in such haste to get her to her rooms, she never guesses she has the wrong girl, and Dolores escapes by the same door.

She goes to Don Johns apartments, warns him of her Father who swears to kill him if he enters their door, and knowing that danger threatens on every side he knows his only chance to save her is in keeping her in his own room over night, till they can flee together and they are to be married *tomorrow* she says and dances & laughs in her joy of being his very own, and she says, "I love him, and will marry him without feeling ashamed even if he is a brother of the King." This was so funny her manner.

Then the King comes to quarrel with his brother and tells him he shall marry Inez of Scotts, and insults Dolores name.

Quick as a flash Don John grasps his sword, but as quickly drops it, remembering his promise to *her* not to raise a hand against the King, just then the Cardinal comes in to defend Dolores name and the King stabs him and while Don John leans over his dead friend, the King tells him he is the murderer, that he is found dead in his room, and tells him he is to tell the world that he is the murderer, but he says, "I will not," then he tells him what will follow to him if he fails to shoulder the guilt, and he still says, "*I did not,*" then he says Dolores shall be bound and tortured and says now who killed the Cardinal? and with pale face and drawn lips he says "I did," and he leads him off to be held prisoner till executed, while she has seen all standing behind the curtains to his bed, she staggers out and falls prone to the floor.

The King goes to the throne room, and tells them to dance, and directly she comes in and he bids her dance, and she can hardly stand from excitement, so the King receives word from the Captain of the guards that Don John has killed the Cardinal, and when they bring Don John in he looks pale but unflinching, and she tells him she retracts her request to defend himself against the King, but he is silent, and the King follows him out, then Dolores steps upon the throne steps and tells them that Don John is innocent, she was there when the Cardinal was killed, she was behind his bed curtains, (and there is derisive laughter from the ladies of the court,) and she heard nothing for she has the full attention of the men, and she pictures to them the hero, dying a martyrs death, an innocent man, and she gets them ready to free him or die, then she goes to the King.

The Princess is with him flattering and the King tells her there is a plot to kill him and enthrone Don John, and she says "only rumors your majesty," but the "Fool" hands him the paper that she had written to Don John setting forth her plans, and he calls her "traitress," and dismisses her from the court.

Then Dolores comes in and she is grand in her dealings with him, she tells him she saw him murder the Cardinal, and she will tell the world unless he write and sign Don Johns release, which he seems to decline to do but knowing she holds his life in her hands he does this, and thinking to trap her he wants her to go over to his desk to get it, but she says, "no you come here," and she stands with her hand on the door, and gets it, hands it to her men out side.

The Cardinal is brought in and confronts the King and to keep him silent he has to promise to give his consent to the marriage of Dolores & Don John, which he does before the entire court to the chagrin of the ladies who have tried to say he never loved her, and to the delight of her friends. Oh! it was magnificint.

Thursday Dec. 13—continued.

I am all packed up, Willard helped me to pack both trunks, then we went up town and I got me material for a coat suit, and we both got gloves, and it is the coldest night I ever saw most, the wind is terrific and we were glad to get home.

Willard went up town since supper and we have had some fun since he came back, and we leave in the morning at eight ten o'clock.

Friday Dec. 14.—1900.

Well here we are in Buffalo still!

We were all ready to leave this morning and we sent for Mr Heley to pay our board, and when he looked for his money it was *gone* and he grew paler and paler as the awful truth dawned on us that *his pockets had been picked,* and the thief had $20.00 and we were *stranded!*

He explained it to Mr Heley and then went up town and I settled my self till morning knowing we would not get away today.

Father came up about five o'clock in response to a telegram Willard sent for money, to see what the matter was, and he seemed awfully sorry for us, paid our bill, gave Willard money and left at 6:12 for Attica. We had told them good bye and as they came in one at a time at noon and saw us here, they seemed awfully glad and surprised too.

Well tonight Mrs Whitman, Misses Nellie and Margaret, Mrs Johnson & Miss Helen, Mr Farrel, and Willard & I have had the jolliest time, laugh? why my cheeks are tired. Helen and Willard flirted and all the rest trying to keep them from it, and to get even Mr Farrel and I would flirt too.

Then the English girl marries tomorrow and the prospective bridegroom came to the house this aft. and while they were at supper, Farrel & Willard talked so they could hear yet pretended not to mean them to, and as they passed the parlor going up stairs they were awfully embarrassed, both laughing.

They all took on so at having to give us up, said every time a couple came that they liked they left, and Mrs Whitman took me in her lap like a child and talked to me in parting. All kissed me, and at eleven o'clock we came up stairs. Guess we will go in the morning.

CHAPTER FOUR

Interlude

Saturday Dec. 15.—1900.

Mr Bissell was all the one to see us off this morning in Buffalo. It was cold and when we reached here we found fine sleighing, lots more snow than up there.

We went to Jessies for dinner and supper, secured board at "The Columbia," with Miss Jackson and came to our new home at nine o'clock. Art Fargo and wife have parted and he is back home, and she is in Buffalo.

Every thing is beautiful in snow, and Batavia is lovely, residence portions.

It seems odd to think of Batavia being our *home* now, for I *never liked it*.

Monday Dec. 17.—1900.

Yesterday morning Willard and I went to church and afterwards walked way out to edge of town, came home, had a very nice dinner, and when we went to our room the gas was awful and I coughed and my head ached perfectly *awful*. I went to bed, and knowing Willard wished me to get out doors. I tried to dress to go to church, but I was so ill I told him to go to supper and I went to bath room and I could hardly get up stairs, when I did get in my room I fell into a chair half dead, and Willard thought I might have decided to come to supper, so he followed me and found me about as ill as I ever want to be, and undressed me, got me into bed, and he rubbed my head nearly all evening, and Miss Jackson did all she could for me too, but I suffered all night terribly. This morning I got up, had breakfast in bed, and came to Attica at 11:20, Mr Jackson helped me to the depot.

Surprised them here, though Grandma said she was awfully glad to see me, and Father had just gone for me to Batavia. He came up at 2 o'clock.

Tomorrow night the Authors club give an entertainment here, and she sent for me for that.

Wednesday Dec. 19.—1900.

Well this house is an *awful sight!*

Last night was the "blow out" and of all the noise and fun they had it all.

First a shadow picture story, then the X'mas tree loaded and an immense basket of other presents were distributed and opened and it was side splitting to see men and women with rubber dolls, rattlers, jumping Jacks, balls, etc., etc. After that ice cream and an abundance of cake was served.

I wore my white organdie with Aunt Evas blue ribbons, for I didint know of this and had nothing but my walking suit here only summer clothes.

Tonight we had Father and Aunt Eva & Laura to spend the evening and enjoy the abundance of cream and cake that was left. We have had lots of fun tonight.

I do wish I could hear from Willard, wonder if he misses me as I do him, it seems a *long time* since I left.

Sunday Dec. 23.—1900.

I staid home this morning and wrote to home folks, and read and this afternoon Grandma and I popped some corn and soon Father came and helped us enjoy it, and tonight we went to the Christmas exercises at Baptist church and it was very entertaining.

This is how I passed the Sunday that I feared would be so lonely.

Have finished Willards picture frame and am going to try to finish my skirt for tomorrow night, for I have written to Willard to come up for the supper at church.

Interlude

"Christmas Eve". Monday Dec 24. 1900.

How well I remember last Christmas Eve. Willard was down to see me, and he asked for me that night, and said Ma had given him the finest Christmas present he ever had, one that he prized more highly than *all* he ever received!

We were happy after obtaining their consent, it all seemed so different to us then, seemed so much *nearer* and dearer to each other.

Well by working till time to dress this evening I finished my skirt, and was dressed waiting in the dining room door when he came, and he said, "Hello Hon," and thats all the way I know he had come, it was so dark.

We were greeted quite cordially by all our acquaintances at the church, and had quite a nice supper, though we got there late.

Just received Gertie's picture and a letter, and Ella Hertzler is *dead,* she knocked her brothers revolver off his desk and it exploded and shot her through the heart and she died almost instantly in his arms.

Maude Cobbs father Harrison Leake dropped dead on the theatre steps the other evening, and left her $20,000. Cobbs will freeze to her till that is gone.

They are all well at home, beautifully fixed up, and have lots of company and good times, and wish me to have a good time, so I feel more like enjoying my Christmas.

Gertie said she never lighted the parlor that she didint think of me, and that she had company every evening most.

Carries fellow was to take dinner with them this year, a fellow that has about taken Willards place down there, but oh! I do hope Carrie wont want to marry for *many years*. We went by to see Father and Aunties tonight and he gave us the $30.00 he paid for Willard in Buffalo, and Aunties gave me $1.00 between them.

I feel so relieved to think we dont owe Father.

"Christmas Day"—Dec 25—1900. Tuesday.

This morning Grandmother gave me a white sewing apron and pair of gaiters [overshoes] that reach to the knee, and I gave Willard a picture frame with my picture in it. He couldint bring me any thing as he hadint drawn any money at all.

104

We have enjoyed his little visit very much, took dinner at Aunt Evas, had splendid one. Had a good deal of fun over my not wanting a Mother in law, and Willard pulled me in his lap and Aunt Eva said if I didint mind that would get him in the notion to get me a new Mama, and I jumped up and said, "Oh! dont, when you feel that way let me sit in your lap," and they yelled, and I felt so teased over it.

He left on the 7:20 train tonight.

This is the second Christmas I ever was away from home in my life, and how I wish I could be there now!

Dec 27—1900—Thursday.

Six months we have been married!

Only 2 of the 27*th*. have we been together, he in Batavia and I in Attica this time. It hardly seems that we have been married half a year, yet in some ways changes have come that should have *taken years*.

Grandma and I have been returning some of my wedding calls, paid three last night and 12 today, still owe two.

Willard and I should be together today and when I go back I am going to *stay*.

At Mr Williams' last night he passed around nuts and candy and we had a real nice time.

It was real lovely out today, so still and the snow well beaten down, nice walking.

Friday Dec. 28.—1900.

Well this morning I received a letter from Ma and Gertie telling of their good times Christmas, and of all they got.

Ma got $200 [$2.00?]from Tom, $100 [$1.00?] from Frank, and facinator [a lace scarf], gloves & handkerchiefs.

Gertie got an elegant silk parasol name on silver handle, and brooch with opals and pearls, that sparkle like diamonds, and a basket of fruits.

Clarence, Willie and baby Louise were home, all ~~gone~~ home but Fannie and I.

Carries fellow took dinner with them and Gertie likes him as she used to Willard, and it makes me blue to think how those good old times will *never* come again, when Willard was my *lover* and came to see me on such occasions and being together constituted our happiness! How devoted he was to me!

Mr Moreford is the fellow *now,* but I certainly hope she wont fall in love, girls are never happy after they do.

Gertie sent me embroidery scissors & emery bag, Ma sent a silver thimble with "M" on it, and Gertie sent a *beautiful* handkerchief. Ma said they missed me every day, and that they did give Willard the best Christmas present he ever had.

Father came over three times today, and got the sleigh ready in case we have good sleighing this week.

Poor Clarence is home and Ma says he seems to have lost all ambitions, and is perfectly discouraged, but I do hope he *will* brace up and try *harder still.*

Dec. 29—1900.—Saturday.

This afternoon I went over to Aunt Eva's, and Father met me at the door and took hold of both hands and pulled me into the house, seeming awfully glad to see me.

They said I must stay for supper and so I did and Aunt Eva and I had a little chat alone while Father was down town and we always enjoy them.

He brought me a letter from Willard written the day we had been married 6 months, said, "I do miss you so much, it is awfully lonesome without you here, and I will be so glad when New Years comes, for you will come back with me that night.

Sweet heart I wanted to give you a nice Christmas present but as the bank broke you will have to take the will for the deed."

Well I know the letter did me *good!*

Since supper Father, Aunt Eva & I have had quite a religious discussion and I feel so sorry he thinks as he does.

Sunday Dec. 30.—1900.

This is the last Sunday of 1900, the last of the 19*th* Century! No one living today will see the close of the next century!

This is a solemn thought, and makes me feel that I am doing *nothing* for my Saviour while the years are flying so rapidly. I am going to try to be better and do some good in the World.

Father came over and went to church with us this morning, and on the way down he said, "I am going to take my girl home with me today to dinner," and so after church we went to the post office, and I found a letter waiting for me from Willard and was pleased for I received one yesterday afternoon, and I said it might not contain good news, and on opening it I did find disappointment awaited me, for he has to work and cant come!

He said, "Six months ago last night darling since our wedding night, how time flies and soon your year as a bride will be up wont it?" Yes, the next time I go home I will be just a married woman, no longer a bride.

He said "Come home as soon as you can sweet-heart I am so lonely without you."

Father and Aunt Eva came and went with me to young peoples meeting and then we went to the Methodist church.

Monday Dec. 31.—1900. New Years Eve.

Father took me for my first sliegh ride this afternoon, and he is a *fine beau.* He kept pulling the robes up around me fastening my cape and looking after my comfort, calling me "little one."

I really think he thinks lots of me, and I do of him. I enjoyed my ride very much indeed.

Then I left on the 3:40 train, both Grandpa and Father took me to the train.

I decided to surprise Willard, so I put away all my things, and got into the closet and waited, *at last* he came, and after he lighted up, I walked out and said "Hello Sweet-heart," and he turned so surprised, his face *bright* and he took me in his arms and kissed & kissed me, and said how glad he was I come.

He patted my cheek and kissed me every few moments and seemed so glad to have me back with him, I am glad too.

Tuesday—New Years day. Jan 1st. 1901.

This the first day of the year, and the first day of the Century, we are in Batavia N.Y. and he didint get today off, but he comes home to dinner, so the day dont seem so long.

Last night we didint retire till 10 o'clock then it didint seem long till mid-night and I was awake when the bells begun to toll the death knell of dear old 1900!

Willard folded me in his arms and wished me a happier year, and we decided that we should be happy since we were *all in* all to each other, so the old Century died and the new one was born in perfect love to us. He caressed and kissed me often while unconcious, and a wife appreciates affection every time if she love her husband.

The whistles blew, bells rang, and many were up watching in different ways something none of us will ever see again.

It was solemn, and how I hope Willard will be brought to Christ this year!

This morning he said, "I love you, of course I do, *my little girl is all the World to me!"* This makes me happy, to feel I am his all, I make his happiness.

I have written home today and it has been a quiet day yet I have been rather happy in spite of the loneliness!

I want this year to be better spent, and I want to be a better girl.

Friday Jan. 4.—1901.

Having been ill we havint been out till last night and there fore have had very little to write about, Miss Evans the tailoress has been quite friendly towards me and has had me sewing in her room and I find I pick up many valuable points in sewing.

There is an elderly man here by the name of Webster that reminds me more of Nat in many ways than any one I ever saw. He came into the piano room while I was playing and said he was attracted to me the first glance he had of me, and a lot of such, but his deliberate way and his innocent way, soft voice etc. all reminded me so forcibly of him.

Sunday—Jan. 6.—1901.

Willard and I went to church this morning and then took a long walk out West Main in the snow and it looked like it was fine sleighing.

Since dinner he read me a lot in "Eben Holden", [*Eben Holden* (1900) by Irving Bacheller] popular book of the day.

We went up to Jessies and she and I took Arts sleigh and had the *finest* ride all around town, and it was still and not too cold and I enjoyed it far more than my first one.

We stayed to supper and it was too late to go to church.

Syms has made up with Cousin Madge now, sat in my lap while reading.

We all planned a lovely trip to the sea shore next summer.

December 1900–May 1901

Tuesday Jan.—8.—1901.

Soon after dinner I went to Jessies and we walked a lot, then came to town and I got some things and she came in and stayed till dark, and I had to write a letter to Attica hurriedly and run to the office, and it was dark and rainy or cloudy.

Havint written home yet either.

Friday Jan 11—1901.

I have been rather busy sewing on my coat and helping Miss Evans, that I have not had any time to run around. Willard has a bad cold and feels too badly to go to church and so we havint been to *one* of the services.

Only got my letter home off yesterday. Mr Webster gave me a red carnation this morning at breakfast, and really he worries me awfully, rather he hadint taken quite a fancy to me, if he has to bore me to death.

Right after dinner I went up to Jessies, and the fog was so thick I could hardly see across the street, and it was damp & cold, and by 3:30 when we started to church the ground was white with snow, and still snowing, and we enjoyed being out in it so much. After services I went back home with her and came back in the falling snow just before the shades of night fell.

Tonight Willard took me to church to hear Rev Davidson preach, and it is still snowing, we tripped through it home and rather enjoyed being out in it.

We heard a very good sermon.

Monday Jan. 14.—1901.

Yesterday—*"Sunday Jan. 13.—1901"* was a glorious day to us, Willard gave his heart to God and means to try to live a christian life, and it has made my faith stronger, gives me courage and I *know* that God will answer prayer. He gave him back to me from the gates of death that trying summer he was in the army and the dreadful fever laid hold of him and threatened his life, and now he takes him as his own child, and we can go hand in hand through life and when one is called away and the other left, the waiting for their call home need not be so weary since they *know* their loved one is safe in Heaven ready to meet them at the gate. Oh! I do pray that I may help my husband in this new life, that I may *never hinder* him.

Interlude

This morning Willard got ready and took me to church without a word, went like he wanted to go, and after services Mr Mason the pastor came to me and said he had seen us here severel times and on hearing our names he remembered having met us in the fall while we were visiting here. He invited us to stay to Sunday school and I asked Willard if he would like to and he said, "yes," so we all went to the S.S. [Sunday school] rooms, listened to a lovely talk by Rev Davidson, after which he went in Mr Farrels class, and I into Mrs Masons class. She is a charming woman so brilliant, yet I think a *true* christian, and, I found her talk very interesting, and the time short. Willard was waiting for me and we came home discussing it all.

After dinner we walked up to Jessies, finding her out we walked way over to Ellicott Ave. and called on Mrs Dodson, cousin of his, and her son Harry is a manly young fellow and they both seemed real glad to see us.

We had an elegant dinner too and Miss Jackson must have made lots of money as, her tables were crowded for over two hours.

Miss Evans and I went to the ladies meeting at Baptist church, and Willard went back to the Presbyterian to the mens meeting.

Thus I did not see him take his start in the christian life, but after we reached our room he took me in his arms and said, "Darling if I have been mad and spoken harshly to you, and made you unhappy since we married, wont you forgive me?" and I told him that was the manliest thing to do, to confess and appologize and of *course I forgave him.*

He knelt in prayer by our bed before retiring and how happy I was, and I asked him if he was a christian if he had started in the right way, and he said, "Yes I hope so dear," and I was *too happy to sleep.*

How thankful I am that he has decided to lead a christian life, and I feel so much happier, dont rebel at being here since it meant his *redemption!*

How many will rejoice with me when the good news is sent them.

The postman just brought me a lovely letter from Miss Margaret Whitman in Buffalo and it did me *good.* I feel real disappointed that I did not hear from home today, for it does seem so long between times I hear.

110

Tuesday Jan. 15.—1901.

Willard and I went to church last night and Mr Davidsons sermon was the ten commandments, and really it makes one feel how sinful they are, how far short they come to the glory of God.

When I see Willard kneeling in prayer by our bed side at night, it makes me feel that a christian husband is better than any riches or social position, it makes me happy.

Have not heard from home in so long. I wrote home this morning.

Sunday Jan 20.—1901.

Have been sewing the past week, and attending some of the meetings in afternoons, and going to Jessie's.

This morning we went to the Methodist church and then went to our classes at the Baptist, but Mr Mason was ill and I did not enjoy it so much.

Warren and Jessie brought Cyrus and spent the afternoon and took tea with us, and our boys took us to the ladies meetings and they went to the mens.

Willard went up to Warrens for me and Jessie and I had had a long talk, having taken Cyrus home early as he was so sleepy. Sunday seems the shortest day of the week, then another week.

Tuesday Jan. 22.—1901.

Miss Evans left this morning for her work in Buffalo, and the house seems lonely. I put on my new tailor suit this aft. and went to church, then around town some and I like it if only I felt it was perfect in the back.

This has been ideal weather, crisp and clear, a day I enjoy walking out in.

Willard and I went to church tonight.

Wednesday Jan. 23.—1901.

I had letters from Gertie, Ma, Fannie, and Gertrude Chester, the latter from Daraimah where she is visiting and out on a three months lark as she said. Also heard from Aunt Eva yesterday.

111

Interlude

Letters from loved ones cheer me up.
Jessie and I have been out all afternoon.

Thursday Jan. 24.—1901.

I had a date for church this aft. with Jessie, and when I called for her I found her ill, has grippe & sore throat.

I went to church, it was hard to find seats, and the talk was quite good.

It is raining so Willard and I could not go tonight.

Friday Jan. 25.—1901.

I went up to see Jessie this afternoon and she is better to-day, and Mrs Wallace and I went to church together and there was such a crowd again.

Tonight Willard and I went, and he preached the finest sermon I have heard yet from him, he seemed so very much in earnest, knowing that he was learning just at the time when so many were interested, and he preached from the text, "The harvest is ended, the summer is passed, and we are not saved," and while I have heard grander sermons on this same subject, still it was *powerful!* Sixty odd people, so many of them young men, went forward seeking the Christ, and it does seem too bad that the meetings had to close now, so much good might have been done if one week more had been given.

It is eleven o'clock and I am so tired. Willard said Wasint that a grand meeting? He enjoyed it, I am so glad.

Sunday "Jan. 27.—1901."

Seven months ago tonight we were married! Never will the memory of that night fade.

We were both so happy in each others love, starting out hand in hand for happier days, I thinking I was Queen of his heart, and that he would devote his life to making me happy, and to prevent my regretting all that I left for *him.*

I am not well today, and Willard went to Sunday School, and Warren & Jessie came with him to dinner.

Since dinner he attended the funerel of a member of the band, the band was in attendance and it sounded *so sad.*

He has read ever since he came home, and it is bed time.

112

It has snowed all day, and must be pretty deep now.

I have been *home sick* today more than usual, and *blue!*

Tuesday Jan. 29.—1901.

Mrs Cavers took me to the missionary meeting tonight at Mrs Masons, and she has such a beautiful home on Main Street, and is such a charming hostess, and the last hour is devoted to social enjoyment, and we played "Clumps" [a parlor game of questions and answers] which is very interesting and amusing.

Had a letter from Attica calling me there to attend both Grandparents in their illness.

Wednesday Jan. 30th. 1901.

I left Batavia this morning on the 11:10 train and found Grandma helpless with sciatic rheumatism, and Grandpa down with a cold.

I dont feel at all well my self, and I know I should have refused to come, they would never have allowed it at home, and yet I came for Willards sake. I felt he wanted me to and that he would not understand my *refusal*. It surprised me that he wanted me to go and be general servant in this way, when he was so indignant at Aunt Lula wanting me to sew for her before we were married.

Sunday Feb. 3.—1901.

Willard came last night and we were invited to dinner at Aunt Eva's today, so yesterday I prepared things so that we could go and leave them here. I made a nice lemon jelly and a potatoe salad.

I always enjoy going to Aunt Eva's, and Father seems so anxious to have us with them.

Tonight Willard and I went to church to hear Mr Davidson, and I held a reception after services, so many knew me and came to talk to me, we left about the last ones.

Monday Feb. 4.—1901.

Willard left at 8:15 this morning and I am lonely of course, dont know when I can go. Father was surprised that I did not go back with him.

Interlude

Last night I spent the evening with Father and Aunt Eva and had a nice time.

Mrs Williams and Mrs Swift came up to the afternoon meeting and I left on the 3:40 for home. Father took me to the train.

Willard had the key and so I was in Miss Jacksons room when he came and after he got in his room I walked in on him and he was quite glad to see me, kissed me over and over.

Friday Feb. 8.—1901.

I called on Miss Congdon, and Mrs Cooley and then spent the rest of the afternoon at the Library. Tonight Willard and I spent a couple of hours with Mrs Cooley, as she told him this noon that I had better hurry up and come to see her, and as I missed her this aft. we laid formality aside and went again.

I like her very much indeed, and we had a pleasant time.

Sunday Feb.-10.—1901.

We went to church and Sunday school at the M.E. [Methodist Episcopal] church this morning, and to the Baptist tonight. 11 more baptized there. This afternoon we took a long walk, went by Harvester works and it was so cold and windy I didint enjoy walking.

Monday Feb. 11.—1901.

Mrs Congdon and Miss Edna took me to the Monday Literary club at Mrs Rices this afternoon and I joined them.

The Pan American countries is the subject for study for the year, and two interesting questions or papers were read, and I found it pleasant so joined them.

Tuesday Feb. 12.—1901.

Tonight Willard and I went up to Jessies and found two young ladies there, and we girls played "Karems" and the boys talked. It is 11:30 and I am tired and sleepy.

Thursday Feb-14 — 1901 — St. Valentine.

Yesterday aft. I spent in reading in the Library and Willard read till bed time to me.

This aft. I went up to Jessies and we all played "Karems" till 2 o'clock when Anna left. I stayed till the whistle blew, then I came home so hurriedly that I was half sick after I got here. We intended going to the Valentine social at Mr Prescotts tonight, but the sleighs left too early for us to go, and too it was so cold and windy I thought.

Had letter from Ethie and Maurice, they wanted me to come this month and said they would take me to the Theatre and I would like to go if Willard could go too. We (Jessie & I) are going to hear Mrs Sanders lecture on Sion ~~this~~ tomorrow aft. (Friday).

We went and my I nearly perished before we got home, the wind was in our faces and I was out of breath most, so tonight we are staying in.

Saturday Feb. 16.—1901.

Mrs Cooley and Miss Fannie Lord called this afternoon and I like her friend quite well, and think more of Mrs Cooley than any one I have met here yet.

Sunday Feb. 17.—1901.

Willard and I went to church and Sunday school this morning and just as we left the church I slipped on the ice and fell and an awful pain in the top of my head was the first I knew I was down, but he lifted me up, and I came home pretending it had not hurt me, but after I got to my room I cried and every body at our table had to laugh because I cried as Willard was so amused. He said I said, "Oh! hon what did you let me fall for?"

Any way my head and back has hurt me all the afternoon, I am lame from it.

Miss Evans came down to spend the day with us or Miss Jackson and she spent a good while in our room and later Mr Saunders came and stayed till supper time and Mrs Baker has been in since.

Willard has read quite a little too to me.

We took our first risk this morning.

Monday Feb. 18.—1901.

I took breakfast in bed and got up at 10 o'clock, and although lame when Miss Congdon called for me to go to the literary meeting I went.

Interlude

It met at Mrs Johnsons and a lovely woman I found her to be. Willard finished "To Have And To Hold" [*To Have and To Hold* (1900) by Mary Johnston] tonight.

Had a letter from Gertie and she thinks of coming in June. Said Anderson was coming in Aug.

She had written to Farrel, he will never forget me, *never!* Seldom a love like that is found. Dear little Pat Brewer is gone to Manilla! How sorry I am, for he is such a sweet boy now and I fear he wont be after he stays there awhile.

She wrote that it was a perfect Spring morning there, and here it is *awful,* snow and ice and mud!

Wednesday Feb.-20.—1901.

We went to prayer meeting tonight and many came to speak to us.

Thursday Feb.-21.—1901.

Tonight we went up to Warrens, and he and Willard played against Jessie & I. We had a very exciting time and while they beat us it was not such a glorious victory as they anticipated.

It is 12 o'clock and I am sleepy.

Sunday Feb. 24.—1901.

We were going to the Washington social at the church tonight, but I was taken with the cramps just as I started to dress and we missed it.

This morning Mr Congdon read my church letter from Centenary, and said he hoped that in leaving a warm hearted southern church and coming to them I would feel no sense of chill, and he welcomed me most heartily in behalf of the church, and then Willard went forward and took the vows of the church and thus we are members of the same church in eight months after marriage.

We stayed to Sunday school and since dinner we have been up to Jessies.

Tonight the blind pupils of the Institute gave a sacred concert at the Methodist and we took Mrs Saunders, and it was very good indeed. They sang, "The Radient Morn," "Lost Chord," and that class of music that requires study from those of us

116

that can see, and it is marvelous how blind pupils can be taught well enough to render such music.

Monday Feb.-25.—1901.

This aft. I returned three calls and had an hours reading at the Library, and it snowed in my face coming home so I feel that I have taken cold, but I do certainly hope not.

I called on Mrs Lewis, Mrs Wright and Miss Fannie Lord, and Mrs Whitlock called on me before I left.

I didint care to go the Literary this evening, it is snowing hard.

Wednesday Feb. 27.—1901.

Eight months ago tonight was our wedding night!

Willard has gone to prayer meeting, I have too much cold to go tonight, and I am *alone!*

This afternoon I spent with Jessie, I tried to stay in but I was too blue to stay alone, so I ventured out.

It has snowed every day since the 14*th* of Jan. and so if I get out at all it has to be in the snow. Had a letter from Gertie and they have had a slight snow and it has been 29 above, and they think that awful, and it hovers around zero here, 2 below or 2 above.

The snow is two feet deep in places where it is packed down, and above my waist in places where it is soft and light.

Sis wants me to go home with her next Fall and I will have been away a year then and I should go back. Fannie speaks of going home too next Fall.

Gertie and Carrie are having gay times. She sent me a great roll of papers that Willard and I have enjoyed very much.

How welcome summer will be, and how happy I will be to see Gertie again, but how *hard* it will be to see her leave!

Thursday Feb. 28.—1901.

Eight months ago since we landed in Asheville, the beautiful bright land of the sky, where the happiest part of the eight months of married life have been spent! Oh! if this summer could only be like *that*. If he would only be a little more like he always was before!

117

Interlude

I was invited to Miss Congdons this evening and am very much dissapointed that I cant go, or couldint as it is too late now. She entertained the S.S. class.

I have a hard cold and it stays just about the same with all the medicine I take, and I am getting tired of the house.

Mr Forpy has been in our room all evening talking of a possible position for Willard as Gen. Agent of Book firm in Buffalo and if he can only secure the position and make the money that he says he can we will both be happy and I *hope* and *trust he can,* we could then be in Buffalo during the Pan American [a fair held in Buffalo from May 1 to November 2, 1901, to showcase the accomplishments of the Western Hemisphere, including Edison's new wireless telegraph] and he can go dressed up and can take life easier and *enjoy life!*

Sunday March 3.—1901.

This is a bright morning the sun is shining like the ground was dry instead of having two feet of snow on it.

Willard has gone to church and Sunday school, and I am still a prisoner because my cold is no better, and I am feeling any thing but *well* today.

Since dinner I have been reading aloud to Willard, "At The Mercy Of Tiberius" [*At the Mercy of Tiberius* (1887) by Augusta Jane Evans Wilson] and he seems to enjoy it very much indeed, and that is my object to entertain him and make home happy for him.

He has written letters since supper, one to Pa. How glad I will be when Spring comes.

Saturday March 9.—1901.

Monday I did venture across the street to Mrs Congdons to the Literary and she and Miss Edna were both very kind, regretted so much that I missed the reception she gave our class Friday evening, and that I could not go to Mrs Dans' entertainment at Hotel Richmond tonight either.

Tuesday there was a tea at Mrs Congdons and I missed that. Miss Shedds paper on Brazil was very good indeed.

Have been in the house all but that day and I am getting restless.

Willard is going to Attica tonight to be gone over Sunday and I know I will be very *lonely*.

Saturday night when Willard was most dressed he said, "Come on and go with me" and as it was only fifteen minutes till train time I said I could not get ready, but he said he would help me, and he *did,* he put my slippers and night dress, and toilet articles in the grip and got my hat and maps for me, and we made it there alright, but I think I dressed the quickest I ever did in my life.

We enjoyed it so much more because we had thought to spend the day apart, and any impromptu thing is more enjoyable.

They were delighted to see us, and Father of course was there to greet us, and they all said they would have been disappointed if I had not come.

We went to church in the morning and to Aunt Evas in aft. and I havent laughed as much in a long time before. Aunt Laura is a Republican and she has read so much of the slanderous trash that floods this section regarding the nigger that she is way *"off"* on the subject, but Father and Willard having felt the same way before going South, had plenty to say in defence of the Southern people and against the nigger. Willard held me close in his arms as we sat on the sofa and being so comfortable we stayed till bed time most and found on going out the wind blowing and it raining hard, dreadful night.

We got home at 9 o'clock this morning. It is too bad to go to the Literary today.

I called on Mrs Cooley this afternoon and then went up to Jessies and stayed till 10 minutes of six and then I was home some time before Willard came. We had cake and chocolate at five o'clock.

Heard from home, letters from Ma & Gertie, and they are having windy cold days now.

Yesterday was so bright, that even if the walks were all slush I went out, returned Mrs Whittacks call and she is lovely in her own house, has a beautiful brick house, and it is furnished so tastefully. She insisted on my paying her a visit instead of a pop call, and as I found it so pleasant I did.

We went to church and Sunday school this A.M. This afternoon we went up to Jessies, and took supper with them stayed till nine o'clock.

I finished, "At The Mercy Of Tiberious" Friday evening at eleven o'clock, and we had both enjoyed it so very much.

Mrs Howland called on me yesterday.

Monday March 18.—1901.

Mrs Cooley called on me this afternoon while I was at the Literary, we met at the parsonage and had a very profitable meeting, and Mrs Rice our president is going to entertain the ladies and their friends and husbands on Monday evening next. We have a very nice time indeed at these meetings.

Sunday March. 24.—1901.

I had a letter from Gertie last Friday and she said Frank was awfully ill, she didint believe he would live a week unless he got better!

This shocked me, for while I know it would be a blessed relief for her, yet to think of him being *lost forever,* seems to horrible to think of, and I do wish he would brace up and be a good noble man, and if he is to die that he would be *saved.* Dear Sister, no one wishes you to be happy more than I! *She deserves a happier life.*

Well yesterday was beautiful, and today is Spring like. We didint go to church this A.M. we had a lot of fun, he got to tossing an orange at me and we got it harder and harder till I missed it and it hit my cheek bone so very hard I fell over on the bed, and he came and lifted me up and kissed the place he hurt, and of course it got better, but we had a pillow fight, and while it dont sound nice yet we neither of us meant any harm.

We had a nice morning, since dinner we have walked way down South Main, up Liberty to Main, and to Warrens where we stayed till supper.

Tonight we went to church and I think he preached the best sermon I have heard yet from him. About the last six months of our Lords life, and it was very *impressive.*

We walked around awhile before coming in.

Friday night the moon was shining and we walked for a long time, then after we came home he asked me to sing some as it had been a long time since he had heard me sing any.

I certainly wish he could secure the position we wanted so much, and leave Batavia.

Friday March. 29.—1901.

Tonight we went to the tailors and then walked around quite a good deal, and then had a four handed game of "parchessi," [four-handed board game originating in India] Miss Jackson, Mr Jackson, Willard and I, and after Monday evening Mrs Rice entertained the ladies of the club, and their husbands, and Mr S—— lectured to us on South American life, customs, etc. We had 28 cards representing cities, states, etc, and I guessed all but four. Then chocolate, reception flakes, crackers, olives, pickles, and vanilla waffers were served.

I enjoyed it very much indeed.

Sunday March 31.—1901.

This is a pretty day, Willard got up early and went for a ~~drive~~ ride on his wheel [bicycle], but came home and we went to church and S.S.

Stayed home all afternoon and evening in the parlor talking to Miss Duncan, Miss Jackson, Mrs Whitlock, & Mrs Baker part of the time.

Monday April 1st. 1901.

Last night after 12 o'clock I waked up by hearing Miss Jackson scream, and I thought she was struggling with a man, and I was so frightened that I could not move or speak till the door closed and I heard her say "He has gone," then I waked Willard and men got up and chased him, policeman came, twice and take it all in all, it was a horrible night. I was ill the rest of the night. I got up when Willard did, but Miss Duncan thought it too windy to go to go [sic] to the State school, as we had planned.

I went to the Literary this afternoon, and I was surprised at the number of questions I answered, it was review, and we took up some of last years work.

Interlude

Tonight Willard asked me if I wanted to learn to ride, he would take Miss Duncan and I up to the State park and teach us, but I thought it a little cool for that, and didint care to, so I declined, and he went out alone, stayed till 10 o'clock, and we walked out Maine, came back and played parcheesi.

I am awfully up set for in trying to right matters, in explaining etc. he said If I *must* know it there was something in the past that, he didint want to think of, it pained him, and made me promise never to refer to the *past* again! At the same time he would not say that there was nothing he did care to forget.

The one thing that will haunt me *always* now is that he loved some one else, even though he married me, and the fact that he lost her, he cant bear to have me speak of the past!

He *refused* to tell me any thing, and if this is not correct, he had better have told me, for *this will rob me of all peace!*

God help me to find the consolation that a wounded heart needs. I went to the altar believing that his *heart was all mine,* that he had no thought for any one else, and to feel this awful thing that I dreamed of once and feared was true since, is *true,* is almost too bitter to be bourn. If he would only tell me that this is *not* the secret, I would not ask him to know any thing further.

He should tell me this much too, for he promised to devote his life to making me happy, and my happiness depends on this.

Tuesday April 2.—1901.

Am not feeling very well today. I wonder if I ever will feel light hearted again?

I have been restless all day, went out with Miss Duncan, then went with severel ladies to the opening after dinner, then over to the missionary society, listened to paper on China, by Mrs Davis, and she and Mrs Rice gave their experiences in Chinese school in Washington, which were very interesting. They served lemonade, fried cakes, and cheese. I sold my picture of the church, thus I will have my Easter offering.

Tonight we went up to Jessies, and played "Karams" till 11:30 and I am half sick.

Tuesday April 9.—1901.

One week since I wrote in this book before, so little happens of interest now that I dont need to write often. Miss Jackson and I went to Miss Sayers opening Thursday evening, and I saw severel bride like hats I would loved to have had last summer when we were looking for hats for that great occasion. Friday afternoon I returned Miss Howlands call, and when I was coming home I saw Jessie & Cyrus leaving, so I caught up with them and shopped, then they came in and stayed till five o'clock with me.

I was in bed Saturday and Sunday, and Willard stayed with me, didint go any place at all.

Yesterday the parade for "Uncle Toms Cabin" [to advertise the play based on Harriet Beecher Stowe's novel, *Uncle Tom's Cabin* (1852)], passed right by the window, and there is two bands, one of girls, other men, Shetland ponies, and bull dogs were fine, and the floats with tableaus in brass figures, "angel hanging to the cross," "Lincoln setting slaves free," and such things were good, but I dont think it could be a very elevating play.

We have had snow since Wednesday, and it is awfully discouraging, poor Willard has to be in it so much he is wishing for good weather, and I do hope we will soon have some.

Saturday April 13.—1901.

Yesterday Jessie and I went for a long, long walk, way out in the country, and I am tired even today from it.

Thursday evening Jessie & Warren came and we played "parcheesi" till late, and Wed. I went up to Jessies and we went to the Cemetary and when we got to her house we were both tired, and the whistles blew before we either of us dreamed of its being six o'clock then Jessie hustled and got tea and wanted me to stay and let Willard come up after supper and play "Karams," and I *waited* till 9 o'clock and knew that he wouldint come then, so I came home feeling dreadfully hurt that he failed to come, but he seemed perfectly innocent, said he didint know where I was, he went to prayer meeting so he just looked at it differently to me is all.

I have had *so many* callers last week.

Ethie wrote me that they were not fixed up yet and so I did not go as I had intended and Willard went to Attica this morning on the 8:15 train, and I thought I was in for an awfully lonely time of it, but I have been going all day.

Interlude

Went to Jessies this afternoon, and we went to the depot to get my hat Willard was to send, and it failed to come, she wanted me to go to tea and spend the evening, but I thought it would be lonely coming in alone tonight.

Sunday April 14.—1901.

At supper Miss Barker asked me to to stay in the store with her, and I did, and she played beautifully for me, then she came and stayed all night with me, we got oranges, and figs, and had lots of fun eating and talking. This morning we had a nice time at breakfast, and helping Miss Jackson to arrange the tables for dinner, then we watched the people going to church, and she played for me, and left at eleven, and after dinner Miss Duncan and Miss Jackson and I went up to the State school [for the blind], and saw little Miss Duncan, who is in the hospital. It is a lovely walk and nice place to go to.

We hadint been home very long when W—— rode up on his wheel, and wonders will never cease, he is going to Savannah [Georgia] on Friday next! Called there on a law suit for the Southern [railroad], and how it makes me want to go South too, and if I could only go as far as Chattanooga, I would be *satisfied,* but I will have to go to R—— [Rochester] instead. Am glad he will have such a nice time though, and that as I *cant* go I have a trip planned for the time he will be away, for it is lonely here.

Monday April-15.—1901.

One month from today is my birthday.

This is a lovely day. I attended the literary at Miss Shedds, Miss Congdon went with me. Tonight Willard went off on his wheel and stayed till 10:30 and I am just so lonely evenings, my eyes hurt me so I cant use them much, reading or any thing, it is *horrible!*

Wednesday April 17.—1901.

Yesterday aft. I went to Jessies and stayed to supper and Willard came up and we played "Karams" till late, and try as we would we could not beat them at all, so we decided the next time for Willard and I to play against Jessie and Warren, and that will be *fun.*

124

I have my hat, and I think it is pretty and so reasonable too, and I am pleased.

Willard will go with me to Rochester Friday and leave Saturday morning for Savannah.

Friday April 19.—1901.

Last night I took tea with Jessie and Willard came up and he and I played against Jessie and Warren and we had the best time yet, and they said I played fifty per cent better with Willard than Jessie. We beat them and the evening did not seem long, but it was one o'clock this morning before I went to sleep and then we got up at six and Willard shaved off his mustache and dressed up and he did look so *good to me,* I hated to loose him, he is so much *handsomer* now.

Oh! I did hate to see him go, but I did not let him know it.

I will leave this morning at 9:14 and I have lots to do this evening.

It is snowing, has been all day & night.

I pray that he may be kept *safe* and return to me uninjured ere long.

Rochester. Sunday April 21.—1901.

I left Batavia at 9:14 yesterday morning and I missed Jessie at the depot, and took a carriage out, blowed 75 cents this way. Then I met Mrs Kneefin, before Ethie came home. This morning we went to her church Methodist.

Wednesday April. 24—1901.

We have been going up town, going through the stores, and seeing the sights of the city and from now on we will devote some time to sight seeing.

We spent one evening at Mrs Terrys, and tonight have been to a musicale at church.

Heard from Willard from Savannah Monday.

Friday April 26.—1901.

Mrs Geer entertained for us this evening and I met her friends in this way, all were nice to me hoped to see more of me the next time I came, and I am glad I have a few acquaintances there.

Interlude

We had ice cream and angel food and sponge cake.

Yesterday we went down on this side of the river to the lower falls, and up on the other side to upper falls, and they are beautiful the angry waves dashed the rocks, and the spray formed rain bows in the sun.

We could see Genesee river coming from under Main Street at rear of big buildings and it seems a horrible risk to think of a street being built over a river.

She showed me the Erie acqueduct, canal running over the river across it.

Father comes up evenings to see us, is staying here looking around for a position.

He seems to think a great deal of me. Wants to hear from Willard but he dont write and I dont know where he is or any thing.

Sunday April 28.—1901.

Last night we had been married ten months, we have been seperated nearly every 27*th*. I weighed 122 lbs. last night on the market scales, the most I have weighed in four years.

This morning Ethie, Lois, and I went to the lake early and stayed till three o'clock in this way saved the annoyance of crowded cars. It is *lovely,* and I enjoyed it so very much. We went on the pier to the light house, saw the coast for miles, and the sky and lake seemed one. Saw the sea gulls.

There are severel hotels, theatre, switch-back track, shoots, toboggan slide, merry-go-round, pavilion, every thing for amusement. We walked around Lake Ave. saw the homes on the bluff, they front lake, and have bath houses right in front, private. We played in the sand, gathered shells, and listened to the waves lap the shore at our feet. It was balmy and nice, and we hated to leave, but when we passed 22 cars jammed, a string of wheels [bicycles], and carriages clear to the city, and found the streets crowded with people trying to get cars out, we were glad to escape the crowd. We went to Central church tonight, and it is lovely there. The orchestra first, then the minister, then, choir of 120, then grand pipe organ, and the music was *beautiful!*

To listen to such heavenly music made me feel I wished the gate would open and let me in, to shut out the discords of this life. God alone knows how I hunger for my husbands love, for *gentleness and affection* from him!

126

The soloists are artists, all and their quartette, duett, trio, anthem, etc was *grand!*

Dr Stebbins sermon was concise, and to the point and very elevating also.

Wednesday May 1.—1901.

Well the last two days I was in Rochester I went around a lot. We went to the reservoy, an elevation, circular in shape, sodded down to the boulevard, and in that mound lies a lake, in the centre of which is a fountain that looked lovely, and a walk around it. We went to Highland park, a lovely place and on the third platform of the pavilion we could see Rochester and surrounding country *fine,* making a lovely scene.

We went through H. B. Graves big furniture store, saw his nine room flat he has furnished on the fourth floor, and I had to rave over it. We went in the front veranda, it had awnings out, matting, palms, chairs, and lion statues, then the reception hall, parlor, library, den, three bed rooms, dining room, and kitchen, all through was lovely, velvet carpets, lace draperies, pedestals with statuary, vases, lamps, clocks, pictures, bric-a-brac of all kinds, taberettes [upholstery fabric], with jardinires & plants, and the most exquisite furniture, solid and massive, but the dining room with window seat, table, side board, every thing the *handsomest, cut glass, china, I raved over!* One room is white, gold, and blue, a perfect *dream.*

And he will furnish any nine room house just as that is every thing complete for 1,000 dollars.

Ethie wanted me to stay till Friday but I decided to come home.

Maurice, Ethie, and Father were at the depot to see me off, and when I got home found Willard came last night.

He had a *grand* time, saw all at Chatt. Knoxville and Asheville that I wanted him to. Mr Rufe Bryant entertained him Sun. afternoon and all night, he was awfully glad to see him, wanted to be remembered to me, etc. Saw Mrs Kilpatrick, and Katherine has been married four months, but not to *Jack!* Poor fellow didint know it till 8 days afterwards, and I fear she will not be happy.

He saw Edd, who sent me a tie and gave Willard one. He heard Miss Webber was married also.

Interlude

He hated to leave Knoxville so much.

Saturday May 4.—1901.

Last evening I stayed to supper with Jessie and afterwards
Mr Stone came in, and we played Karams, and Willard came up
after the "Veterans" meeting was over, and walked home with
me. The moon was shining beautifully and the walk home was
nice. Willard is going to Attica this evening to stay till Sunday
eve.

Today is beautiful.

Sunday May 5.—1901.

Willard came home to supper and we took a beautiful walk,
up Main, and coming home we saw the awfulest run away, two
buggies colided, the horses kicked loose, and ran, sparks flew,
and other horses scared and for awhile it looked like general
destruction, and one lay flat in the street all cut up, but I was
so frightened I came home.

Monday May. 6—1901.

Willard took Miss Duncan and I to State park hill to teach
us to ride, and it will be fun if we only can learn well.

Tuesday May 7—1901.

This afternoon Miss Duncan and I took the wheels up to
the park for an hour and a half I jumped on and off that wheel,
but as we started home I got on coming down hill and rode to
the foot of the hill! I was so surprised at my self and she sat at
the foot of the hill laughing heartily at me.

After supper Mrs Saunders, Miss Duncan and Earle
Barker, and Willard and I went to the park, but I saw things
were going *dead wrong,* so we came home.

Such emotions as I have tonight *kill!*

Thursday May 9.—1901.

Yesterday morning we went for a ride and rode down hills
and easy places, but this morning we rode from 9 o'clock till
eleven, around town, up to Jessies, up and down Washington,

and Ellicott Ave's, way out Main St. Had lovely ride, both enjoyed it immensely.

Friday May 10—1901.

Miss Duncan came down to early breakfast with Willard, heard his regrets at her departure, and with many good byes she left, but none to *me*.

CHAPTER FIVE

Discord

Wednesday May 15.—1901.

This is my birthday but it has not been noticed, and I feel the contrast in this first birthday of our married life and what I always fancied it would be and what it was always before.

Since I last wrote it has been *one heart ache!* I keep hoping that this coldness and lack of attention is thoughtlessness and that it will be right yet, but each day brings fresh wounds, all are disappointing. Oh! could I have seen into the future this far last May how much unhappiness could have been saved.

He isint happy, and I don't believe I can make him so, for he wont let me pet him or love him, I havint it in my power to, although I feel I would give any thing if I could, while he could so easily make me happy but wont.

Any thing for an excuse to get away with wild boys, and since he has been going to Attica running around with those toughs he is very different to me, *like another* boy.

He has left me five Sundays and plans to go again next Sunday.

The thought of how to please me, or how lonely I must be, never seems to enter his mind, yet he *swore to devote his life to my happiness,* I should never regret it.

Well we went up to Jessies tonight and had a *very* nice game of "Karams," and cake and lemonade.

Sunday May 19.—1901.

I have been in bed since Thursday morning and today is the first time I have taken my meals down stairs. I have been quite ill, and alone most of the time, with little attention or sympathy.

Tuesday May 21.—1901.

Mrs Johnson called yesterday and wanted me to wait on the table at the supper tonight at the church and I may go.

I havint heard from home in three weeks and I cant think what the trouble is.

Willard didint go to Attica Sunday as I was ill, but was sorry he didint after I was able to go to the table, and he is going next Sunday. We wont be together much more now.

Wednesday May 22.—1901.

I went over to the church yesterday at 4:30 and worked till 7 o'clock, and I was tired out, waiting on table, and Willard came then and we ate with Mr & Mrs Squires, but those elegant salads and cakes were gone by that time, and I knew Willard would be hungry, but he said he ate supper here first so he was alright.

After we came home Willard took his wheel and went riding, and Jessie and Warren came down and spent the evening with me. They think it is awfully funny that he leaves me so much of the time.

I heard from home this morning, and it seems that they have written to me before, they are well and no one said any thing about not writing for so long, so I think letters must be lost.

Friday May. 24.—1901.

While at breakfast this morning Mr C——brakeman on N. Y. Central brought a note saying for me to come up to Attica on the first train, and so I must bustle.

Monday May 27.—1901.

Eleven months ago today we were married, how happy was *that night.*

Mrs Bacchus left Saturday night and I did not get any sewing done by her, but I will pitch in and make what I can my self. Willard came and he and I took her to the train, then went by the Dr's. Last evening Willard pulled me down in his lap in a big arm chair and nestled his head up against my cheek and teased me for awhile, then he lay quietly back and I rubbed his head and put him to sleep, when supper was announced he picked me up like a baby and carried me to the table.

He teased and acted so much like he used to that it gave me *hope* that he would change.

He held me in his arms all night and petted me, kissing me in his sleep severel times.

I will have to stay here all week to get my dental work done.

Saturday ~~May~~ *June 1st*

Last Sunday night while Willard was holding me in his arms I told him eleven months ago at that time we were rehearsing and he laughed and asked if I had been tied on to him that long, and I said does it seem that long? He said *"no it does not hon."*

I saw Aunt Eva and Father quite a good deal this week, and found Willard at the depot to meet me.

It seems good to be back home again. And my teeth are all good now that is a great relief.

Thursday June-6.—1901.

Tuesday and Wednesday evenings, Miss Duncan and I had Willard take us out wheeling, both evenings we rode two miles, and had lots of fun too.

This morning I went out for a spin alone and had quite a nice ride, but I took the wheel back and this ends it till I get another wheel.

Willard and I started up to Jessies and we met them coming down street, so I went to the dress makers with Jessie and Willard went with Warren, and so by the time we got back to the house we had very little time to play "Karams", but it was a close game, the boys beat us though.

Friday June 7.—1901.

Passes from Washington to Chattanooga and returns have come, and yet *I cant go home!* I didint give up till this afternoon, and I just had to take a big cry I was so disappointed.

I had every thing ready to pack up, my clothes ready to put on, and then to be put out seemed too bad.

132

I went with Willard to the depot, and hated to see him go, when I thought all the time that I was going with him.

Jessie and Warren & I walked around and heard the band play, and I sat awhile with them, and how lonely it seems all alone in this room.

Sunday June. 9.—1901.

I put on my blue silk, new white & black hat and went *alone* to church and Sunday school. Of course I had lots of explaining to do, every one was surprised to see me, all thought I was *home* by now, etc.

Since dinner I returned Miss Carr's call and found her away, is in Canada, but having only Sundays in which to call, I am releived that it is at *last* paid.

Jessie came for me to go to childrens day service at her church and we rather enjoyed it. Mrs Cooley came home with me and since tea we have been up to call on Jessie. Mr Cooley went with us, we found her out but staid till 9 o'clock with Warren.

We came by "Mother Cooley's", had a very informal and jolly time there.

We had bananas and Mr Charlie took his Mothers pumpkin *pie!*

Monday June 10.—1901.

I put on my violet silk waist, and black silk skirt, wore a white chiffon rosette in my hair, and some were so jealous that I looked better than they, that they told me white looked alright for evening but black was best for day wear.

I look better fixed up a little is the reason this was said. Well I had the Literary with me today, and had a very nice time. I went over and got a wheel tonight but it was too late to ride before I got it home and dressed, so Miss Jackson, & Miss Rogers & I played "Parcheesi," till late. Heard from Willard today.

Tuesday June 11.—1901.

I got up this morning and was out riding by 9 o'clock, went by Jessies, and out in the country for three miles, and coming back my wheel ran into a rut and threw me *hard,* hurt my knee pretty bad.

I enjoyed riding on Washington Ave. and around town very much.

I found a letter awaiting from Father inviting me to go to the Pan American Friday, and of course I am going.

Thursday June. 13.—1901.

Last night I rode up to Jessies, found they were at the wedding, (Jessie Curtiss') and I went over to Miss Hopkins, had a very nice little visit with her.

This morning I have had one of the nicest rides yet, Miss Congdon and I got up at 6:30 and was riding at seven o'clock, we went out Ellicott St. stopped at Mrs Prescotts and came back, went up to park and had a *lovely ride*.

Friday June 14.—1901.

I took sick last night, and of course I missed my trip to Buffalo, and I heard from Willard this morning and it will be impossible for me to get transportation to Washington, so that is another disappointment. Had a letter from Gertie, telling how bitterly disappointed they all were, they met all the trains Sunday & Monday, and she had tickets for me to concerts & receptions, as she was on so many committees, but Carrie went instead.

After supper I was sitting on the veranda looking for Willard every moment, and at 8:15 Mr Barnett said he would not be here it was too late, so he rode away, got to the corner, came back smiling and I said "he is coming," and here he came, and with a new style straw hat he looked so odd.

The band concert was right at our corner & we sat out on the veranda and had a lovely free concert.

Saturday June 15.—1901

I had written to them that I was ill and could not join them, so they were not looking for us at all, but Willard decided to go, so we went up on the 8:48 train, went over to the Erie depot in Buffalo and met them, and they were so *delighted* to see us, and *surprised!* Father & Aunt Eva did some shopping and Willard and I went down to see the friends at the "Waldemar," and we found some more surprised people and they seemed awfully glad to see us. Mrs Whitman said, "Well bless her heart I thought she would come to see me, I have thought of you so much and could just see you right before me," and she hugged me in the old fashioned way. After dinner we took an Elmwood car and passed through a beautiful part of the city, got to the grounds at one o'clock, and I could never describe the beauties of the flowers, the avenues with trees, seats, & statuetes on either side, and the court of fountains with electric tower in rear & center with an arch of beautifully tinted buildings form a *glorious picture,* indescribable.

We skimmed over many buildings, went on the midway and heard [John Philip] Sousas band play awhile right in front of the court of fountains. We went to the temple of music heard three selections on the immense pipe organ, heard a phonograph in our building and at five o'clock Father & Aunt Eva left us, then it was getting ~~dark~~ cool and we strolled around, enjoyed it so much went back to the midway found a lot of it we had missed earlier in the day, all of Mr McConnels attractions, 8 in number, and we met him, he came forward smiling in his old deliberate way said, *"Well when did you get here, when did you leave Chatt? I was thinking of you the other day, wondering when you would be here,"* and I interrupted him by introducing my "husband". He looked awfully funny said he guessed congratulations were in order, he hadint heard of it, and I told him it was an old story, we had been married a year.

He was lovely, walked around with us, and told us to call at his office at 8 o'clock and he would make us out a trip pass to the red star route, 8 shows, 2 coupons to each.

When we found our train left at 8:40 we met him again and told him, and he said never mind he would extend them to us the next time we came, and he took us in to see the Phillipine village, and incomplete as it is I enjoyed it. He was in manners so like he used to be, the same old Emmett, but in looks he has changed, he is not so handsome and does not dress so nicely.

We did hope to catch a glimpse of the illuminations but did not.

It was 10 o'clock when we came home, we have had hot tea, fruit, crackers, and a very nice lunch, & have talked it over like girls.

Discord

We did not get up till 12 o'clock, then he got up in a teasing mood and I could hardly dress for him, but we had dinner, a good one, at 1:30, after which we sat out on the veranda in the cool, took a walk, went by Jessies, and since supper we have been to evening services.

Today has been a happy one, more as they all should be, we have been companionable and found our pleasure together.

Monday June 17.—1901.

Willard was in a big way last night, he tickled and pinched till I was wild, and I tried to keep even with him, and it was late by the time we quit laughing and went to sleep. Tonight we had a nice ride, would have stayed out longer but a rain came up and we got home just in time, it poured.

Thursday June 20.—1901.

Tuesday evening we went up to Warrens and Jessie and I came very near beating the boys at "Carams", but they won it, so as they go out to the farm next week we want to beat them *once* any way, and we decided to go back tonight. Last night we were going to prayer meeting and Father came, and we had a very nice visit with him, he stayed all night, and left on the 9:30 this morning.

We have gotten pretty well acquainted with each other, and he likes me I know.

This is dreary, rainy weather for June, but it is so similar to this time last year.

Fannie Lord had a bad day, but it was lovely last night. Today is rainy, his day.

Friday June 21.—1901.

Well we *did* beat the boys last night and it was the *best* game we ever had they said that , for it was so close all the way and they got so excited they both took off their coats and played hard, and when they saw they were beaten they were so surprised and looked so sheepish that Jessie and I hurt our selves laughing.

136

The neighbors must have thought something was happening from the noise we made.

Tonight Willard and I went riding.

Saturday June 22.—1901

I took a nice ride on my wheel, and got a bunch of daisies, since dinner I dressed up all in white and went to Barkers store and to Jessies, after supper Willard & I went out in town got soda, and then he went out alone and the awfulest thunder storm came up, and Mr McGee and I sang glee club songs and Miss Jackson and Mr Barnett listened, and we had lots of fun. Willard stayed out till eleven o'clock, when the storm was over.

Sunday June 23.—1901.

I got up and got Willard some berries and cake, had my breakfast and went back to bed and we slept and rested and then played and enjoyed ourselves till 12:30 had a nice dinner after which we went to call on Mrs Cooleys friend Miss Long, and Mrs Le Deur came up too, and she took us to her dear little secure cozy nook on the veranda, and served sherbet, two kinds of cake, and grape juice.

I enjoyed our aft. We enjoy our veranda too, we get the papers and read and watch the people passing. We went to our church to hear Rev. Congdon preach the baccalaureate sermon, the church was decorated in class colors, and flowers and the class came in two and two, "every lassie had a laddie."

Monday June 24.—1901.

Tonight Willard and I took a ride on the cinder path towards Leroy and I got two of the hardest falls, both were miracles that I was not *killed.*

We had bananas and wafers after we came home.

Miss Christine Duncan arrived tonight.

Tuesday, June 25.—1901.

We wheeled up to Jessies tonight and she and I beat the boys at "Karams", which did us *lots of good.*

Sis is not coming until September and *that* knocks me out all around.

Discord

I went over to Mrs Swifts and met a Mrs Lenix of Leroy, another cousin, and she is teaching me to make a shawl, and it takes me out in the hot sun so much.

Wednesday June 26.—1901.

Tonight Willard and I took a nice ride out Main and Oak streets, down Walnut and stopped to see Mrs Lewis, the moon is beautiful and I enjoyed the ride so much. One year ago tonight we practiced for the wedding.

Thursday June 27—1901.

Our first anniversary!
We would have celebrated it no doubt if we had been South, but not up here, every one is rushing for the *dollars* and think little of sentiment or romance.

I gave Willard a lovely watch fob with charm attached, and he thanked me and kissed me for it, seemed awfully pleased with it.

We had a lovely ride on the cinder path towards Bushville, went four miles, and then we rode up to Jessies, and the moon was beautiful.

They beat us the first game, and we had 23 to their 5 and we started home and we were laughing at them and Willard took off his hat and said they would play out the 50 points and we did, but got beaten.

It is 12:30 and I am sleepy.

We enjoyed our evening even if he did feel that he didint want to lose the time to go to the Falls or the Pan American.

But how happy I was my wedding night! What a perfect success it was, and I will never forget that strange thrill of happiness that came to me as we knelt for his blessings and Willard, *my husband,* pressed my hand closer and closer in his. I felt that he loved me above all else and was happy that I was his very own.

It is hard to think that my year as a bride has flown and I had to live like an old married woman all of it most, didint get to enjoy it like all brides do most. I was treated only as a bride the first *two months!*

Friday June 28.—1901.

A year ago tonight we went to Asheville and how happy we were while there, and I would ask nothing better than to go back to Asheville and be as happy as we were then!

I pray that God may grant us such happiness yet!

Thursday July 4.—1901.

Every evening we have been riding or going up to Jessies to play Karams and getting soda cream, and last night he rode to Attica, came home at noon, and went up to Jessies, took bananas, peanuts, & candy, and we had lots of fun, even if our drive was spoiled, and we had planned to go to the Falls, Pan Am. or Mamton Beach.

We played "Karams," and sung, jollied & after supper shot off fire works and had a romp. Willard lifted me off the high veranda, then put me back again, and was in a high way.

We rode home and had cream and got home at 12 o'clock.

All voted it a jolly fourth after all.

Friday July 5 —1901.

Tonight was the band concert, but it was on opera house balcony and we could hear and Willard took my wheel apart to fix and I fixed peanuts and fed him while he worked, it is an awful job and he cant finish tonight.

Sunday July 7.—1901.

Willard went to Attica last night and of course I have had a lonely time.

I went to church and Sunday school, and he came too late for us to go tonight.

He had a narrow escape going up last night he ran into a boy and was thrown 6 feet over his handle bars and lay for a half hour unable to move, and he is lame and sore now of course.

If he breaks his neck going to see her [Mrs. Thomson, Willard's grandmother] leaving me alone every Sunday she may wish she had been less selfish.

Discord

The Misses Shine and I went for a nice ride this morning, and Jessie, Mrs Williams and Mrs Swift called this aft. and Warren, Jessie & Cyrus spent the evening with us, and we played parcheesi, Jessie *beat*.

Thursday July 11.—1901.

I had a date with Jessie for last night and Willard wanted to go to prayer meeting so we went, and tonight we couldint go for he went to Attica with Ronnie Lee Last and I spent the evening with Jessie.

They came home at 1 o'clock, and my heart breaks most when I smell liquor on his breath, for when a man drinks he does every thing else bad.

Monday July 15.—1901.

I took sick Thursday morning and Friday Jessie came by with Arts buggy and took me driving, and that night Willard ran for Dr Le Deur for I was unconscious and very ill, and Sunday aft. I had another hard time with my heart.

This aft. Jessie came and took me for a drive, and fine thing she did for I had to stay alone all evening. Willard went riding.

Wednesday July 17.—1901.

Willard and I went to prayer meeting and took a ride afterwards.

This little dunce Belle is making a darn fool of her self and Willard is joining her. A man that is old enough to marry should be old enough to know how to act to keep down talk.

Friday July 19.—1901.

Miss Duncan, Willard and I rode nearly to "Horseshoe lake", but it looked like rain and we came home, and Mr McGee and all of us sang but Belle and she sneaked out on the veranda to be with Willard. She is cracked over him and wants him to know it, she cooes around him in a way she thinks no man could resist.

Tonight Miss Duncan, & I were going to ride to the band concert, but Willard had to chase off and stay so late, she went away, and so we had a little ride and heard a few pieces by the band, then came home, and as soon as we began the music Willard & "Belle" got together on the veranda, all the rest in the parlor.

They are acting disgustingly and *every body* is talking, yet I cant say any thing to either one, if I do *I am jealous* they say.

Sunday July 21.—1901.

Last night we rode to the State park and had a very nice evening, Willard came up about 8:30 and we rode way out Ellicott and had a nice ride.

After we came home we had music and *of course* she stayed out with Willard all the time, and when he is away you cant keep her from the crowd, she sings and is one of them, but no she wont leave him if she can possibly be near him, *little fool!* Miss Duncan wanted Willard & I to go home with her, and she had to poke along too. I walked with *her* up there though.

We went to church & Sunday school and after dinner he found for the *first* time that the corner in front of her door was a nice place and she came up, saw me out there too, so she went in her room, and when Miss Duncan called me to sing I knew just as well what they would do as though I was there, I heard them talking up there, and when I started to go to the park as we had planned to do, he & Miss Duncan, & I, he paused to talk to her and I said what are you waiting for? He said, *"Miss Belle,"* so I turned and walked away to Miss Duncan, and the little idiots didint know they had been snubbed, they poked along too, uninvited, and spoiled the evening for Miss Duncan & I.

Then Mr McGee, & Miss Mary were going to the lake and Willard said we would go too, and I found he was going to rent a tandem, and let her go too, and he tried to fix up Lizzies wheel too, so she could go, and goodness knows any thing to get away from her silly cackle and disgusting ways, so I determined not to go if *she* did, and as I left the room, Miss Duncan told her she was going to be talked about if she didint *call a halt,* and she was furious, never would speak to any of the three again, *never.*

Well we went on alone, and under some circumstances I would have enjoyed it but how can I enjoy any thing the way he treats me. He ignores me *utterly,* speaks to me in the ugliest way, and causes every one to know that he *hates* me! My God how can I be patient under this?

We got out there before sun set on the water, Willard rowed us for an hour on the lake, and we sang songs, and we came home around Main St. long hard ride, but we got here all right. Then Belle was standing with a crowd on the side walk when we came home, I heard her telling them that it was none of *her* business, and she should never speak to any of the three again, yet no sooner were they gone than they sat down, and Willard invited the crowd to "take one on him," and she changed her mind already, she went, but I kept by Willard and as there were six of us she had to pair off with Miss Jackson, but after we came home she saw Miss Duncan at the piano and said "I am going up stairs," no one begged her to stay, but Willard who said, "dont run off and leave us like that," and she could not stand it, she *had to come down* and I was playing the piano, but while my back was turned I knew he was fanning her and they were making eyes at each other and sure enough they were acting so it added to the *talk.*

Monday July 22. —1901

We rode out to Aunt Nells tonight, Mrs Gur and Grandma were out there.

I had a glass of butter milk, and bread & butter, and lots of cold water and we got home at 10:30, made good time I thought.

After we came up stairs she called him to unfasten her dress for her, and I am not alone in believing *now* that she is a little "chippy".

[lower half of page cut out]

July 26.—1901.

Many are the utterly wretched hours I have passed this week and especially since Wednesday night. I had heard so much to make me believe Willard was not true to me, and every rumor that reached me and I would try to make my heart trust on, his actions towards me would carry out those very rumors, and so at last when I heard a full conversation while laying down on the hall couch, between Barnett & Willard I could keep still no longer and of course in the condition I am in I said more than I intended, and things have gone from bad to worse.

He not being in a good humor with me I could not be very bright or entertaining and that evil thing exerted her self to keep his attentions turned to her, and so *now every one is talking!*

[lower half of page cut out]

It is killing to have my husbands name connected with that thing, and oh! the things that are told me about my own husband, and how I have to fight for him and stand to him and then to be snubbed in return is awful!

I was to go to LeRoy [a town south of Rochester] over Sunday but I heard too much and I determined to *stay.* I knew she had laid plans during my absence and while I was told *he* had too with her, and lots that was awful, still I meant to be fair to him, and when he came home he said "tonight would have been a fine night to have gone to LeRoy." Miss Duncan and I tried to get him to go riding with us, but he made excuses and put my wheel out for me, and when I hesitated he said, "Wont you go unless I do?" and was mad because I wouldint go right on, so I *bluffed,* I went off with her, and turned and came back and instead of trapping them as some would have done, I let him know I was here, and as I came up she said, "She's come back to watch him, we cant go", "I bet she has" Mary said. I saw he was mad when he found I was back, and he told me it would be an hour and a half before he could go, yet in five minutes he pushed his wheel out the side entrance angry as could be, and *she* went away *furious* as I had broken up her little game.

A man told me they had planned to go out to Horseshoe lake tonight, and I busted it up, just as I meant to do! But the pain at my heart is no less, for if he *meant to,* it is as *bad!*

He went to the P.O. and was gone some time and they passed him *alone* near here, he rode slowly and looked after them, but he came on to us and after the music ceased Miss Duncan & Willard, Mr Barnett & I rode around some. I asked Willard about the plan to shake me and get out with her, (and of course a girl that would slip off with a married man, would go for *no good,)* and he *denied* it over & over, he had never had a date and so I told him what the talk was and of the *lies* she was telling on him, and how people were saying she was making a fool of him, and asked him to help me to put down this talk! People censure me for ever having gone out with such trash, and I asked him if he thought it *fair* to me to act in a way to cause his wife to be talked about.

Now if she is lying on him like that, I cant see how he *can* treat her pleasantly, for she will *ruin him!* I will give him *every chance!*

She acts like a sheep killing dog, she is so nervous she figits when I look at her hard and if ever there was a *guilty woman she is!*

Sunday July 28.—1901.

Well she looks rather crest fallen, she has made her brags that she will part this couple, and she has been insolently triumphant, but today the day she felt he would be here *all day,* and I *could not* be near him all the time and she would have such a chance is gone and she has had no chance to do any dirt at all.

We went to church and he sat out in the yard till dinner time, then I did not give her any chance to talk to him.

After dinner we spent in our room and he teased and played with me, was in a good humor, till he took something out of his trunk and put in his pocket before he would let me in there and I begun to scuffle in fun but when he looked so determined to never let me see it, I thought of the *"note* business" and the longer we fought for it the worse each got and then I had to tell him what I thought, and he showed what it was his "loan book", and of course he was mad and while I know he should be more frank with me, and tell me all, so there would be no room for doubt, yet I felt sorry that I had misjudged him, I appologized to him, asked his forgivness and he *said* he did.

Monday July.-29.—1901.

What a relief! They have been gone all day with the Huggins' notorious chippies Kit & Mother both, yet intimate friends of theirs, birds of a feather, flock together.

We had two meals in peace, and since supper we rode to the Library and up to the State park, and we passed them in that wonderful trap with the "Huggins'." They came back while we sat on the veranda, and they stood close to him and talked, and he did not offer them his chair or invite them to sit with us, so they went up stairs, and thus another day has passed without any startling developments. She cant set the World on *fire!* Willard is not well, fears typhoid fever.

Tuesday July 30th.—1901.

Willard and I had a lot of fun last night, a real good time, but he said he bet he would have typhoid fever before the week was up, and I know he has not been well for a long time, and I have feared this summer he would have fever.

I am awfully uneasy about him now!

Tonight we rode out to Jessies and it was fine coming back, came in 27 minutes.

Jessie walked to the foot of the hill with me and Willard rode down and we stood and talked over an hour.

Wednesday July 31.—1901.

Tonight we left *them,* went out to Benhams and after we rode five miles found they were not at home, we rested awhile on the cool veranda, got some cold water, and came back in the moon light.

Found Mr Jackson, & Miss Duncan here, and we sat out on the veranda and had lots of fun.

Thursday Aug. 1.—1901.

I have been hearing many awful tales about Willard & *that thing,* and some things seem to be so true that it has made me awfully unhappy, I will not soil this book by writing the *many* many things that have been told me, but if he acted differently I would not believe a word.

Tonight we had to go the the train to meet Laura Moore and see her off on the Boston sleeper, and he wanted me to go on and let him come on later, but I saw *her* game and I stayed with him till he left.

We had a ride after the train left.

Friday Aug. 2.—1901.

This has been the *worst* day of all to me, it seemed that the very things people told me to watch, was done today, and if I allow my self to think him guilty it means no more peace of mind for me, a *ruined life!* I have cried over it and been nearly *wild,* I am getting so thin and feel awful, this is killing me!

Since we came in from the bicycle shop tonight I have told him what I have heard and we have had the most satisfactory talk yet.

Sunday Aug. 4.—1901.

Last night I came home found "Shines" were going off for supper, and so I went up to Attica on the train, but Willard thought I was wheeling and when he came I was hidden, he said, "Has Madge got here?" and they seemed surprised that I had started and he said, "She started first, I didint pass her," and was for searching for me but Father couldint stand it he said, "Oh, she is here boy", then they all laughed. I started over to see Aunt Eva, and he had started to see if *"his girl"* had come, and I was wheeling when I met him, and he I said, "Hello", "Hello", then the third time he knew me, and he came to me said he wondered what little girl that was that thought she knew him. He & Aunt Eva went over home with me to see the others.

We went up to see Uncle Elliot, Aunt Emily, and Uncle Fargo. She is quite a bright girl and Aunt Emily is very jolly.

We went over to see the house since it has been painted and a veranda added and it is a pretty place, looks like a new house. We had lunch and started home at 6 o'clock rode 12 miles and got home 20 minutes to 8 o'clock.

The road is pretty and it was a fine aft to ride, every thing looked pretty.

I had berries and cake, then later the crowd got into the chicken that was left, and I enjoyed it for my ride gave me an appetite.

Monday Aug. 5.—1901.

Tonight Willard and I rode out to Jessies and thought the moon would light us home but it did not and we came four miles in the dark, but Willard was very kind he rode by me and slowly and we made it all right home, then he got bananas, & fruited crackers.

146

He is acting as he should now, and it helps me wonderfully, he pays no attention to them, and that is the way to stop all this mischief!

She feels very much defeated, I can tell she feels worsted, and I guess she knows by now that she has not been dealing with a fool, and that there are slower people in the World than *me!*

We will come out victorious if he will only keep on as he has started.

Wednesday Aug. 7.—1901.

We went to prayer meeting tonight and talked out on the veranda a long time alone, and I wish we were keeping house and could be alone more, and none of this discord in our lives that arises from living in such a place as this boarding house.

Friday Aug. 9.—1901.

Tonight Mr Fitch and Mr Barker came and spent the evening with us, and we played games, but did not have any music because they didint want to go to the parlor with the rest of the crowd.

Monday Aug. 12.—1901.

Saturday I was ill and Willard got a card saying Grandpa had fallen and broken a rib, so he wanted to go and I told him to not mind me, to go on up, so he got Miss Barker to stay with me, and he brought me some oranges and bananas before he left.

I had a pretty hard night and she did too, she tried to get some one to run and get whiskey, but no one was here, and so I suffered on till morning.

He came back Sunday morning, and stayed in my room all day till I told him to go for a ride.

Tonight we went up to spend the evening with Mrs Cooley who has two guests, we played "Karams", and Mrs Brooks & I, beat Willard and Mrs Cooley. That house is grand and I always enjoy it.

Tuesday Aug. 13.—1901.

Tonight we went over to Miss Barkers and Mr Fitch came and he plays and sings divinely and we had some exciting games, then she served lemonade and cake, and we passed a very pleasant evening indeed.

Friday Aug. 16.—1901.

Last night Willard kept trying to find Dr Snow and he came back, and they were all on the veranda and he came right to me, sat on the arm of my chair and put his arm around me and it nearly killed her, she was *wild,* to see that after all her boasting of her powers over him and what she would do etc.

Tonight we rode an hour then he went to the Drs and was up there an hour or more, and he came back and sat with me on the veranda till later, and we rode down to the concert and had a very pleasant evening.

Monday Aug. 19.—1901.

Saturday aft. I had a ride with Miss Duncan who told me so much, and when Willard came home I told him all and after we had supper we decided to go to Attica, get Father to go with Willard to get a position in Rochester and leave here.

It was getting dark when we started and so we rode 12 miles under difficulties, but reached there at 9:12 and found them glad to see us. We were locked out of every place but one room over the library, and we slept there, then went over to Aunt Evas for dinner, and had a very lovely day. Of course we had to tell them the state of affairs here, and they thought as we did to leave it all would be best.

Willard wanted to tell the folks good bye, so he rode 18 miles to do it, and I came home on the train.

Mr Barnett & the barber were very kind, they opened the door for me, and I had a cup of tea & some cakes on reaching here, and then I sat out on the veranda after I came home, and talked with Barnett.

He told me lots of amusing things of this "thing", we have here, and lots that did me *good.*

We had quite a talk Willard and I, after we went to bed, he met Grandma on the way home and she *of course* dont care what *I* suffer, just so *she* is pleased and she gave me fits, and told him not to leave her, and so I think he means to *stay in this hole* for *her sake!*

I was so tired and sleepy this morning that I didint know any thing till he kissed me on the cheek as he started away this morning.

He is getting more thoughtful I think, he listens to what I say so much more than he did, and I *could* be firm about this and he would go to Rochester, and I may insist on it yet, I dont see why she has to have her say every time.

Wednesday Aug. 21—1901.

Willard and Father went to Rochester this morning. I went to see them off and then met Father this aft. Willard staid to see Maurice and Ethie and the girls. Miss Duncan and I had a nice ride this aft. I have waited till 12 o'clock for him and I guess he means to stay all night. He did not finish his business I guess.

Thursday Aug. 22—1901.

Willard did come home last night and the good folks around here were all excited over it, "Mr Leland had gone, and Mrs Leland looked for him all night and, he had deserted her!"

About 3 o'clock Miss Duncan and I were talking and Willard walked in and we had lots of fun over it.

He has secured a position with the B. R. & P. rail road [Buffalo, Rochester & Pittsburgh Railroad], and goes down the 3rd of Sept.

Tonight we walked around then went to Mrs Swift, she had Mrs Watts, & Mrs Montrose visiting her, we had a very pleasant time.

Friday Aug. 23.—1901.

Bealah Phelps and Margurite Grinell spent the morning with me and they sang and cake walked, and amused me for a long time, bright little girls.

Tonight Willard has read & written & we have enjoyed the band concert from our room, it was on Opera house balcony.

Saturday Aug. 24.—1901.

Mrs Mittower spent the afternoon with me, and since supper I started up to the library for another book, and Miss Healy and Miss Whitman came, the latter to spend the night.

Anna McKinzie has been in too.

Discord

Sunday Mr Healey came and Margaret went to his relatives and we invited them for the evening, and we went to church. After dinner we rode out to Jessies found Anna McKinzie out there, and we had a very good time, came home to supper and as I got off my wheel I was taken very suddenly ill and have been in bed ever since with pleurisy and am far from well now, but had to be up today, as we leave this place tomorrow.

Mrs Mittower, Miss Barker, Miss Duncan, and Miss Smith have been coming to see me daily, and been so kind to me.

Mrs Mittower had invited us to spend the evening with them Wednesday and Jessie Thursday and this last week would have been lovely, but instead I had to lie in bed.

Willard was going to take me to the Pan-American tomorrow and on the lake Sunday, but he is going to Rochester as I start for Attica.

I must pack up now.

When I went to pay Miss Jackson our board I told her we were going to leave and that I felt we had not been fairly treated in regard to the Sine [Belle's last name] affair and she got to telling me things she heard I said of Belle that she knew was untrue, and when I said it was certainly *true,* she was furious, called them in and I had three angry women going for me like wild fire, and yet I feel that I held my own pretty well.

I told them to wait and talk to my husband, and they seemed anxious to, but tonight Miss J. had decided to say nothing, it was none of her businiss, she *refused* to talk, and Belle had skipped out. *Cowardly curs!*

Miss Duncan came down her hour, and I walked home with her. I told Mrs Congdon and Miss Edna good bye, and Willard & I went to Barkers and Mr B——was so kind and fatherly, and May Belle was lovely, we came home at eleven o'clock and the swell dance had ended, after we left and they thought they were not annoying us, it was not fun any longer.

We had breakfast and Miss J. [Jackson] stayed out of the way, and it looked like we would have no chance to talk to them and give them the lie, but as Miss J. brought their breakfast to them Willard said, "Miss J. you three women gave my wife the lie this morning, now I certainly *did* unfasten her dress!" then commenced a scene the like of which I hope *I* will never again be mixed up in, but I *had* to defend my self & Willard, yesterday morning and he defended me nobly today. He told her she *lied,* and when she said she thought him a gentleman but had changed her opinion of him, he said, "*I have never* changed mine of you!" She said I wouldint have you, he said, "you would have me darn quick if I would have you. You have flirted or tried to flirt with me after I quit speaking to you, while my wife lay up stairs sick but I wouldint notice you." She said your wife is jealous of me has been all the time, and he said, "she had no reason to be, I only treated you politely and you took it differently, you know you would part us but you *failed dismally*".

He told her to tell me any thing she could to make me feel bad, she had circulated reports concerning him and her, "now tell my wife, make her feel bad," and she could not.

It was firey and we said our say and got out, left them chewing over it. Willard was lovely to me the *last,* and he got my ticket, checks and every thing, and it hurt me to see him leave, he was so pale and I felt I did want to go with him.

Jessie came to the train with her buggy and took me home with her and brought me to the 6:30 train, so I came up at seven o'clock!

I feel like I was going to be ill, I am so worn out with that horrible affair. I need love and sympathy now if I ever did, and he is far away.

Sunday Sept. 8.—1901.

Grandma took me riding Tuesday and Mrs Bacchus came Wednesday and we have been sewing hard all day, and riding after supper.

Had a card from Willard Tuesday, he was well, was erecting machines at the Davis Mch. Co. I have hoped a letter would come but looked in vain.

I havint heard from home either, & I dont want Gertie to come till I know she is.

Mrs Bacchus wants us to go to the lake and I want to, if she can go too. I think we would enjoy it.

It has been beautiful, and this is a grand place, so roomy, and so pretty, flowers, trees, and lovely lawn.

Discord

We have been sewing on the lawn and veranda.

Sunday Sept. 12.—1901.

President McKinley died after a weeks illness yesterday morning at a the home of President Milburn in Buffalo! Shot down by an assasin. [Milburn, a lawyer, was president of the Pan-American Exposition.]

I have never heard of a death that has caused such universal gloom, and his death was pathetic.

The parting with his wife whom he has so tenderly loved and cherished was *so sad,* but she has that to always comfort her, she knows he did love her truely.

Thursday. Sept. 19.—1901.

Today is memorial services all over the World, and those held in Presbyterian church here, participated in by all the ministers, and singers of the place ~~was~~ were fine. His favorite songs were used "Lead Kindly Light," "Nearer My God To Thee," and "Oh Lord Thy Will Be done", the last words he ever said.

I had a letter from Willard Monday morning he wrote Sunday aft.

Sis says she is coming but she cant say when, hopes to be with me before time to write again.

Sunday Sept. 22.—1901.

I wrote to Willard Thursday I was ill, and I got a letter yesterday morning saying he would be up next Sunday instead of today and while I want to see him, yet I am *glad* I will be well when he comes.

Surely Gertie will be here by *then,* I am getting restless, I want to go.

I want to be with Willard before I go home for so long a time.

We used to count the days till we could be together, and now we are married we are seperated so much of the time, it is not right and I dont mean to do this way any more.

Wednesday Oct. 9.—1901.

I spent the night with Aunt Eva last night, Father has gone to Seneca Falls [west of Rochester] and we christened the new bed room suit, and I was just getting ready to sit down to sewing when a messenger came to tell me some one in Buffalo wanted to talk to me, and I danced with joy. I found it was Gertie and I took the 10:30 train to Buffalo.

It was most one o'clock when I reached the Michigan building [at the Pan American Exposition], but she ran out to meet me from the crowd, as she could see me first, and every one seemed glad that two people could feel so glad to meet again, and it had been so long since I had seen her, I was very happy. She introduced me to the Michigan crowd she had been with and I took lunch with them.

We went by our selves most of the aft. and saw the entire grounds, but we were eating supper when the illumination came on, and while we saw it yet we feel we want to witness it come on.

We came home at 12 o'clock *tired out.*

Thursday Oct. 10.—1901.

We went to town, and since dinner Father, Aunt Eva & Laura called on Gertie and they said I had a very sweet, lovely sister, and I think she likes my aunties too.

Friday Oct. 11.—1901.

This morning Gertie and I took a drive, I took her by the Stevens farm and the country looked beautiful, leaves turning enough to be gorgeous. We drove till nearly noon, then as we were invited to dinner and supper at Aunt Evas we dressed and went over. The old lady pretended she had not heard us invited, and had gotten dinner ready for us, but she *lied.*

We had a lovely dinner after which we took a delightful walk, down to a little bridge that spans a stream where the ducks were bathing.

It was as balmy as spring, and we had a very nice walk. We had a nice supper, came home at bed time.

Sunday Oct. 13.—1901.

Willard came up at 12 o'clock Friday night, the old lady kept him down stairs talking till after one o'clock then when he came up to our room he was mad, and I knew the reason.

Discord

We went to the Pan American Saturday and rather enjoyed it but he was *all wrong* all day, and Gertie had to see the *result* of *her* interference.

We were all too tired to go to church and we had a very dull time, but after supper I took him to my room and had a talk with him and he seemed so much more natural, he stayed with me till train time, then I went to the front with him, and he told me to sell my wheel, he was going to get me a new one in the spring.

He kissed me several times, left me in good humor, and she was *mad*.

I fear Gertie is not having a nice time but there is nothing here to do.

Tuesday Oct. 15.—1901.

The old lady has been mad, but she had refused to let me have the horse to go to Batavia, so I wanted to give her every chance to be mean, and I asked for the horse, she was angry shrugged her shoulders and said, I have nothing to do with the horse, dont ask me, so I asked Mr Thomson, and he hitched up, and in spite of her we went for a nice ride, went through the Cemetary, and around country roads, and had a nice ride.

We went to the Library, was shown through by Aunt Laura, then we went to town, and over to Aunt Evas.

All morning we sat in the cold & sewed but Frank Fargo & wife came and the furnace was started, and even the gas stove, and we nearly melted.

They are from Lake Mills Wis. and Mrs T. shows plainly she does not want us, so we will go our way.

Thursday Oct. 17.—1901.

I had letters from Jessie & Ethie, both inviting me to visit them, and we are all too glad to get away from here, we will go in the morning.

We had cleared up the dishes and were starting to town this morning, and Gertie said, "we are going for a morning constitutional," and she said angrily, "I take mine in the kitchen," and this is only a sample of the uncalled for things I have had to make me miserable. I have told Willard I would *never* come here again, and I *will not!*

154

I am not feeling well I may not be able to go tomorrow but will run over and see if Father has a valise to let us have, before I tell her I am going, she will be glad to have us leave.

When we got to Aunt Lauras, she insisted on our staying to supper, and it was not pleasant over here, so we stayed till eight o'clock. When we got home, Father offered me a seat by him, and when he started to go he said, "Well Madge are you going in the morning?" I said yes at 8:15. Fargo asked where we were going and Gertie said aloud while no one else was talking. "We are going to Rochester in the morning", she heard it first in this way, I intended telling her privately so she could not make any thing out of it.

Friday Oct. 18.—1901.

We left at 8:15 stopped over in Batavia left my wheel at the dealers, and went up to see Jessie, she said for us to write when we were going to leave R——and come to her.

We got out to Ethies at noon, met Maurice at the gate, and they soon made us feel at home.

Maurice wrote Willard a note to come to supper, knowing I wanted to see him and he came early.

We had "Carams", and a jolly time and it seemed odd to have a call from my husband then go away home, and leave me there.

Saturday Oct. 19.—1901.

Ethie got tickets to Baker theatre for we three to see, "The Game Keeper" [possibly *The Gamekeeper at Home,* a play by John Richard Jeffries], and Sis was ill, so Lois went with us, and I enjoyed the play *fine.*

The game keeper sang well, and, "You, you none but you!" was lovely, it is ringing in my head now.

I came ill after I got there, but I took a tablet and staid up all evening.

Willard came out and spent the evening we had lots of fun playing "Carams."

Gertie is learning and she makes the fun for the crowd, every time she gets a man in it tickles her awfully & it does one good to hear Maurice laugh.

Discord

Willard came to dinner, and we would have gone to the Lake if Willard had saved any money but he gave me all he had. We went to Central church tonight and he liked the sermon & music, said it made him feel he wanted to go again, and I hope he will. We walked home in the moon light and had a very nice talk.

We had the jolliest supper out in the kitchen, we never could have had that much fun in the dining room, but it was informal and enjoyable. It is after 12 and Willard is just gone.

Monday Oct. 21.—1901.

Willard came out and the evening has passed very pleasantly playing "Carams."

Tuesday Oct. 22.—1901.

Ethie and Gertie and I went to the mattinee to see "Naughty Anthony" [*Naughty Anthony: A Farce in Three Acts* (1899) by David Belasco], Gerties treat, and we had lots of fun.

We walked around town, and Willard came tonight and Sis talked to him on the veranda, then we had the best game of "Carams" we have had yet, he was nicer to me, very different all evening.

Wednesday Oct. 23.—1901.

This afternoon was lovely and we went to Highland Park, and Mount Hope, and saw the acqueduct on Erie canal, the stores and Post office etc.

Willard came tonight, and we got a telegram from Jessie saying for us to come Friday, so we will stay out our week, Ethie had been begging us to.

Thursday Oct. 24.—1901.

We walked to the terrace this morning and to a physical culture lecture in afternoon which was quite good.

Willard came and we were invited to Hams for the evening, men played cards, and ladies "Carams", we had fudge. They had let Lois stay with the Hams so that Willard could spend the last night with me, but they did not invite him so that he felt they wanted him, and yet he wanted to stay the most kind.

156

We stood out in the moon light and talked till one o'clock, but I think we understand each other better than we have for some time.

He said "I love you as well as I could love any one," and said he did not suppose there ever was a couple that felt just as they thought they were going to before they married, and I dont think they do either, so if that is all that is the matter with him, that is all right, for, I dont feel towards him as I thought I would.

Friday Oct. 25.—1901.

Ethie took us to the train, and Maurice came in the coach to bid us good bye and as the train crossed State street we saw her going home.

We reached Batavia at 12 o'clock, met Miss Barker first thing, she was so glad to see me, invited us to spend one evening with her. Also met Miss Shedd who invited us to the Literary social Monday evening.

Jessie seems cheerful & Warren is doing all he can to make us welcome.

Saturday Oct. 26—1901.—Niagra!

Sixteen months ago tonight we all rehearsed for our wedding, and today we have celebrated by visiting one of the seven wonders of the World Niagra falls! I had read and heard of its wonders and seen many pictures, but one has to see it to appreciate it, and I could not describe it were I to try all day. It is *grand* and the longer one looks at that rushing, hurrying, volume of water dashing on the rocks below and foaming white, and the spray forming rain bows, the more magnificent it becomes. We spent the day pleasantly looking at the Falls, American, and Horse shoe, on both Canadian & Am. sides. We went to the Waldemar to see Miss Whitman, took dinner there and stayed till 9 o'clock. Mr Farrel was real nice stayed home to be with us. We had music, Prof Healey, Miss Margaret, Gertie, and they even made me sing.

Sunday Oct. 27.1901.

Sixteen months ago today we married, and how I wish we were as happy now as then, if I had never come North!

Discord

Tonight we went to temperance lecture at the Baptist church, I wished Willard had been with me, if he had loved me as he did in Asheville. My heart aches for true love, and I yearn for him to be a loving husband, but God may pity us, and bring it right yet.

Monday Oct. 28.—1901.

We went to town, saw Miss Barker, & Mrs Johnson, and found a letter from Willard on my return home, he wrote me the same time I did him yesterday, went to Central church again I am glad. He sent me $9.00 all he had and wrote me a nice letter.

We went to Literary social at Mrs Johnsons and all the ladies said it was good to see me back if only for a little while.

They welcomed me warmly, and wished me many good things in my new home.

Wednesday Oct. 30.—1901.

In passing Mrs Whitmans this aft. she called to me, took me through her new house, said she was so glad to see me every body had missed me, and her daughter had said she had no idea how much life Mrs Leland made at the Columbia, so many had left, and the house seemed so lonely since I had gone. She sent regards to Willard. We came to Attica tonight, and I went in as usual spoke, but she was *mad* hardly spoke, so we shall stay here very little.

Friday Nov. 1.—1901.

I packed up yesterday morning and we went over to Aunt Evas to supper, and today we took dinner and supper there.

While down town this afternoon we got a card from Willard saying he could not come tonight as I had expected him, and I was awfully disappointed to think I could not see him again and we have been seperated two months now.

We fixed up lunch over there, stayed till bed time, and found the door locked here when we got here, and she was so mad when she let us in that I did not tell her Willard was not coming.

She has the heat turned on plenty that she wants the room warm for Willard, but *we* can freeze.

158

I forgot to tell her, but she does not deserve any confidence in return for her treatment of me.

She thinks I lack spirit, but I have tried to get along with her for Willards sake, she is mean as can be, and has never treated me right and I am glad that I leave this place *forever* in the morning.

Saturday Nov. 2.—1901.

The crisis was reached this morning in Attica, and I will never have to endure insults and ill treatment at her hands again, there can never be any question of friendship between us again, for I shall never darken her doors again or speak to her on earth!

She insulted both Gertie and I and accused me of many things I am perfectly innocent of, and we were *ordered out of her house,* but she waited till we were ready to leave any way.

She said she had raised him, done every thing for him, his duty was to *her,* and when I said "A mans first duty is to his Mother then?" she said when a man has such a wife as *you* it is, never been any thing but a burden to him, and when I said I had done my duty to him she said, "I am glad you *think* so, I know you havint."

She read Gerties letter home in which she said, "Margaret said as we came up the walk the other night, this is prison my cell is on the other side," and they made every thing out of that, old man said, "*you* vacate your cell, the sooner the better," and they told me to go home and *stay* there, that the time for me to have gone was when I made Willard leave Batavia. They told him not to humor me by going to Rochester, and he *did* go to *please* me, and the selfish things have been mad ever since.

She said she pitied Willard if he ever had to live with me again, and called me names.

She had the nerve to say she had waited on me more than any one that ever came there and that she had sent out and gotten things for me to eat, any thing I expressed a desire for.

She *lied* about both in fact I have found her to be a liar long ago any way.

When I told her that she talked to Willard made him different, she smiled and said "perhaps." She said Gertie came to make trouble and had succeeded admirably, and Gertie said, "since you feel this way Mrs Thomson I cant accept your hospitality and if you will make out my bill, I'll settle," she said in the most insulting way "No I thank you, I dont take boarders, and if I did I would choose who came to my house!" the grossest insult she could have offered any one! I will *never forgive it*.

Father was so cut up over it, he went to town with me, to get my letter and money from Willard, and the tears rolled down his face, he is *crushed over it*.

Both Aunts were lovely in their sympathy and love to us both, we did not eat at Thomsons, ate at Aunt Evas, and she said any thing comforting she could think of, and Father and Aunt Laura went to the train with us, watched us leave. We left Batavia at 11:35 got to Buffalo at one o'clock, and I got my ticket for $15.00 and we came up to the "Waldemar", to see Margaret Whitman. We leave at 6 o'clock on our home ward trip. What a different home coming to what I fancied my first visit home would be, when I left a happy bride, secure in my husbands love, expecting his protection from storms and troubles, yet have just under gone a trying ordeal, at his Grand Mothers hands, and I am not *sure* of the stand he will take!

CHAPTER SIX

Separation

Sunday Nov. 3.—1901.

Home again! We left Buffalo at 6 o'clock got to Cleveland at 9:50, reached Cincinatti this morning at 8 o'clock left at 8:30 and arrived here at 6:30 found Frank & Willie at the train to meet us, and when we got to the house Pa was standing at the gate, and I said, "Hello dad" and hugged him before he could realize it was I, he said brokenly, "I am so glad to see you, go in the house they are wild to see you" and then Carrie ran out, and Clarence, Louise and then they called Ma and she nearly smothered me with kisses, they all did, no one ever received a warmer welcome, and it seems good to be *home*.

Friday Nov. 8.—1901.

I have not been out of the house since I came, and I have an awful cold, I dont feel like doing any thing.

I have written 24 pages to Willard and told him all, and I am anxious to hear from him, I feel restless and unsettled till I hear from him.

I have also written to Father, Ethie and Jessie, and hope to hear from all *soon*.

I dont care to go out any place or see any one yet.

Sunday Nov. 10.—1901.

This is a lovely day but I have felt too bad to go out any where. Miss Sophia Albert called, and spent the afternoon with

161

us. Mr Johnson, a young man who came to meet Carrie last Tuesday evening, called Friday evening and I sent he and Carrie to town to get some quinine for my cold, and he brought me a box of candy and was very nice to me, so I met him at the door tonight and he tried to get me to go with them to church tonight, but I felt too bad and too I stayed with Ma, we had a very nice talk.

Mr Johnson told me to be down there when they came home but I was not.

Monday Nov. 11.—1901.

I have not heard from Willard yet, and I am feeling rather blue over it, but he may have waited to write Sunday.

Mr Johnson telephoned to take Carrie to the show tomorrow night, asked about me and said he certainly did like me.

Tuesday Nov. 12.—1901.

Gertie heard from Homer this morning and I felt awfully disappointed that I did not get the letter I had been looking for, but this afternoon I *did* get it, he sent me my weekly allowance, and said he regretted the disgraceful actions of his Grandparents and he hadint thought there was any unpleasantness other than *she* wanted us to go to house keeping, and if he had known it I should never have stayed there at all. So I feel that he is going to prove to every one that he is a *man,* and will *defend his wife!*

He has been most dead with a cold too for over a week, and I have been too at same time, but I feel uneasy about him, am glad he likes his room, trust he will be comfortable and have good health this winter.

Thursday Nov. 14.—1901.

Last night Mrs Albert and Sophia took me to see "The Belle Of New York," [a musical by Hugh Morton] and it was *splendid,* and it seemed like old times to listen to the music & see old familiar faces, and I wore my blue silk, and knew there were many who knew I was Mrs Leland of N. York. I was introduced to Mrs L. G. Walker but I never cared for her, she saw I didint then tried to be nice a little.

162

November 1901–April 1902

The Opera house is *lovely* since it has been remodeled, it is similar to the "Baker Theatre", of Rochester.

This afternoon we went to town and saw so many I used to know, and all seemed glad to see me, say I am looking so well, and Anderson just shook my hand so warmly, and looked like he really was delighted to see me.

Monday Nov. 18.—1901.

Hallie Barnes called yesterday aft. said she was so glad to see me it looked like she never would see me again.

She is a swell little trick, and pretty. This morning I went to town and got my hat it is an $18.00 pattern hat but I got it greatly reduced, it is a black and pink creation parma [violet] & chinelle.

I hope Willard will like me in it.

I have a dainty pretty pair of shoes too. I went in to bother Mr Johnson and Carrie last night and sat him out. I am anxious to hear from Willard.

Tuesday Nov. 19.—1901.

I got Willards letter this morning his cold is better, it has been awful cold and so much snow all week. He says there is a nice crowd at the boarding house, they have pedro every evening and a good time generally. Says he will hear *her side* when he goes up Thanksgiving! Not a doubt in my mind as to that, she knows how to *lie!* She has ruined our happiness for 14 months, will she succeed in ruining our lives as she is trying to do?

Gertrude called this evening, and we went to see Carlotta this afternoon. She has been away three months having great times.

She and Will are happy yet.

Friday Nov. 22.—1901.

Tonight Ma & Pa, Carrie, Mr Johnson, Gertie and I went to hear Col. John B. Gordon [commander of the United Confederate Veterans] in his lecture, "The first days of the confederacy," at the Opera house.

Mel Gardner came and sat with us and we had lots of fun, he said I was brilliant and that I was as pretty as ever. He came home with us in the moon light and said I was as jolly as ever, and it certainly did seem like old times.

The lecture was good, and I enjoy going to this pretty theatre.

Wednesday Nov. 27.—1901.

I had a letter from Willard today that caused me so much trouble, I have wept as bitterly as at any time since we married.

Seventeen months ago tonight we stood at the altar and before God and man swore to love, honor, & serve each other so long as both should live.

I believe both were perfectly sincere in vowing to forsake all others and cleave only to each other, yet since early Spring things have been going from bad to worse till today I have received a letter that has caused me to shed as many bitter tears as any yet wrung from my aching heart.

God knows my heart and knows I am willing to do my part to get along with the husband I have chosen, but I cant *make* him see any thing for old Granny influences him all the time.

Friday Nov. 29.—1901.

Tonight we all went to hear A. W. Hanks on "Sunshine and Shadow," it was fun from the rise of the curtain to the fall of it. Mrs Arnold sat by us and we enjoyed it very much.

Wednesday Dec. 4.—1901.

Thanksgiving we had a nice dinner and all were here but Fannie, but I never see any contentment, I am perfectly miserable, and well I may be, for Willard is certainly acting the scoundrel with me.

He tries to excuse Granny on two trivial matters, but passes over the main insult, and I can see plainly he is taking her part in the affair.

He says people comment on his improved health, that he is gaining flesh and feels better than for a year past, and they tell him it certainly agrees with him to have his wife away. He continues, "Our land lady made the remark the other day that a married woman had no business in a boarding house where she had nothing to do, for all she did was to make mischief and stir up strife, and she didint want any around her," he said "So you see married ladies are not wanted here." He says "You speak of my getting lonely, how can I when every one is so full of fun around the house."

I had told him that when he wanted me and would tell me I would come to him, and it seems to have scared him nearly to death, he takes pains to tell me I am not wanted.

He thinks because I have been so fair with him, and forgiven snubs and told him I was willing to love him and do my part if he would help me, that he can treat me any way and I will still love him, but if he cares for my love at all, he had best be careful, for I can hate him as cordially as I ever loved him.

God only knows where this will end since he seems determined to do wrong all the way through.

Wednesday Dec. 11.—1901.

Gertie and I went to see Mrs Underhill and shopping this afternoon, and tonight we went to see "Sapho" [*Sappho*, written by Alphonse Daudet and adapted to the American stage by William Clyde Fitch], it is *grand*. It has been a long time since I saw any thing as fine, and it is true to life. A couple love each other devotedly till his people come between them then he leaves her and breaks her heart, and in after years he returns to her, but it is too late for she has given him up forever and has no place for him.

Thursday Dec. 12.—1901.

Tonight we all went to hear Geo. W. Cable on "Parson Jones," ["Posson Jone'," a short story first published by George Washington Cable in 1876] but I did not enjoy it much, had neuralgia too bad and was restless.

Friday Dec. 13.—1901.

Today is Pa's birth day he is 71 yrs. old, and Will and Louise were here to dinner, and Clarence was off too.

Mrs Allin came in just at dinner and stayed till 3 o'clock, she said the dinner was *fine*.

I had a line from Willard this morning, said

Separation

"Dear Madge,
Enclosed find M. O. for four dollars.

Respt.
W. C. Leland"

Of course this adds to my respect for him. I cant see what he means.

Friday Dec. 20.—1901.

Gertie left for Ga this morning and I know she will have a nice time, but we miss her.

Havint heard from Willard yet, dont know what he means to do.

Saturday Dec. 21.—1901.

Tonight Carrie and I went to town and Mr Johnson and Mr Clemmons took us around, we had lots of fun, shocked Smith, Anderson and some of the other clerks by promenading together.

"Cliff" treated us to cream, and bought us some candy, we had lots of fun, and I like him splendidly.

Sunday Dec. 22.—1901.

A perfectly awful day! Frank came in at eleven o'clock and says he had vertigo and ~~fle~~ fell down the stairs and this morning at three o'clock Pa waked and heard him groaning, and soon Clarence he and I were working with him, and I will *never forget* how he looked, bloody as he could be, black eye, & ear, cuts on nose, lip, & chin, and blood oozing out of nose mouth and ear. I bathed him and at 6 o'clock we got him into a chair, and at 9 Willie came and we got him into bed up stairs. He is awfully hurt, was unconscious till noon.

I am worn out but went in to see Mr Johnson awhile, he had the blues and wanted to talk to me.

His Aunt had spoken to him about the life he was leading and it put him to studying. I felt that I was not capable of helping him, but I would do any thing to help him. I certainly like him.

166

Christmas Eve. Dec 24.—1901—Tues.

Mr Cliff had asked to come out and talk with me last night but as Carrie was going away we decided we would better not keep our "date."

Today we have been up town all morning and are tired down, for Mr Johnson took us to town tonight, and we burned all evening, had lots of fun.

We had cream, orange phosphate candy and he bought fire works, had fun in firing them off to scare Kid, then we sat on the railing and talked till late.

I saw Mrs Mill, Carmelia, and others I had not seen since I came home.

We have fixed up the presents for *all* in the parlor, will try to enjoy Christmas.

Christmas Dec. 25.—1901. Wednesday

In spite of every thing we have had a very enjoyable day, this morning we all went in the parlor to see what we had received and there were surprises for all.

Pa had a cane silver mounted from Sis & I, ties from Fannie & Clarence, kerchief from Ma, tooth brush from Carrie, cigars from Will.

Ma got ½ doz silver desert spoons, beauties from Sis and I, a doz linen napkins and dressing saque from me, gloves, kerchief and throw from Fannie, hair brush from Clarence, kerchief from Carrie.

Clarence got two books from Sis & I, tie from Fannie, kerchiefs from Carrie, & Ma.

Carrie received the handsomest silk parasol with pearl and gold handle I ever saw from Mr Johnson, elegant drawn work kerchief from Lillie Alley, & lace trimmed one from Gertie, and book from me, lace protector for collar from Lillie Condra, facinator [a scarf] from Fannie.

I received a beautiful picture from Gertie another from Ma, kerchief from Carrie, dresser scarf from Fannie, and two pound box of candy and basket of fruit from "Mr Cliff."

We had a fine dinner, after which Mr Johnson called and tonight he took Carrie to the show, and Mrs Albert took me, to see "Other peoples money" [*Other People's Money* by Edward Owings Towne]. It was splendid and Mrs Walker, Mrs Albert and I sat on the back row and "Cliff" kept looking back at me when any thing good happened, and the music was *fine*.

Coming home we had lots of fun all of us together, Mr Albert acting jealous of Johnson and we found a whiskey bottle on the gate post at Alberts and he said, "Johnson you left that on the wrong gate it is next door you stop."

Thursday Dec. 26.—1901.

Mr Johnson telephoned me he was coming out tonight and he has just gone, he wanted to tell me his troubles, and Carrie left us at 9 o'clock, he stayed till 10:30, and told me all about Susie. He has never loved her but she is determined she will marry him in spite of every thing, even against his will, and she is so desperate and determined that it worries him most to death.

He likes me fine and considers me one of his very best friends, and my heart goes out to him in his trouble.

His mother is dead, and he has no home and he is lonely and craves a home, says he feels at home here, and feels like I am kin to him, and that he has known me all his life, I feel the same towards him.

Friday Dec. 27.—1901.

Mr Johnson phoned me this evening he was "in for it" with Susie, wanted to talk with me, so he came right up and talked it over with me, but felt he could not refuse to go out and be manly, said it was not in him to be cowardly and he grasped my hand held it a moment and bade me good by and left. I feel awfully uneasy about him for I think they mean to trap him.

Carrie and I went to the recital by the pupils of Southern Conservatory of music [directed by Professor Cadek] that was fine.

Saturday Dec. 28.—1901.

"Cliff" phoned me early this morning, he said it was worse if any thing than yesterday, had the blues, wanted to see me tonight, I told him if it did not rain tonight I would be up town, he said he would meet me at Millers.

Poor boy is in deep trouble.

As it kept on raining he knew we could not go so he phoned us instead of seeing us.

November 1901–April 1902

Sunday Dec. 29.—1901.

Mr Johnson came out tonight and was in so much trouble he did not care to attend church, and wanted to talk to me, so Carrie talked, played the piano while he talked to me, we sat either side of him on the sofa and had lots of fun even if he was so blue.

"New Years Eve." Dec. 31.—1901.

Well today has been a blue one to me the contrast between this and a year ago when I went to Batavia to surprise him and he was so happy to have me with him, he said I was all the world to him, and we were happy together, and it has been over three weeks since he wrote me a line, even when Christmas cheer was abroad in the land, he did not even send greetings or a word, and he knew I was ill, yet has not cared whether I lived or died.

He has ruined my life if this is all he cares for me!

Mr Johnson ran up to see me a few moments tonight to ask my valuable advise, and Mel had said he would be up but he was bidden to a banquet, so failed to appear, but I dont blame him.

We had planned to observe watch, but there wasint any thing going on in town so Mr Cliff just came out and he is happy, having gotten out of his scrape. We played parcheesi and had lots of fun together.

New Years day. Jan. 1.—1902.

This has been so far rather a gloomy beginning of the year.

Mary Relyea's father died yesterday and Carrie went over there early and Ma and I spent the morning in the kitchen and I have felt so little like doing any thing this afternoon.

Mr Johnson has just phoned me, but the boys were teasing him so, he said he would call me up again later.

Carrie and I are wild to go to the play tonight, "At Valley Forge" [*At Valley Forge: A Comedy Drama of 1776* (1901) by William Lynch Roberts].

Mr Johnson called just now and said if I would be at the theatre he would show me the prettiest Georgia girl I ever saw, and Carrie and I feel slighted for we wanted to go, but Carrie acted too independent last night, while we were playing Cringle [a parlor game], so cross etc, he did not know what to think, and

I think he is showing her that "there are others" who will treat him nicely he can take to the shows.

Wednesday Jan. 8.—1901 [1902].

Mr Johnson has been coming out about every other night and we three having lots of fun, we have jollied about us going to New York together, finding Carries ideal and bringing him to her, etc, but tonight she was tired and didint want him to come, so she left at 9:30 and we had quite a little chat and I found that all said in jest may not all be jest after all.

I am fortunate in having met such a fellow now, when I am in the very deepest trouble that a woman can have. Willard has proven that he does not love me and would be glad if it was all over between us, has quit sending me money.

The family are in reduced circumstances and I wont burden them or live here where so many would rejoice at my unhappiness, others pity in a contemptuous way the girl who thought she was making such a brilliant match and it had turned out disastrously.

Unless Willard supports me, and does his duty I will not remain his wife, I am too young to allow him to ruin my life in this way, yet I have to *live* in the time that I am suing for a divorce, and I have no money or any way to get along but to start out in the world and make my way.

This is where he is so valuable, I know he cares enough for me to go where ever I do and protect me from harm.

The insults, that fall to a woman who battles with the world, are what I have dreaded, and with this honest fellow that would shield me from all harm in a strange city, I need not fear any thing from that source.

Willard said in the letter that came today, that, "he was sorry he ever married me, for he had come to the conclusion that he was not fit to be a husband. He would give any thing if he could place me back in my home where I was before he took me away." This he can never do, and since he has done as he has I will have to suffer humiliation, and untold regret and remorse.

Why should I struggle in the world for a living and remain his wife in name only, rather than get a divorce, when if I was *free*, I could marry a man that would love me devotedly, be good and kind to me, proud of me, take good care of me and not talk about his efforts in my behalf like it was a hard ship for him, but instead take pleasure in exerting him self to make me happy in every way possible.

Will God call me guilty if after all my efforts to be true to my husband, to do my duty to him, and he *will not* have it that way, if I find contentment in another love? If I marry him and lead a pure life as an honored wife, instead of running the risk of poverty and discouragements causing me to drift perhaps. *Which is right?*

Thursday Jan. 9.—1901 [1902].

Last night we three went to Presbyterian church as we thought to prayer meeting, but we found a business meeting, and refreshments served in dining room, but we left, didint stay of course, and had cream at Live & Let Live [the most popular drugstore-meeting spot in Chattanooga] on the way home.

This aft. I met him at corner of Market and 9*th*. and we took a ride to Rosswell [a subdivision of Chattanooga] and back, and he told me many things that comforted me. He came nearly home with me and I enjoyed the afternoon.

Friday Jan. 10.—1901 [1902].

I wanted to hear Bob Taylors lecture, and phoned Mr Johnson to get my ticket as he had my pocket book, but all the tickets were sold, so I stayed home and at quarter to 10 o'clock Carrie got mad left the room huffy and I made it right with him [Cliff Johnson?] or tried to.

Sunday Jan. 12.—1901 [1902].

I would hate to feel that I had knocked Carrie out of any pleasure by going in the parlor, yet she feels that I have, and Mr Johnson liked her as well as ever while she treated him right, but she has snubbed him unmercifully of late and I guess it is over, our pleasant times together, and I am sorry.

This aft. Mr Johnson and Mr Clemmons called we had music and lively times, and tonight we all went to the mass meeting at the Auditorium and while there he talked to me, and coming home Carrie didint say one word to him and he stayed till 10:30 and she let me see him to the door, hardly told him good bye.

Separation

Monday Jan. 13.—1901 [1902].

Tonight Prof Foster lectured on liquid air to crowded house at opera house.

Pa and Ma, Carrie and I went and Mr Johnson sat behind us and came home with us, he and Carrie had rather a little more to say to each other than before and I wish they would be sensible and make up.

Tuesday Jan. 14.—1901 [1902].

Carrie and I spent today at Mrs Otts had very pleasant time, and enjoyed the dinner so much.

We came home was looking for letters, but found none. I was crazy to go to see, "The sign of the cross" [a play by Wilson Barrett], but couldint, Carrie went. Mr Johnson wanted to see me so much he could hardly give it up, but I could not let him come.

Wednesday Jan. 15. 1901 [1902].

This morning at 9 o'clock Bess Snodgrass was married and she passed here in carriage going to the train, looked beautiful.

I got the sweetest, dearest letter too and had just finished reading when I had a chat over the phone with "Cliff".

My letter is due now, hope to hear this afternoon. This dreary world when love is gone! Oh! Willard you cant know what you are doing to act like this.

Thursday Jan. 16—1901 [1902].

Tonight Cliff wanted to call and I suggested going to entertainment at the Unitarian church by school of expression, and he brought Mr Charlie Clemmons an awfully handsome fellow, and as he did not want to go we stayed home. Had lots of fun and yet we got a chance to talk a little privately too.

Friday Jan. 17.—1901 [1902].

Gertie came in at 12 o'clock last night and this morning at 10 o'clock I was called to the phone and it was Uncle Dave at Lee station, said Grandpa was dying and we begun to fix Ma up to go, and we all went to see Pa & Ma off at 2:30 this aft.

Poor Mother is frightened, so afraid she will be too late to see him *alive*.

We went to Baptist church to Needham meeting to hear Oscar Seagle sing.

Tonight Cliff had a date thinking he could not come out here, and when I told him he could, he said he would give $50.00 to get out of the engagement, but he wanted to see me if only a *moment* so I let him come from 7 till 8 and he certainly hated to leave me.

Sunday Jan. 19.—1901 [1902].

Grandpa died yesterday at six minutes past one, and will be buried today, Pa phoned us and this is all we know.

Cliff came out to see me this aft. and Walter Trueheart came so as they took him up stairs, and I knew it would never do for him to know I was entertaining young men, I had to leave my dear boy and stay with the crowd some, but I dislike to miss a moment of his time.

Tonight Frank and Gertie, Carrie & I went to the Auditorium to union services, and we saw George & Leonard in the choir so a wild desire seized them to join the choir, and I followed too.

I saw my boy sitting in the congregation and I watched him, he behaves beautifully and seems serious. I wish he would be a christian, bless him I love him dearly!

Carrie and George started off after church, Gertie went back to find her furs she left with Frank, and Clemmons came to talk to me, and Gertie joined us and still Cliff did not show up, but when we started home he was waiting out side for us, and we just came on home *alone,* asked no one any odds.

George didint come in so Cliff and I had the parlor alone till quarter to eleven! I believe he loves me dearer than any thing, he says I am his *life.* Says he never loved before, never will again, I am perfect in his eyes, if I have a fault he cant see it, all he wants to make him perfectly happy is *me,* the sooner the better, he wants me the very *first day I am free!*

He says his *whole heart is mine,* his life work will be to make me happy.

Monday Jan. 20.—1901 [1902].

This morning Uncle Pyott phoned, he was at John Pyotts, wanted to know how Grandpa was, he and Aunt Mary were on the way over, said they wanted to see us, so we went, Pa came home just as we were starting. They insisted on our staying to dinner and as it was so far home and getting cold we stayed, and had a splendid dinner.

All very nice but Cora and she hasint any sense, never did have.

We came by Mrs Mulls and had a fine chat with her, she has a mother-in-law and knows what it is to *suffer!*

We were waiting at Live & Let Live for time for Gertie to go to womans chorus and I saw a man come in that the moment I saw his face I said, "Why that is Dr Vickers" and he walked back in the store, and when he turned I bowed and he came to shake hands, said he thought he knew us, had asked the clerk but couldint catch the names, and he seemed so delighted to see us.

He looked natural and seemed like old times to chat him.

Wednesday Jan. 22.—1902.

Monday night Pa was taken ill and Will stayed till 12 o'clock, Clarence sat up all night. We were awfully uneasy about him came near phoning for Ma to come, but last night we feared today would be dreadful for her to drive through the country, so we wrote a card for her to come home, look for her any time. Dr Nolen said Pa was not bad off, he was more frightened than was necessary.

Cliff wanted to come last night but Pa was too ill, so he had a date with Carrie tonight and he came early but I didint go in till 9 o'clock.

He is so dear, he loves me devotedly.

Thursday Jan. 23.—1902.

Uncle Pyott and Aunt Mary came to spend the day and we had a very nice day considering all things.

Cliff called at eight o'clock, at 12 o'clock and I left the dinner table to go and it was lucky he called then, while they were down stairs, could not hear us talking. When I went down to dinner Gertie said "Is she going this afternoon?" I said "yes," and it passed unnoticed.

He called at 7 o'clock and I asked Pa if he could come and he said yes, so I have had my boy all evening with me.

174

He loves me truely I feel sure, says I am all that makes life dear to him, he would not care to live if I was taken away from him, and that *nothing* in this world could make him love me less, he tried to keep from loving me but he could not help it, he loves me better than him self, and if he *does,* that is a love to be *prized!*

He says i am the sweetest thing in the world and all he needs to have a happy home, a sweet resting place at close of the day, is *me,* he is perfectly happy when with me, *home* would be the dearest spot on earth to him if I was there to greet him noon and night.

I would never have to ask him to stay home evenings, it would be his delight to be with me, a privelege he hopes to have ere long, *bless his dear heart.*

Sunday Jan. 26.—1902.

I have been ill since Thursday night and Cliff has been inquiring for me each day. This aft. he came at three stayed till five, came tonight and Carrie stayed in till 9:30 so we only had a half hour together, it was provoking.

Gertie took Carrie to task about it, but I havint. Tonight we have been chatting he says for me to just consider it *settled I am not going away,* and he means it.

Dearest boy in the world I know.

He never wants me to leave him, wont leave me even for his health.

Miss Cora Lee Palmer brought a young man out ~~last ni~~ tonight (Monday). He is jolly and about 38 I would think but I dont trust him, I think I am on to his little game alright, at any rate I shall keep my eye on him and be doubly careful from now on.

When he gets any proof to blast my name to the intense satisfaction of those old demons he will know it!

I received today the most insulting letter I ever heard, no man would have penned such lines to a lady, nothing short of a fiend would have done it.

The war is on now, its fight to the bitter end!

Tuesday Jan. 28.—1902.

It is bitter cold today and ice and sleet over every thing yet my boy is out in it working hard. I havint heard from him this morning he may be worse, I hope not though.

Separation

Cant see him till tomorrow night for Pa says Sunday and Wednesday is enough to see him, but we cant hardly endure it not to see each other every evening. Of course it is best to be prudent, it means safety at this time.

Wednesday ~~Feb.~~ Jan. 29.—1902.

Tonight my boy came and of course we had lots to talk about, enjoyed the evening very much indeed. He says I dont love him like he does me that I am not so foolish over him as he is me, says there is not a quarter of an hour passes that he dont think of me.

Friday Jan. 31.—1902.

This afternoon Carrie and I went to town and going from one department to another I heard Carrie say, "Hello Mr Clemmons" and I looked over my shoulder saw Charlie C. and Cliff, but I went on, but directly Cliff came and asked us to take cream with him and we four had lots of fun.

He said he was so blue he would give the world to talk to me two hours, he *must see me,* so he phoned Gertie to ask Pa if he could come, he said *no,* till Cliff said he was going away then he said he could come, but he forfited his date for Sunday.

He was ready to leave in the morning at 9 o'clock, but after talking it over with me he decided not to go, said they would not believe he left on account of his health, they would think he left rather than stand by me in my troubles, and rather than have me have *24 hours* of trouble on his account, he would stay here and die. I could not change him, he would not go at all. I know he loves me devotedly to risk his life for me.

Sunday Feb. 2.—1902.

We wanted to know if winter was over or if six weeks more of winter was to be endured, and while it snowed early this morning the sun shone a good deal later, so we can expect winter weather awhile now.

This has been a long day to me and I know it has been to him.

Gertie and I went to Vespers at the Unitarian church at 5 o'clock, and it was quite interesting.

Tonight we three went to the Stone church to last of the Needham services the house was crowded, and we went to the gallery, and Cliff came late, we moved over and he sat with us, we had a little consolation after all being together, even though we could not talk very much.

He walked home with all of us and left with a good bye, it seemed hard.

Monday Feb. 3.—1902.

This has been a very busy day to me and quite interesting too.

I cleaned up the third floor, bathed and washed my hair, then at 3 o'clock Gertie and I went to see Doctor Rock, ~~spirtet~~ Spirit medium [the Hindoo Seer, one of several spiritualist mediums in the area], made a date for 6 o'clock. We burned an hour, spent from three till 5 at studio, womans rehearsal, then went to musical tea at rectory of Episcopal church, and was back at 20 Oak at 6 o'clock.

He [Dr. Rock] told me my married life from beginning till now. Said the time was that he [Willard] worshipped me, I filled his life and he was true, till I failed in personal magnetism, then he turned from me to a dark, low, well rounded beautiful woman, and he was living with her he *saw them together.*

Said I had a dark magic life before me, I was like a fly in the spiders web, and the answer to what course I should take, "Consult the medium".

He said he could bring him back to me, give me absolute control over him, and change the conditions in my favor. Said I trusted a woman that played me false, etc. I think I can remember all the rest.

I gave him the case, and am to go back tomorrow, no Wednesday.

Cliff phoned the moment I got in and he said I was changed, and I know it seemed to me he had come from another world, out of the past.

Tuesday Feb. 4.—1902.

Tonight Ma, Carrie, Gertie and I went to hear the "Mendleshon Quartette," at Opera house, and it was *fine!*

Separation

Miss Marguirite Smith as child impersonator was bewitching, and the concert bright, sweet, and finished.

Norman and his girl were there and Elmo and his girl, Mr Walter & his, but I looked in vain for "Cliff" my darling! It was so good I wanted him to enjoy it too.

Mrs Arnold sat by us asked so many questions about "Willard", hard to answer.

Wednesday Feb. 5.—1902.

I went over to see the Hindoo Seer this morning and found him *gone!*

All my hopes were shattered by that house devoid of the sign, I knew he had skipped, and all the help I had hoped to get from him, was a mistake.

Then I remembered all the dark events that he said were crowding in upon me, and that all this I have to face *alone,* without any knowledge of how to begin.

Cliff is coming tonight and I am so anxious to see him again.

Thursday Feb. 6.—1902.

Cliff laughed heartily at my beleiving "that old scoundrel" as he called him and it amused me to see him laugh.

He said he lied if he said his motives were not pure, and didint *dream* that I had taken any thing seriously till later in the evening, when he quit laughing and talked seriously enough.

Said *I knew* he loved me foolishly, that I was all he had to live for, all that life held dear for him was me, and that he would if he could lead me out before the world as his own, his acknowledged wife! He couldint ask for greater happiness than that, and the sooner I could be free so he could prove his intentions, the better it would suit him.

This afternoon Carrie and I shopped till 4:15 then I went up to the studio tea, at Conservatory of music.

Found Miss Cora Lee Palmer & Mr Sherman there and I had bushels of fun, for while I dont trust the man, at the same time I have to laugh at him he is so full of fun. The womans chorus was prepared with three vocal selections, solos, vocal, piano, & violin, were given at intervals during the two hours from four till six o'clock, and tea, whipped cream, and cheese wafers were served.

I enjoyed it very much, and we came home to supper, then George Bectel called tonight. He, Gertie, & I sang most of the evening, had a jolly good time till 9:30 when he bade us good night very nicely. Said he was indeed glad to have met me hoped to see me again *often* and get better acquainted with me.

Saturday Feb. 8.—1902.

I heard from Willard and Jessie yesterday aft. and Father the day before. Willard said he had been ill, had intended sending me some money but couldint now. Said he had no decision to make, signed him self "Yours with love - W." The meaner I talk to him, the more he turns, the better his letters are.

I want his answer, *must have it.*

Gertie and I went over to see Minnie this afternoon, and met Cliff at Millers, he walked with us to Pam's then back to Lovemans, and had to go to Rossville [a town in Georgia], but it was pleasant to see him that short time even.

Disappointed tonight, missed the show.

Sunday Feb. 9.—1902.

This afternoon Gertie and I went to the sacred concert at the Auditorium, Cliff, Elmo, and Charlie Clemmons were there but of course he could not come to me without attracting attention, and we had to just fore go the pleasure of a chat. The music was good and Cora Lee Palmer, came to Vespers with us. Tonight Walter Trueheart came at the time I expected ~~you~~ Cliff, and I was disgusted to think he had come to spoil our evening, but when he heard "Carries beau" coming he and Gertie ran up stairs, so we three stayed in the parlor till 9 when he left, and that left us *only one hour!*

He says he cant express his love, all the love that God gave him is given to me, that I am dearer to him than *his own life,* I am *his darling* and he will *never* give me up.

Tuesday Feb. 11.—1902.

I have written a good long letter to Willard and I hope to rouse him from his sleep, enough to get him to commit him self.

Separation

Gertie and I went to church last night, sat by Mr Sherman & Cora Lee, had lots of fun, yet enjoyed the service too. I like the evangelist.

This aft. Will Clemmons phoned to know if we were going to rehearsal tonight, and we had lots of fun.

He admires Gertie very much, and jollied me about Mr Johnson.

We had a very good rehearsal then came by church heard a part of his sermon. Church was awfully full but a half dozen men got up and gave us chairs when we got in.

Wednesday Feb. 12.—1902.

I had a long pert letter from Ethie this morning saying all the trouble between Willard and I was my awful extravagance, and she didint think we ever could live happily together again and I was better off with my people. I have been furious ever since I read her letter, I shall give her fits when I answer too.

Cliff comes tonight.

Sunday Feb. 16.—1902.

Friday it snowed all day and yesterday morning there was great sport for those sleighing and coasting.

Mr Johnson phoned me that he was sorry I didint go to the show the morning before for he wanted to show me his "Janeen". He had begged Sis and I to go, he would bring us home, and when he phoned this it made me furious. Charlie Clemmons talked to me a long time then said it cost Cliff $7.00, tickets, roses, and carriage, and then Cliff talked some more. Wanted us to go to town he wanted to see me, etc, and he said for me to go to hear Sam Jones at Auditorium this aft. and he would come to us, but we went in the choir and on our way home in passing Miss M^c-Gregory's I did not look till I had passed then when I turned round I saw him with her, the curtains held back, both rubbering!

Well when he came tonight I just told him what I thought of him, told him he need not prepare any such elaborate jokes for me for I failed to appreciate them, I didint care how many young ladies he took to the theatre, but when he intended to I did not care to have him beg us to go, that he might see us home. I told him if he was tired of our friend ship, he need not resort to such means to rid him self of me, a hint to the wise is sufficient.

He actually shed tears, and looked hurt to the quick, said he had no such motives, nothing like that was in his heart, he thought it was decided I could not go before he made the date with her. Said he was not angry he was *hurt*.

He did every thing to prove he was the same, said his love was so great he could not express it, I was all he had to live for, he would always love me.

Monday Feb. 17.—1902.

Tonight Mr Johnson and I were chatting pleasantly over the phone, and he wants to take dancing lessons on Wednesday evening, and wanted to call two evenings a week instead and I know Pa would never consent to it, so when he asked what they said I said they didint see any reason to allow him two evenings instead of one, especially since he had taken our regular evening for some one else and that they had said a plenty, he got mad, said too much talking over nothing, if that was the way they were going to do he would call his days off from out here, he saw through the whole thing, and the more we talked the worse it got so we "rang off."

I never was more surprised at any thing than this, it has shocked me, makes me ill, the thought that he may be a fraud, and the Hindoo *right*.

Tuesday Feb. 18.—1902.

He had asked to call tonight, so I phoned him to come out I would not go to the rehearsal, wanted to talk to him, he said he would come, then at noon he phoned to say he could not come out, he had no date but just couldint come, I said, "I shall not insist; but I prefer it", he said he would come, but about six o'clock he rang up to say he could not come, he would not come to this house again, he didint have to beg to go to the best houses in this town. I told him "if I had doubted that, he could never have come to ours", he would tell me if he ever saw me again, and I told him that could not be if he refused to come out tonight, that no gentleman would refuse a lady an interview, he was ugly, nothing to be gained by talking further, he had carried it as far as he cared to, and rang off! Thus I find I have been duped by the *greatest scoundrel yet!*

Separation

Such shocks as this kill, I never yet had any thing to tear me up worse for it was so sudden, so unexpected. Had he done this Sunday night I would not have been surprised, but after his actions when I had given him every chance it stuns me!

We went to rehearsal, Will Clemmons handed Carrie an envelope containing my ring, asking her to hand to Mrs Leland.

I wouldint let Clemmons see there was any thing wrong, I was as bright as ever.

Wednesday Feb. 19th. 1902.

Gertie and I went to church to hear Dr Broughton, Sherman came to us and sat by us, soon Elmo Johnson and his girl came and sat by me, he is *sweet* looking, has a good face and seems to be so gentle and good, he looked at me and they left first and in passing us he looked down into my eyes, and smiled, I returned it cordially.

Friday Feb. 21.—1902.

Last night we three girls went to church, tonight Carrie and I went to the farewell services, and Gertie went to the basket ball game, but I wouldint have missed Dr Broughtons last talk for any thing hardly. He is the sweetest spirited man I ever saw, and his sermon on the second coming of Christ was the finest I ever heard, it opened up to me a new line of thought, and made plain many points I have thought over often.

He is funny, but refined and not in the least sensational.

Mr Johnson came in and passed me, I barely knew him, and he is not happy one bit, he never will be he cant be and tell all the lies he does, if he has a conscience.

Sunday Feb. 23.—1902.

Gertie and I went to the concert this afternoon, saw Mr Johnson, spoke and we went way around from him, but Charlie Clemmons sat behind us, we talked and I think he wanted to find out how we were taking it about Cliff, but if he was he found we were *living* just the same as ever.

We went to "Vespers" at five o'clock and to Stone church choral service sat in the gallery, Johnson and McGregory came in and sat right under us down stairs.

He is not attentive at all to her, paid very little attention to her, he looked all over the church but right above him to see us, but he spoke as he passed us after church. He can act as he pleases but he wont ever be a contented man, he cant be.

Friday I had a kind letter from Father saying he had done all he could in mine and Willards affairs, things had reached such a crisis he was powerless.

Saturday I heard from Willard, he said his decision was "that the *sooner we parted the better, he would not furnish me any more money* etc". He casts me aside for "Granny," and I am helpless without money, yet too proud to stay home, or to work here. I shall appeal to Father to help me to a position where I can make a good salary. To think that boy would ever for sake me, the Madge he seemed to worship for years, the girl that was his whole life, that made life even endurable for him, after all *his vows of love and protection,* then to desert me for no cause on earth only that *she* wants him to.

Monday Feb. 24.—1902.

I have written a long letter to Father [Mr. Leland], I told him all, asked him to lend me money to enable me to study six months in N.Y. city to be a milliner. I told him the memory of those first happy days before we went North would never leave me, and that in my heart there was, for that tender devoted young husband, still great tenderness and love.

I know he will never do right while she lives and he listens to her, for she hates me and has determined to seperate us ever since we left Batavia.

Wednesday Feb. 26.—1902.

Last night we went to rehearsal and the entertainment is to be given April 7*th*.

This morning we went up town and I phoned from Live and Let Live that I wanted to speak to him a moment, so he came over and walked down Market to 4*th* up to High street, and I talked to him calmly yet quite emphatically, determined to know the kind of man I had been fooled by. I certainly never was more duped in my whole life than by him. He was lying to me yet he hopes we will be good friends he will always think of me, hopes to see me in New York, will have my well fare at heart etc.

Separation

I told him I didint ask to see him to scold him, all I wanted to know was if he had only changed for some cause or other, or if he had lied to me all the time, and I had found that he had only been playing a part, and he knew what he was as well as for me to say it.

He said that all I had said to him all my secrets should be locked in his bosom and *die with him,* his own brother should never know that he had ever called on me.

I came home, and we girls took Louise to University to see the funerel of Loveman Noa, the only military funerel procession I ever saw and it was strangely sad to me. Any thing military reminds me of him.

We spent last Saturday night with Mr Sherman and Cora Lee Palmer, they had two boxes of candy and we had lots of fun, he tried to steal my pon pon out of my hair and teased a lot.

We didint know till Sam Jones was at the Auditorium Sunday before last that Lillie McKinley was a widow, we were in the choir and we saw her in mourning, and I knew he was dead.

She looks prettier than before.

Sunday Mch. 2nd. 1902.

The Prince of Prussia [Prince Henry] was in the city from 7 till ten this morning and people went crazy to see him, but we none of us tried at all.

He was duly honored, being taken to all points of interest, and given a thousand dollar album of the city and surroundings.

Gertie went to see a Royal Rogue [*A Royal Rogue* (1900), a play by Charles Klein] last night and when she came home, found a telegram from Farrel saying that they would be here today, so George came out with them, and I met Mrs. Dagley at last.

She is no bodys pretty child but is industrious no doubt and will make him a good wife.

They seemed devoted to each other and are well suited.

Mr Bechtel came back this aft. and took them to the train at 4:40.

She sang so much, and has a loud voice but while she has been graduated in music, she is far from being a good singer, she knows *nothing* compared to those who pretend to sing in the cities, and as for being a pleasing singer she is far from it, it being a positive relief when she *stops!*

He doesint know it how ever and is very proud of her accomplishments.

We went to the choral service at the Stone church tonight it was fine. Mr Bechtel had two selections.

Monday March 3.—1902.

Tonight Carrie and I are going to have the privelege of hearing the Royal Italian band, the finest that ever toured the United States.

Cliff Johnson phoned me this morning, said he had been thinking of me all day, and he wanted to talk a long time, but I was busy and rang off.

He said he was taking two lessons a week, hoped some day to dance with me, said I could give the soundest best advice of any one he ever knew, and I had had the best influence over him, he would be my friend till death etc, etc.

He talks like a crazy man.

Tuesday March 4.—1902.

Words fail me when I want to tell of my delight last night when I heard the most exquisite music that it has been my pleasure to hear.

It was *grand,* and that director felt every note that he heard, and his every motion was full of grace and his attitude when some grand climax was reached was so expressive.

It would seem that he was pleading then threatening, his face pale, and Mr Albert went into the box to see his face, but said it was painful to see him. At times I would think it was as grand as it could be, yet it would rise higher, increase in volume, and by the time it had reached the climax of grandeur, I was ready to yell with enthusiasm.

The audience was spell bound, and I thrilled, and had often heard of it but it was my first experience.

I wouldint have missed it for any thing. We are invited to Sallies party tonight.

Wednesday March. 5.—1902.

We three girls went to the party last night even though it poured rain, and while the crowd looked nice we did not enjoy it, no congeniality.

Separation

Sebie is Willards double, I found a great pleasure in watching him, he is not as good looking, but is about his build and is dignified and his actions are similar. The girls all like him and especially Lucy Dillard, she made her self ridiculous over him.

Mrs Becker had her dining room very pretty a long table with fruit, flowers, ices & cakes, we found Mr & Mrs Winn the only congenial people there and he knew Willard at Knoxville, so he talked to me all the time we were at table. We played cards too, came home at eleven.

Tonight we are going to hear the Bostonia Sextette club.

Thursday March 6.—1902.

Ma, Carrie, Gertie and I went to hear the Bostonia Club last night, and it was the most heavenly music I ever heard, the dreamiest, sweetest, and so entirely different to the Italian band, that was *grand, magnificent.* Ma and Gertie went to the mattinee Tuesday.

Mr Johnson was there with Miss McGregory, he kept peeping around in every way to see me Carrie said, but I didint look in his direction and they got out before I saw how she was dressed, like a pea cock Carrie said, and I wanted to see.

But that divine music made me dream of Willard and not Cliff. I believe I turned to him for comfort in my trouble with Willard and I fancied I thought more of him than I did, for all my intense longing for my husbands love and tenderness has returned and it is he who fills my thoughts, and the realization of my position is even more bitter than before.

I finished my black silk in time to wear tonight, and he bought it for me in Buffalo and I regret that I never made it up for him to see.

Tonight Gertie and I went over to see Mr and Mrs Winn, he talked all the time, she had very little chance to get a word in edge wise.

In a picture taken before her marriage she looks like a belle, far above him at that time, yet he is so handsome and has so much better chance to be entertaining and look nice, he looks the superior of her now.

Mrs Burks and Mrs Hudiburg called this afternoon.

I had a long letter from Father in response to mine for aid, his money is tied up in stocks that the market price is against,

186

and if he sells now it means a loss of $120.00. and above that he has only enough expenses of living, so he cant help me, he sent my letter to Willard and a copy of the one he wrote him to me, he appeals to him to do right by me, tells him to write to me to forgive him and come to Rochester and try it over again, says "if you care for me or my good opinion I ask you to do this, I cant bear to have you cast Madge aside as you have." I cant hope that he will though.

Friday March 7.—1902.

This is a quiet night, we are staying in the first time this week.

Will Clemmons called for Gertie and Johnson rang him self in to have a long talk, asked how they all were out here, etc, and she said who is that? He said "Cliff", and she told him she wanted to talk to Mr Will and he had to go way back and sit down! He acts so funny, tries to talk out here so often, it looks like he might be regretting his actions, it wont do him any good to though.

Monday March 10.—1902.

I was half dead with a cold yesterday and it was the most beautiful day I ever saw, too lovely to stay in, but these spring days remind me so forceably of the Spring two years ago, when I was planning my wardrobe and dreaming of the happiness that was soon to be mine, reading his letters of love, and he was counting the days till he could fold me to his heart and call me his very own.

The lonliness of my life seems harder to bear, the hopelessness of my position. If I had never been happy as his wife it would be easier but to recall the tenderness and love of those first sweet days, when we were as happy as any couple could be, then realize it *is over forever,* I am forsaken by that same man, it is killing me, and death is preferable to such misery!

Cliff came near being killed yesterday aft. he had gone to take Miss McGregor driving, and as he started to get in the buggy the horse plunged forward throwing him against the front wheel and the buggy passed over his head, and she was thrown over a fence. He was taken to the hospital and was not conscious till about nine oclock this morning then partially.

Separation

Mr Will Clemmons came by a few moments tonight and said they thought he was going to pass in his checks, but he was sitting up.

Mel came by this aft. and made me the most generous offer, said any time I wanted to see any thing at theatre to let him know he would take a great pleasure in letting me have the tickets if he had them.

He will get me transportation on any Rail road I want too, and I will certainly visit some since I *can*.

Wednesday Mch. 12.—1902.

Gertie and I started to see Mrs Bectel, had long talk with Ollie Williams, and met George, he turned us back, as his Mother was too ill to see any one. We walked, nearly to Mrs Cauklings with me. It is a beautiful day.

Thursday March 13.—1902.

Cliff calls up so often wants to talk but we are chilly to him, and Tues. evening he called to talk about his accident thinking he would get lots of sympathy, but he got *left*. I told him I heard he was dead, and I talked as lightly as though it was *nothing*, and soon said good bye, without a word of kindness, hopes for his recovery or regret for his accident, and I hardly think he will call again.

While down town this aft. we saw Mrs Connelly and Lillie the widow, and I would rather meet snakes any time. We had quite a long talk though. Saw Pearl Sykes and she looked an awful sight, worse than she would to go to the kitchen before her marriage.

Tonight a messenger brought two tickets for me to see "Joshua Simpkins", and I took Carrie. Mel came in after the 2*nd*. act and sat with us, and we went to take cream at "Live & Let Live" and we wouldint let him come home with us and miss the last car.

It was tame but beat staying home.

Monday Mch. 17.—1902.

Yesterday was the hardest day I have spent since Willard wrote me what he did. This beautiful Spring weather recalls so vividly to mind that Spring two years ago, when I was planning to be his wife, and dreaming of having him to walk with pretty Sundays, and to have a gallant fine looking husband.

Now I am the lonliest *widow! deserted!* Carrie and I walked out by Erlanger hospital and Vine, and it seemed my heart would break, but I didint tell any one.

Mel worked hard to get me a ticket to see "Faust," there was such a "rush" at the office, but he sent it up about 5 o'clock, and after I asked to go with the Alberts, they took Carrie too. We were fortunate in seeing this.

Lewis Morrison was Mephisto and a fine one he is too.

Faust tempts Marguerite, and she yeilds to him through her *love* for him, and from the night she sins all happiness dies, their love is a *curse,* and the devil claims Faust and he sees Marguerite being taken to Heaven by Angels, the most gloriously lovely thing! She is Morrisons daughter and a fine actress too.

Every young man should see this and girl too, there is a fine lesson in it.

Thursday March. 20.—1902.

Tuesday we went to rehearsal, yesterday to the openings, saw every one, and Will Clemmons had been talking to us, he went up stairs told Johnson we were down stairs, and he came down, stood in the same aisle close to us, and I moved on away from him talking to Mrs Chester, and when I turned he was still looking, I bowed and he came up shook hands with Gertie and I called Mrs Chester to look at those elegant suits on models, and never looked at him, and as Gertie and I left the store, he and Will were standing at the entrance, I never looked as I passed.

This aft. we went again, and as we passed he was sitting in the window at the office, he tipped his hat, but we walked on unmoved by so great a favor, and I rather think he has come to the conclusion I am not as muchly smitten as he imagined! We found lots of mail from Sherman on coming home, a letter for Hobbs & Leland, pocket book from him to "sister" Miss Sloan, and Cora Lee's photo for Hobbs, his photo for Leland. His letter was characteristic of him, full of fun, and he is going to be at Battery Park Hotel, Asheville till Monday, hopes to hear while there.

He will be in New York city April 1*st*. and I want to keep up with him, he might be a great help to me.

Dear old Asheville! Would that I could recall the past two years and relive them, knowing what I do now.

Sunday March 23.—1902.

This morning I wore my black silk to Centenary, went alone and had to go down to the front seat.

Mr Belk the evangelist preached a splendid sermon, on "As ye sow, so shall ye reap". Said we reaped what we sowed, the crop was greater than the sowing, it takes longer to reap than to sow, and the harvest is *sure* to come! He made good points on all the divisions of his sermon, and it was especially good for young people.

This afternoon we went to the concert at the Auditorium, it was unusually fine.

Monday March 24.—1902.

Gertie and I went to Mrs Dr Hall [a spiritualist medium] the trance medium this morning for a test reading, and I am going back for a full reading. She told me very much the same that Dr Rock did, described the woman that stood between Willard and I, and Miss Duncan answered the description, but she will tell me the name and if they are living together openly or if he goes to her secretly, and she says, I will be in court next month but for me to do nothing till she gives me instructions.

I had a long nice letter from Belle Barker and she said the Duncan girls were so cozily domiciled in the Pan American block, that she spent the night with Christine last week and they talked so much of me, intended writing me a joint letter but didint get up in time, and they were both out on cases. It must be some other woman, that is dark, well rounded, beautiful, dimpled and with dark hypnotic eyes.

She says I must go to Denver or New Mexico City, that I have lung trouble resulting from female affections, and I will rue it unless I go as she advises.

Tuesday March 25.—1902.

I had been to town this morning, and was sewing on my Easter suit when Mel called me and said, "lets take a car ride,

I'll be on the corner of 6th and Lookout at quarter to five and we will go to Hill City," I was there on time and we walked to the bridge took the car, and to my surprise we did not go to Valambrosa, but to the end of the line a mile and ¼ beyond the bridge, we walked as much further to a hill covered with pines and sat down to talk, but our time was so limited we hardly begun till we had to leave, we missed the car and walked to the bridge three miles, and had a nice talk. I told him my great troubles, and he said, "the cur ought to be killed, and I'd like the job!"

He said if he had only married the girl he loved he would have been worth something, he would never have been dissipated, and would have made the most of his time and opportunities. He said Mag you and I should have married we would have been too happy for any thing, I said, "No it would have been like you and Minnie, you loved the other girl," he said *"but you are the girl I loved!"* I was surprised altho' he has tried to tell me often of late years, and he said, "yes I loved a little girl in Virginia when I was a lad, and then I met you on coming to Chatt. and I loved you better than any one I ever saw, and never have loved any one since I met you, and *I love you better now than I ever did!"*

He says he is going to help me, and for me to do nothing without consulting him. I came home at dark, and Gertie had been looking for me and had the door open, so Pa wouldint know I was out. We dressed and went to rehearsal and then the lecture by John P. D. John, "Did man make God, or did God make man?" [president of Indiana Asbury (Depauw) University]. It was magnificent.

Wednesday March 26.—1902.

This morning Leone and brother Dr Lutz of Ohio came, and they want to go to the mountain and Park, but it is raining, I want to finish my dress and make Carrie a green silk waist for Sunday.

Saturday March 29th. 1902.

Thursday it rained all day and Will Clemmons called in the evening and we had music and a real nice time. Yesterday it continued to rain, and in the aft. the Dr went to get tickets and could only get three in the gallery, so Carrie and Leone went to see Julia Marlowe in "When Knight hood was in flower".

This morning Gertie went with them to the mountain, and at eleven o'clock Carrie and I went to Voigts to join them for the Park trip, Dr Lutz drove up in a double stanhope [a light carriage], rubber tired, with match horses, and we certainly did have a fine outing. The horses ran all the way and we took in so much of the park, orchard knob, National Cemetary, West side of town, and they took the 4:45 train home!

Mel was standing by the Rossmore [Hotel] and I spoke to him, he came, shook hands and we had quite a chat.

On the way to the train we met Cliff, he tipped his hat so cordially. We saw every lady today most.

We came home and took Ma for a drive in style, and this is certainly one fine day we have had, it was just *right* for a trip to the park.

"Easter Sunday" March 30—1902.

This is a beautiful day and I had every thing new for Easter but was sick all night, so didint go out this morning.

I had a communication from Willard Friday he said he would be only too glad to have his pension granted and when it was I might have half of the back pay, and half of each payment as he received it.

Said he was sorry he could not let me draw his back pay from the state but it had been drawn and spent some time ago, it went as all his money had this winter. This is just what has hurt me so, to have him act mean, blow the money I should have on other women, and torture me to death, yet him to have the sympathy of every one and they tell me I am to blame for my extravagance has put him away from ~~him~~ me. *It is cruel as death!*

Tuesday April 1st. 1902.

Tonight we went to rehearsal and only have one other before the oritorio concert.

Will Clemmons came home with us and came in stayed till ten, invited us to the reception tendered by the Y.M.C.A. by B.Y.P.U. [Baptist Young People's Union] tomorrow night.

November 1901–April 1902

Thursday April 3.—1902.

Will phoned today to know if we were coming and I said "yes", and we *did* go, but of all *stale* times we had it.

He didint introduce one person to us and every one was strange to us nearly.

Johnson and his girl were there, they sat in front of us and turned around repeatedly to see us. They rubbered hard when we decided it was too slow for us, and started home, and it rained all the way too, we dont think we will repeat the experiment.

Ice cream and cake was served and quite a nice program rendered.

Friday April 4.—1902.

Mr Winn brought his wife over to call tonight and they stayed till eleven o'clock! Rather lengthy call, but he seemed to enjoy him self immensely.

He had us sing a number of tunes and sat on the sofa by me cutting up all the time, and I simply would hate to have a husband like him.

Will phoned to know why we were not at the hall, I told him we had company.

Sunday April. 6.—1902.

This morning Gertie and I went to Centenary, she wore her new black lace hat I made, her black silk skirt and green & purple silk waist, and I donned my easter rigging, and certainly created a *sensation right*. The way people stared, some couldint keep their eyes off of that dress! Well it *is* beautiful, and I never had a suit that I was as proud of, and I would give any thing if Willard could see me in it. I believe he would feel proud of his wife, after all.

Mel walked home with us, and we passed McGregor's, "Mary" pulled back the curtains and *stared* at us all the time we were crossing the street and passing her house, and I had the satisfaction of knowing that as exquisite as he thinks her, she never looks any nicer than I did, so I didint care if she *did stare!*

Mel came out tonight, stayed till ten and we had a fine talk, though the time *flew* by, we had just begun to talk when it was time for him to go.

Separation

He loves me *above every body else,* and is my *best friend,* will do any thing to help me, and a friend like that is too valuable to slight.

I enjoyed the evening very much and I *know* he did, his life is so empty and he has always loved me, and he thinks how different life with me would have been, cherishes all memories of the time we were sweet hearts, free to have linked our lives together, yet forever separated now. I dont feel the same.

While young I was infatuated with him so much so that probably had he said as much then I might have been his, but he lost his chance and lost opportunities never return.

Tuesday April 8.—1902.

I wanted to see Joe Jefferson tonight but it was obligatory that we all be at the final rehearsal, and after practicing all winter we none of us felt like missing the concert Thursday night.

The festival chorus will not go to the recital tomorrow how ever. Music club will.

Thursday April 10.—1902.

Last night I took Gertie to see "Nell Gwynn" by Una Clayton Co. [*Nell Gwynne* (1884), a musical by Henry Brougham Farnie] and Mrs Albert took Carrie, they sat in a box and Gertie and I had lots of fun.

It was a fine little company and we enjoyed it very much.

Tonight the oritorio concert came off. We wore white and no doubt it looked pretty from the audience, but I feel I would regret having paid 75cts. for no better entertainment. We did not have the orchestra, only organ and piano, and while it is a high class of music, it fell flat I think. So many left early in the evening, others looked bored to death. Chatt. people will have to become educated to that before they will want to give that price for many such concerts. Earghotts recital may have been fine, the chorus did not go for they felt he insulted them.

To compliment the music club when they refused to aid him in giving it, then slight the very organization under whose auspices it was given was *dreadful!*

Sol Moyses took us to get cream at the Live & Let Live, and brought us home.

194

Friday April 11.—1902.

Mrs Albert took Ma & Carrie, and Gertie took me tonight to see, "A Persian Princess," it was good, and I laughed immoderately at the ludicrous climaxes.

Saturday April 12.—1902.

This aft. I took Louise to see, "Little Miss Military", the first time she ever saw a play. She got tired, but I amused her till it was over. I am so tired I can hardly sit up, I am so thankful I have none, it is the hardest work I know of to care for a baby.

Sunday April 13.—1902.

As tired as I am Gertie and I went to church this morning, and Centenary was so hot, no ventilation, then coming out in the air I took cold.

This aft. we went to Baptist church and the doors were opened, wind blew on my neck, back of head, and it has nearly finished me.

We called on Mrs Barnes afterward.

Mel called up, was coming at eight and I had to tell him *no* for Pa didint want him to come.

Wednesday April 16.—1902.

The pupils of Conservatory gave a recital and Gertie had a solo with violin obligato, (Prof Cadek playing) and she did *fine,* this being her first time, I think she deserves great credit.

Thursday April 17.—1902.

I have been feeling so dreadful all day I didint dress till some one rang and of course it was Mel, couldint have found me when it would have taken me longer to get to the door parlor. He and Gertie had lots of fun. He didint tarry long and some way I did not enjoy his call this time.

Tonight Sol Moyses called without an engagement, and Gertie wouldint go see him so Kid and I had to sit up and entertain him, or be bored by him, till 10:30 and I was half sick.

CHAPTER SEVEN

Return

Sunday April 27.—1902.

Sunday last I didint go any place till night, then we went to Walnut St to church. Wednesday night Gertie and I went to see Lawson Whitaker and Thulie Thomson married at Presbyterian church, and it was very pretty, but she wore a veil, and I know I looked the best as a bride, though my dress was not any thing like as elaborate.

That was the first wedding I have been to since I married, and it has been twenty two months ago today! Then I was the *whole world* to him, now I am *nothing!*

Mrs Smart played Shum aus Traumin [possibly intended as "Schön aus Traümen" from Richard Wagner's *Lohengrin* (1850)] and it was while that music was being played softly, that we took our vows, and it recalled how earnestly he spoke those words, and the tender pressure of his hand, and then to think how little he cares for them now. We went to the last lecture of the course, Father Stafford in his fine reading of "Julius Ceasar," and it was magnificent, as is any thing he gives, he is a grand actor, and so intelligent, can handle any subject so masterfully.

We were invited to a reception at Centenary last night, too tired to go.

Mel came up awhile Thursday afternoon and we sat on the back veranda and it is delightful, in the shade, we had a nice chat, we wanted to go to Atlanta with Gertie today but Frank went and he backed out.

They left at 7:20 this morning, and I am indisposed, will stay home I guess. Mel phoned about 11:30 to take me some where this afternoon, but I told him I was ill, and Will Clemmons phoned to call too this aft. I told him the same.

Heard from Willard Friday, he said this trouble between us had caused his Father to altar his life insurance, making Eva the beneficiary instead of him.

He wants to know if I come back if I am going to be suspicious of him, Jealous of every woman etc, makes the terms as hard as he possibly can, but I will fight this out I believe.

Monday April 28.—1902.

Well I answered Willards letter and I reversed things, refused to accept his terms and stated mine, it is left to him now, *he* is to decide whether I return and the world be none the wiser that a tragic under current exists, or whether it is all to be made public, and I go out to fight my way.

My letter will probably end it all between us, for he will be furious at my telling him I knew who had circulated reports to injure my character and disgust him, and that if any other than C. S. Thomson asked him laughingly about those charges I was bringing against him, he or Mrs T.—— had told him, and had him ask ~~you~~ him for *effect*.

I would much prefer going back if he would do right, but I cant promise to be deaf and blind to any kind of a life he may chose to lead, and unless he promises to treat me as he knows I have a right to be treated, then I cant get the consent of my mind to go back.

God knows *best,* and will lead me through this vale of sorrows I trust, and teach me the *way.*

Tuesday April 29.—1902.

I finished my letter, went down to mail it so it would go off on the 10 o'clock train, and I found Sol Moyses on the veranda with Carrie and Sophia, he proffered to take me to town and bring me home, and I had them go with us, and we had lots of fun, they teased us for going behind, he taking my arm etc, so Sophia called her self Mephisto & Carrie her little "Imp", and we fooled away the evening quite pleasantly while it would have been a very dull one other wise.

He took us to Live & Let Live for cream, and Johnson saw me in there, went up to the back window and then came back and stood on curb to watch us leave the store and he looked *hard* at us far as he could see. Sol wants to take me driving, to his farm and all around, I would like the drive but the company *nil*.

We worked *hard* till one o'clock today, then Gertie and Homer came, and I am tired *out,* made one table cover, hemstitched it and fringed it this morning, and her pretty one with wide drawn work, I made in three and a half days, it is a beauty.

Homer is so thin and frail, but if he *was* larger he would be very facinating. We tease Gertie.

Wednesday April 30th. 1902.

Gertie had to go to womans chorus rehearsal at 2 o'clock, and Homer and I went up to meet her, and while waiting we went to see my picture at Mudges, it is the very lovliest one I ever had made, and Nellie Brown was there, she said they considered it the finest bridal picture they ever made, and I would be surprised at the favorable comment it had excited.

She said she thought every thing of hers, she had one, thought it the sweetest thing in the world. She wants to give me one of her photos before I go back, and I certainly will prize it, *such a beauty!*

She is a perfect *dream* of beauty, and always seemed to love me so dearly, and I have her too.

We three had cream, and while enjoying it, a party of six came in and I recognized one as the man that shared his seat with me from Batavia to Rochester last April, and soon I saw that he knew me, but neither of us spoke, it would have been jolly if he had been *alone.*

We went to Orchard Knob, stayed till sun set, every thing looked so peaceful, it seems strange that such a tempest of emotions wages in a heart, when all nature bids us be calm, and peaceful.

Will Clemmons called tonight, we had music, and at 10 o'clock we went down and had cream at Fountain square on "Billie," having heard he was stingy, I took him up at once. We jollied all the way down, and he sang some of the cutest coon songs [from the black minstrel shows] at the gate, so we had a nice evening.

April–August 1902

Thursday May 1st. 1902.

This has been a gloomy May day and I have sewed all day, and have felt just as *blue* as could be.

The future looks awfully *dark*.

Friday May 2nd. 1902.

Tonight Homer and I Will Clemmons and Gertie went to the Synagogue to services tonight, to hear the handsome new Rabbi Mannheimer, and we heard a fine sermon from him too.

Sol came right to us, sat behind us and was lovely in his welcome to us, and he looked handsome in his Sunday best, white vest etc.

Homer and I didint want to come home with them, we walked around and went to Live and Let Live for cream, and my cameo silk raises sand every time I wear it, store full of young men.

Sunday May 4.—1902.

Homer and Gertie, Frank & I went to the Stone church to hear Bishop Warren this morning, and it was a splendid sermon. The altar was more beautifully decorated than at any wedding I ever attended, palms banked, and festoons of roses and smilax from gas fixtures, over altar rail, and vases filled on stands, making it a dream.

My beautiful dress creates so much admiration every where I wear it.

Tonight we went to the Auditorium to the mass meeting of the Bishops and the music was very good.

Monday May 5.—1902.

We went to Baldurs parade this afternoon, and tonight he took Carrie, Gertie and I to midway, where we had a *jolly* time, saw Capt. Garner, Walter Martin, Allan Jacoway, Will Clemmons, Mel, and we rode on the golden chariot, went into the streets of Cairo and had lots of fun. I was offered *free* ride on donkey.

Tuesday May 6.—1902.

Ma, Carrie and I went to McKee Campbells to see the flower parade, it was beautiful, and yet nothing new.

Return

We had a picnic dinner at home, and Farrel phoned from the Southern that he and Leone were here, would be up in a few moments, and they came but I saw a difference in them, Gertie did too.

They seemed to be impatient with each other, and I fear discord will arise. We were to meet them on mid way, at Voigts first and all go together, but Homer and Gertie went off and left us to wait till they phoned, and I knew they wouldint do that, so I told Carrie to come on and we would go any way, and we did, and Sol came as soon as he saw me, took charge of us and right after we got in I saw Mel and we walked around then we wanted to talk, so we went to 9*th*. took a car out, and got off at Rapid Transit station near Avondale, and waited a half hour there for car, so we talked a lot, and as we so seldom have a chance to be alone we enjoyed it *immensely*. He loves me madly, yet it is so hopeless to him, he says I run him *crazy,* but I am the only girl he ever had a thought for, his *first* and *only love!* We came back to midway and watched for Carrie & Sol, they had gone, so we came by Voigts took cream, and on Vine met Sol coming back from seeing C—— home, he said I was a dandy to lose him that way, and he was going to strike me off his list, so he is angry with me.

We knew the others were home and were afraid we might get into trouble, but I came up without waking any one and found the girls had just come in. He was so sweet tonight, some of the old tenderness returned.

Wednesday May 7.—1902.

Homer and Gertie went to the mountain this morning, and Leone came out to dinner, we had a cozy chat both before and after dinner, and she told me a great deal, that I know they are waking from the blissful state to the practical life, and it always wounds a young wife to see the change in her husband from the ardent lover to the practical, indifferent man.

With her, she would always be as ardent, and the honey moon would last forever, she has thought it would, and resents the change in him, and the more she does that, the faster he changes, till they both wake to find the dreams they cherished during court ship have vanished, the change has come, but neither can say *when*. I feel sorry for her, hope they may be happy yet after they come to understand each other better.

She left at four, before Gertie came home, and she wants us to visit them week after next.

Homer, Gertie & I went to mid way tonight, and we got with Mr & Mrs Winn, and Miss Merriweather to the Vienna gardens, had beer, and then took a ride on the wheel, threw so much confetti, and took chances on every thing, saw so many people we knew, then we got with Mr Benjamine and Paul Manker, and had lots of fun bumming on street fair.

I like both gentlemen very much.

Thursday May 8.—1902.

Homer went home this morning, and Gertie is lying down, I know how she feels, I was always so lonely and blue after Willard left me every time.

I have just heard that Mel wasint at work yesterday, and I fear he has foolishly tried to forget his troubles and hopeless love in drink, but I *do hope not,* I feel I am to *blame.*

Frank says he is out drinking, oh my! He took Ma and Gertie to midway [part of Spring Festival] and Carrie and I went alone, but Sol and Walter Trueheart cornered us and we lost them, went into midway and as Gertie was waiting for them to do the shows, we three threw confetti and chatted, but tired out, we went to a booth in the street fair to rest, and Walter Martin came and wanted us to go to midway with him, we had beer then rode in the golden chariot, saw the tight rope performer ride across the wire on a bicycle illuminated with incandescent lights, saw Speedy dive then came home. I had the poorest fun tonight of any time yet. Worried about Mel.

Friday May 9.—1902.

Every one says the Coronation was a mess last night, and we went over this morning to see Carlotta and she was kept busy phoning, every body telling her how far short it fell of her efforts, and it has *made* her I think.

This aft. we met Mr Benjamine at Voigts had straw berry cream, went to mid way, rode in the golden chariot, went in to see the dog and monkey show, "the Japs," cycle whirl & Niagra, and Wild Minnie.

Return

We saw Speedys dive, and Sandys feats, came home 6:30 and while he insisted on our going back tonight, we are too tired to enjoy any thing.

Mel was sober this aft. and Lou Warner sent him home, told him to come to work tomorrow, and they would be his friends but to "cut it out," stay sober, and he will have to quit for he has worn their patience out most.

I do trust he will stay sober!

Saturday May 10.—1902.

Well I havint heard from Willard yet it seems I am as unsettled here at the close of the festival as I was three months ago. I hope to hear soon that I may *know* what to do.

Frank says Mel is not sober, is in trouble, and dear me I am so dependent on him. No passes as long as he stays this way. We all went to the street fair for the close of a jolly week, but it was too crowded for any thing, saw Mr Benjamine & Seeluck.

Sunday May 11.—1902.

Well the festival is over, and I am in a fever of impatience to go away, and unless I *do* every one will know I am deserted by the man that was supposed to adore me! Last week I entered into the spirit of the festival, forgot my position for the time, and was as vivacious as any one perfectly happy, certainly had a jolly time, but the reaction has come, and I feel *keenly my position*. Surely could he realize for one moment his sin in marrying a girl, then treating her so cruelly, he would change and not *allow* those old demons to *rule* him. If Mel had kept straight it would have been better for he could get me passes to visit till I could make other arrangements.

Sunday May 18.—1902.

This has been an uneventful week that has just passed, lived in *hope* that the clouds that have settled thick over my path may drift away *soon*, and my way made clear to me.

Each day when the postman passed without a letter from Willard I kept hoping it would come, and when Frank returned each evening to hear that Mel had sobered up, but as yet things are where they were last Sunday.

202

I feel sure Willard is in Attica today and my letter will be disected by those old demons, and I will get his answer this week, as it will be three weeks since I heard.

Had a special delivery from Leone this morning inviting us to a dance Wednesday.

Walter Trueheart called this aft. and Sol Moyses this evening, we three sat out on the veranda and entertained him and Gertie was teasing him and kept Carrie & I convulsed, for we dont manage him like she does.

Friday night we attended Hickmans commencement at Baptist church, Ethel Allin played a violin solo, and for two recitations piano selections.

Sunday May 25.—1902.

I attended all the graduation exercises last week, all very good.

Sol phoned this aft. twice to take me riding but Nellie Brown had said she was coming, but didint and I missed my ride. Tonight we went to the choral service at the Stone church and Mr Paul Manker came home with us.

Monday May 26—1902.

Tonight Carrie went with Sophie to hear "Wang" [*Wang* (1891), a musical by J. Cheever Goodwin], and Cliff and Gertrude Chester, and Miss Moneypenny joined them and they occupied boxes.

Gertie and I went to the farewell reception tendered Dr Taber and wife, and we had a splendid evening, the program was bright and refreshments bountiful and delicious, strawberry and lemon sherbet in cakes, with every kind of cake.

George, Mr Manker, Mrs Underhill and Mrs Murphy & daughter added to our pleasure. I wore my pretty dress.

Thursday May 29.—1902.

Gertie and I were invited out to spend the day at Mrs Allins on the side of the ridge and I had one of the pleasantest days I have had out there.

It was cool and the view is so fine, and they entertain so well, then Ethels music is so charming, and the dinner was splendid roast, salad, macaroni with tomato sauce, beans with cream dressing, rolls, coffee, and cherries with icing and sponge cake with cocoanut icing. Every bit so delicious, so appetizing.

We came home on the six o'clock car saying it had been a fine day.

Tonight I went with Sophia to see "The Chimes of Normandy" [*The Chimes of Normandy* (1877), a comic opera by Robert Planquette], and enjoyed it splendidly.

Have heard nothing from Willard and getting desperate, wrote to W. W. Finley at Washington for an extension of my pass.

Frank left for Memphis at 10 o'clock, and Pa comes home from Nashville tonight, went over last night.

Friday May 30—1902.

Carrie and I went to the dramatic school commencement tonight, it was quite good, one girl had two studies from the Spanish and she recited, sung, and danced in appropriate costume, and I have seen much on the stage that was no better, she certainly should go, for nothing else would suit her. One hardly appreciates such how ever in a church, so *unusual*.

Have heard nothing from Willard yet and dont know what to think.

Sunday June 1st. 1902.

Pa fell on a peach peal in front of Centenary this morning, and broke two bones and dislocated some in his left hand. Dr. Nolen came out this aft. and set it and he is suffering quite a good deal.

Carrie, Gertie and I went to the Baptist exercises tonight, beautifully decorated for childrens day.

Saturday June. 7.—1902.

Monday I went with Gertie to get her summer out fit, she traded $38.00 before dinner, we stopped for cream at "Live and Let Live," met Mr Holt, Franks friend, and he wants to call.

Wednesday I took sick and for two days I suffered dreadfully, had Prof. Prescott who is *grand,* he just eased that awful pain *so soon,* and was so tender and kind in his treatment of me I just love him. [Prescott ran the Southern Sanitarium and Magnetic Institute.] He came twice, and I want to go to have him cure me before I leave.

Yesterday I sat up all day and last night Mr Holz called and brought a quart of cream, peach, we *all* had a large saucer, and it was so nice and refreshing.

He thought of bringing candy too, but didint want to kill us, he dont touch any thing sweet.

We had a very jolly time, I like him, but got so nervous because he stayed till 11:30 and I knew Pa wanted him to go at ten.

He is going to take us all driving Sunday week, said if I left before that to phone him, we would go.

Mel is in Knoxville and I was almost in despair when the postman brought me my pass extended 60 days to Washington & back, just as I asked.

This piece of good luck got me in a good humor, if I could hear from him.

Sunday June 8.—1902.

Yesterday aft. Mr Trueheart came out to tell us Mrs Trueheart was at the depot and they were going to Paduca Ky. to live, have sold their home at Buford Ga, and were to leave at 9 o'clock for Ky. We went down and Walter told us he had taken his mother to the Rossmore [a hotel] she was ill, and we found her in bed. We sat on the side of the bed and had quite a chat, I hadint seen her for so long, she thought me changed, and when Walter came and sat by me on the bed she told Gertie that Walt had always loved me better than any one.

I wore my black waist, silk skirt, and she said dont her arms look pretty through those sleeves? He said "yes I'd like to bite them," she seemed pleased to have me know he thought so much of me, while she used to fear that I would think he did, always telling me he never would love any one but Maude. It amused me, as I have never seen the day I would think of him other than a friend. The waiter brought up three sherry cobblers that were *fine* so frosty.

Walter came home with us, and wants to come out and tell me all his troubles, he and Edna are going to seperate.

While at supper Mr Holt phoned for us to come down at 9 o'clock and have some peach cream, and he would see we gothome alright, we did, and he came home with us stayed till eleven o'clock.

He certainly likes us *fine*.

Sunday June 15. 1902.

Thursday and Friday we attended the closing recitals of the Southern Conservatory of Music. Seeluck sang and it was interesting to know who won the medals, Gertrude or Rose for piano and Rose was the fortunate one. They said a New York friend sent a medal to the school and that went to Miss Chester, but there was no honor in that, since it was not stated that it was a tie between the girls, and that Gertrude had won it as fairly as Rose.

Gertrude returned it with *thanks.*

Yesterday I went to Prof Prescott and he is going to cure me, I feel better already. Last night Carrie and I went up town and Platt Holt called us in and treated.

Prof. wanted me to go to Willard and as absolute quiet is necessary for a test, he came out this aft. and yet it was too noisy for me, and all he got was two men talking, Willard said, "I would like so much to have Madge come back if she would be like she once was!" He tried repeatedly to get there so fully that he could tell the place, names, *every thing,* but conditions were not favorable.

Mr Holt came and took us to Centenary to hear George Stewart. He preached on the text "As ye sow so shall ye reap," made a fine talk, one that we all need to bear in mind, it is hard to do right, but it pays to sow good seed. Mr Holt said it did him good. He sat next to me, and Mr Dix fanned Carrie and chatted over her shoulder to her.

We went to get cream after church and enjoyed the evening ever so much, for we all like him.

Monday June 16.—1902.

We took our moon light drive tonight and I never enjoyed one more in my life it was the jolliest one I ever took I know. We laughed from 7:30 to 11:30.

Tuesday June 17.—1902.

Last night we went over the Crest road to Rossville, the city looked beautiful, but the drive was lovely, the lights and shadows made the whole evening a dream.

We went to the spring, then through town to Hill City and way over there we had bushels of fun.

206

He handed me on to the front seat and we teased the girls all evening. He told them to pick blackberries awhile, go to sleep, and Gertie said she saw a kerchief on the bridge, if she knew it was a lace one she would go get it, he asked her if there wasint two of them, and all such that kept us laughing.

It was a perfect drive to all.

Friday June. 20.—1902.

Mr Holt called tonight and took all three of us to get cream, and we had bushels of fun, I wore my new dress just finished, and Johnson was there with his girl, he *rubbered.*

Sunday June 22—1902.

Yesterday we decided to go see how Carlotta was so after tea we went over and found her jolly and happy and wouldint take a million for her prospects, we went on down town and Platt got off at 9:30 and came to us at Millers and bummed the rest of the time with us.

We went to Bukofzers for cream & it wasint good either.

Coming home it was late, and we had car loads of fun, he is so funny I can have the jolliest times with him of any fellow I ever saw.

Tonight we went out to Prof Banatts, his wife died last night, found them bearing it splendidly.

Went to Centenary, then came home and took my letter to mail to Willard.

Platt took it for me, so he could stand out side and chatawhile.

I have been going to town every morning for treatment, and Platt always calls me in to drink some thing. I certainly like him fine.

Wednesday June. 25. 1902.

Two years ago tonight Willard came to stay till he took me away, *his own.* I had callers all day and Mrs Arnold had come to stay too, was to practice over her music after supper and I went up stairs to light up the parlor and ran right into Willards arms in the reception hall, he said he couldint wait till the next day, he had to come to his darling!

Well we practiced and had lots of fun that night.

Return

I have written him a nice love letter, and do *hope* to get a nice one in return, I asked for it for Friday.

Thursday June 26.—1902.

Two years ago tonight we practiced at Centenary for the wedding, Edd came down at 6 o'clock and Willard brought him out so he went with us to the church, severel friends were there to see it, and we had quite a nice rehearsal. Mrs Chester said she *knew* I would do my part alright without practicing any.

Mrs Pyott, and Mrs Chester were wondering which was *the one,* the little one or the tall one, and I was happy to tell them the fine looking one, though Edd is now married and I *know* his bride will always have the best of care, and he will stand to her against the world if need be, she will never be deserted without a cause, so *looks* are not *all.*

Had such a sad letter from Jessie, she is heart broken over the death of her little daughter.

Also heard from Father.

Jessie says she hopes to hear soon that all is well between us, she cant believe it is any thing but a misunderstanding, for she thinks we both *care for each other!* How comforting!

Friday June. 27.—1902.

Two years ago tonight we were married! Early this morning Gertie and I went to town, Platt was waiting for me at Voigts to go to McFarlands lake, and I had decided not to go as some one might *talk* about it, so he joined us for a "bum", and as usual we had lots of fun, at "Kress'" he bought me a large rose to wear and acted a monkey generally there at the Novelty store. Prof. said I was looking well and bright.

We took grape juice at Voigts, and pine apple sherbet at Live & Let Live. He came home with us, and we have enjoyed the morning finely.

I have relived all that happened two years ago today, we were happy in each others love, perfectly so.

Two years ago at that home there was a bright wedding, and today there is a funeral, Lewis Hall he's dead!

The change that has come into our lives in this time is *dreadful,* and it is hard to bear, this second anniversary is bitter indeed, *no home,* no husbands love to make my life bright!

Saturday June 28.—1902.

Last night I could not bear the pain in a courageous way, I gave way to it and when the hour came that represented the one where he met me at the altar a proud bride groom and took me for his own, so *earnestly,* so *tenderly,* then led me out the aisle so happy, my grief was uncontrollable, for I have written him lovely letters, begged him to let me know what he would do, and wanted a letter to cheer me on that day, and nothing came at all!

How he *can* treat me this way I cant see. Prof. tried to cheer me up this morning, keep me from being blue and did help me wonderfully, but still my position is a hard one indeed and it is hard to prevent worry.

Prof. thinks in one week more I will be perfectly well "as sound as a bullet". If I only can have perfect health and gain flesh and then go to him I may regain his love, I want to be handsome looking when I go.

When he used to rave over plump girls realizing how thin I was it made me feel *awful.*

Sunday June 29.—1902.

Two years ago today we went to "The Bon Air" in Asheville where we spent our first month of wedded life in *perfect bliss! Never* will I forget it, and the memory of those days makes me lenient to his faults now.

No other honey moon could be so sweet, no other husband so dear, I can hardly bear to give him up, to let the step taken by both in such seriousness be the ruin of both our lives, that is why I have forgiven so much, and laid aside pride to beg him to let us begin anew, for if he only *would* do as I am willing to, we could be happy yet, and could bless the day we married, and each anniversary would be so sacred we would renew our vows and be *sweet hearts again!*

As yet have heard nothing from my letter, and if today he takes it up to show *them,* I wont hear or if I do it will be a *failure.*

Soon I must go and see what can be done by seeing him, and if nothing, begin the battle of life.

While writing the above Willie brought two letters and one was from my husband at last, written the day of our second anniversary, mailed at 7:30!

209

It is the first I have heard in over two months, but he says if I am willing to live within his income, save money, and keep house he will send for me as soon after he receives my answer as possible, and if I do accept he hopes and trusts every thing will turn out well, says he is glad my health is so improved, and that I am having such good times hopes I will continue so long as I am here. He adds, "as for me I will treat you as near right as I can, and no one can promise more."

As I am perfectly willing to do all he asks I unhesitatingly wrote and accepted his terms.

I do earnestly desire to be all to him he ever dreamed I would or all he expected, and I want us to love each other dearer than ever!

I pray for wisdom, to know just the right step each time, want a sweet even disposition, and to be cheerful, unselfish, bright and winning, that I may possess his love.

This has relieved my mind so much, and others will rejoice too.

Dear Prof. how grand he is!

Monday June 30th. 1902.

Prof. was delighted when he heard the victory won, considers it wonderful, since he hasint been working on him, but he rejoices and has given me some good advice, he wants me to let the past go entirely, and begin anew for a happy future.

Wants me to be happy all the time and quit worrying, not allow any thing to make me mad.

Wednesday July. 3.—1902.

I went to Prof. yesterday and again this morning, he thinks I am getting along nicely can go to Pikeville now, so we plan to go Monday.

We have had Platt out to six o'clock dinner today, and the table looked beautiful, cut glass sparkled and the salad garnished with egg, fish with lettuce, tomatoes lettuce & ice, and makroni with tomato dressing, pickles, jelly, preserves, etc. made a nice spread, water mellon for dessert.

He seemed to enjoy the evening fine.

210

Sunday July 6.—1902.

Friday Platt took Carrie to see Gertrude Chester, and I had the bag finished tied with lavender ribbon and he raved over it, thought it beautiful, said he wouldint take any thing in the world for it.

Yesterday we went with disappointments, Pound refused Gertie passes and refused Mel one to Pikeville so I cant go, and they will think so hard of me. I hope we can go to Harriman though.

We went over to Mrs Underhills tonight for a little while, and she invited us to dinner next Tuesday.

Platt had us take cream with him. Will hasint brought me a letter from Willard as I expected today.

Tuesday July. 8.—1902.

We spent the day with Mrs Underhill, had a splendid dinner, veal chops, irish potatoes, corn, cucumbers, tomatoes, home made light bread, ice tea, peaches and pound cake.

I enjoy being with her so much, we have so much to talk about.

We came home at five as Mel came to see me. His mother is dead and he dont feel like talking of his grief to many, but he wanted to tell *me*. I felt so sorry for him, but it may be a blessing, for he says he wont drink any more, her last prayers were for him.

He hopes to secure the passes for us to Harriman, and I *do* hope he can.

Mr Holt came to take Carrie with Mr Whittle & Lillie Condra up to meet two visiting girls, but he wanted to stay here with us, we always have so much fun together.

Wednesday July 9th. 1902.

We girls all went to see Miss Julia Leach and Mr Anderson married at 8:30 this morning, and on coming home I found a paper from Aunt Eva, and letter from Willard waiting me, the paper contained a notice of his departure for Lake Mills Wis. and his letter came from there!

He has a good position there, says he dont know how I will like it, it is a small place, but he has a nice room, and we will take our meals three doors above. He is glad I am coming will send for me by the 1*st* of Aug. Asks me not to write that I am going to him to my Northern friends, for the old people dont know it, and they think I am *left,* wont know where to write him. I can see her gloating over it, but when she hears I am there, she will change her tune. If he has gone away that he may be free to do right by me, we will get along *this time,* no danger of *failing!* I am happier than I have been for 18 months, he is away from their influence, and I feel that we will get along now.

I believe Willard loves me yet, by his leaving them and sending for me after all they have said against me.

How thankful I am for this.

Well I had to go tell my benefactor the glorious news, he was delighted, thought every thing was coming my way, and he is certainly one of the *best friends* I ever had.

I came sick on getting home and am surprised at the pain I have.

He made me a present of my *health,* hopes I will be perfect before I leave him. He has never refused to see me, has given me more time than any one else, each treatment has been so thorough.

I do hope we can go to Harriman. I would have prefered that Willard go some other place, where the climate would be better for us both, but I am too glad to get him away from that evil influence to say a word.

He is working for Frank Fargo and has a finer position than before. I want to go on the Mississippi as far as I can to reach Madison.

Thursday July 10.—1902.

Tonight is the lawn fete at the Court house, and band concert by the 7*th*. Cavalry band. Carrie is to assist Mrs Charlton at her table.

I dont believe I can go, dont feel well enough.

We all did go to the lawn fete, and band concert tonight, but having no special friends interested we didint have a good time.

Monday July 14.—1902.

Yesterday I looked for Nellie Brown as she wanted to come over to see me, but had too many to claim her time, so I was home all day, all went to Centenary in the evening.

This morning I went to be treated, but Prof. came up to tell me he was too ill to be treating, had to give up and go home, and he looked so white and haggard that I feel uneasy about him.

Thursday July 17.—1902.

The postman passed and still no letter from Willard, it was a week yesterday since I heard and I hoped to hear every week now, but may be not.

I went to get Nellies picture and it is a swell picture but doesint do her justice, she is far prettier.

She and Grace go to Rock Springs tomorrow and they had so much to plan for their trip, I left them, but enjoyed so much the time I was there, they are lovely girls, and too it recalled the trips Gertie and I used to have.

No nearer Harriman than last Thurs.

Saturday July 19. 1902.

Yesterday morning I had another treatment by Prof. he talks so much to me of things that he has had to read and study to gain, it opens up new lines of thought to me, I find him interesting.

I received a letter from Willard this morning, he doesint know whether he will like it there or not, it is small but his two cousins have the finest houses there and move in the best society. He dined with one last Sunday, and had a row on the lake, gathered a boat full of water lillies.

I will try to be pleased, but hope he will secure a position else where.

Little towns try my very soul, give me a city, *and some life!*

Sunday July 20.—1902.

It has been so awfully hot here for days and we have hoped so for rain, yet it does not come and today promises the usual amount of heat.

This has been an unusually hot summer. Willard says it has been dreadfully warm there too.

Only one more Sunday in July. I wonder if I will leave Aug. 1*st.* if so I have only eleven days more.

Would like to run up to Harriman for a few days but I should take all the treatments I can before going.

I feel far from well today, and I know he would be disappointed if I was ill like this even now.

Monday July. 21st. 1902.

Walter Trueheart phoned Gertie that his father died yesterday, and they would be through with him tonight as the interrment takes place at Buford Ga. She, Carrie and I went to meet the train, and she is awfully dazed, was quiet and hardly seemed to know any one. They all seemed so.

We stopped with Platt and had cream. It is an ideal night beautiful moon light, and I wore my short sleeved dress and it seems grand to live in such a climate as this, but I have very few more days here.

Tuesday July 22.—1902.

I went for a treatment this morning and came home after ten o'clock, and for a moment it seemed too late to go to Mrs Lipps as we had planned to do, but I decided that unless we *did* go we would not find any better day, so late as it was we went and I am *so glad we did*. We found her alone and so glad to see us, and I enjoyed the whole day so much. She got a nice lunch of ham, tomatoes, light bread, jelly, ice tea, and canteloupe, and we enjoyed that immensely chatted over the lunch till 2 o'clock.

Mrs Durham came in and interrupted us in the aft. but when Mr Lipp came he said it looked like old times to see us, and they insisted on our staying till after supper, and we did, had lots of fun, were glad we stayed, Mrs Lipp was sorry I hadint been out to spend a week with them, and she wanted us to stay till tomorrow aft.

She had fried chicken, ham, biscuit, coffee with cream, jelly and canteloupe.

She seems to regret my leaving and I love her better than ever before.

Wednesday July 23—1902.

Gertie and I both went to Prescott this morning, he is happy over my progress, thinks there is no danger of my not being well in time to go.

214

Carrie has gone with Sophia out to see Miss Moneypenny at Gen Warners summer home, they say it is *lovely*.

Willard got my letter yesterday and I hope to hear by Sunday, want to know *when* I am going.

If I had not been here so long and every one talking about my staying so long, I would stay and go to Ga, and to Grandpa's and Harriman.

I could enjoy it so much.

Sunday July 27.—1902.

Twenty five months ago was our wedding day! We have been together very little of that time, but I hope we will live together long enough to get acquainted this time.

Rather expected a letter today but Will hasint come from office. Last night Ma and I went out to see Mrs Barnes and Hallie in their new home. They are pleasantly located at 808 E. 9*th*. St.

I have been to Prof. every day last week for treatment and he thinks I will be well enough to leave the 1*st*. Friday.

We are making our traveling pillows and if I hear from Willard and he wants me to come the 1*st*. I can go then.

We were exploring the new brick house across the street after supper and we saw Dr & Mrs Barnett, they joined us then came over and stayed till late.

Tuesday July 29.—1902.

Dr Barnett & wife came by for the big three to go to the Brewery, tonight we did so, stopped at the Armory awhile and they stayed on the veranda till late, Dr telling funny jokes on his Father.

Thursday July 31st. 1902.

Carrie and I went over to Mary Relyea's tonight because she had set the night and said she would have some one mighty nice to meet Carrie, but I hated to go since it was Gerties last night here, to go to stay with strangers instead I didint like it, but Carrie had no one else to take her and fearing to offend Mary by absenting our selves, I went, but wasint I provoked to find she had done nothing to entertain us at all!

Return

We came home at 10 o'clock *mad*.

Any other evening we would have enjoyed it. She had fudge and we played Karams. Sol took us over there.

Friday Aug. 1st. 1902.

Gertie left this morning at 6:45 for her Ga trip. I will be here till next week rather glad I am not going today.

Sunday Aug. 3.—1902.

Yesterday morning Carrie went with me to see Prof, and he *gave* her a fine treatment, she looked better all day than for weeks past.

I bought material for a skirt, black kersey [a woolen fabric], think it will make a very handsome skirt, and as I have so little time here I am anxious to get at it.

Carrie and I went over to call on Dr Barnett and his wife this aft. we ate grapes and sat out in the back yard till late, came to tea at 7 o'clock. Yesterday and today have been *awfully warm*.

Tuesday Aug. 5.—1902.

Yesterday I took my last treatment of Prof. tears came in his eyes when he was talking about my leaving and how much he had enjoyed my company, said he thought more of me than any patient he ever had. Told me *never* to forget him and I could always think of him as one of the *truest, best* friends I ever had.

I spent today with Mrs Mull, met three young men boarders, Mr Johnson, Mr Smith, and Mr. McManus.

She told them I was her pet *first* and I was going to have a glass of cream, and I *did enjoy it*.

We talked all afternoon, she said she enjoyed it so much, and I did.

Mrs Barnett phoned that they would be over so we spent a very pleasant evening.

Wednesday Aug. 6.—1902.

Since supper Ma, Carrie, Sophia & I walked out to see the Confederate arch at Cemetary and it is lovely, and I was agreeably surprised in the Cemetary, it is laid off in walks and looks like a beautiful park. We went to the Russell house balcony to watch the crowds at the lawn fete on the lot where the Carnegie library is to stand.

No doubt it will be here when next I come home.

Didint hear from Willard so I hardly think I will go Friday.

Friday Aug. 8.—1902.

Well I worked hard on my skirt yesterday and today and still it is not finished, and I am glad I did not leave today for I have no way to sew boarding.

Then I am sick tonight and would hate to be traveling now. Mrs Charlton called tonight.

Saturday Aug. 9—1902.

Had a letter from Willard today he is in Milwaukee and will send for me on his return to Lake Mills.

I wont have to hurry so now.

Sunday Aug. 10.—1902.

Dr Barnett brought his wife and Mr O'Leary to call tonight, I had wanted to go to the Baptist church, but had to entertain them.

I like Mr O'Leary very much he is witty and wide awake having come from N.Y. and being a lawyer he is naturally bright.

We had lots of fun at their pranks, I wish he would take to Carrie and make her have a good time.

Monday Aug. 11.—1902.

Carrie and I went over to call on Mrs Barnett at her new home on Fourth St. She has three boarders and seems to get along nicely, I think she is brave to attempt it.

Some way the evening bored me.

Tuesday Aug. 12.—1902.

I went to Prof again he thinks I am getting along wonderfully well just gaining as fast as any one can.

I went to see Carlotta and the baby and stayed to lunch. Sallie Mae Hudeling is visiting her during Mrs Ray's absence, she is pleasant but awfully ugly.

217

Ma and I called on Mrs Pratt since supper and Carrie, Prof Lovejoy, and Miss Cliff Ray came while we were there, they are such cordial people, and Mr Pratt is so jolly.

Thursday Aug. 14. 1902.

Yesterday afternoon Mel came out to see me, he was dressed up and looked awfully nice.

He amuses me, always talking about how desperate he is getting about me, and he hates to see me leave, wishes he could keep me here.

This aft. we are going on a picnic.

Friday Aug. 15. 1902.

Mrs Duncan, Ma and Virginia went in the phaeton [a light carriage drawn by two horses], and Mrs Charlton, Carrie, Bessie Bicker and Carrie Squires and Duncan and I in the "tally ho" [a large carriage pulled by four horses]. We left home at three o'clock and it was the hottest day of the season 101.9 at one o'clock but driving we didint mind it, then too it clouded up and we had an ideal time for our trip.

We went to Stringers branch and enjoyed the spring there then went to White Oak Springs for supper and how we all did enjoy that spread.

Fried chicken, ham sandwitches, chipped beef, salt rising bread biscuit, crackers, stuffed eggs, sweet pickles, olives, tomatoes, blackberry jelly, plum jelly, lemon jelly cake, gold cake, lady fingers, vanilla wafers, ginger snaps, jelly snaps, sweet milk, basket of fruit, assorted candies, (fudge, and coconut candy, home made) fruit was grapes, pears, peaches, canteloupes.

How different it was to a public affair. The three girls ran a race for a young man in N.Y. and Carrie Squires fell down in the race and we yelled it was so funny.

We drove home in the moon light and ate all the way home, I certainly enjoyed it.

I went to see Prof. this morning and he says I have stayed till I am well, that he cant see any reason at all for me to suffer or not to enjoy perfect health from now on, said I would have to take care of my self, I would never be robust and able to do as some women for I was delicate and constituted for a "lady."

He gave me many parting words, it was hard for us both to say good bye, he said I could always feel he was my *true good friend,* one of the best I ever had, but he said for me to come tell him good bye when I started home.

Saturday Aug. 16.—1902.

I have cleaned the kitchen, range, and up stairs this morning and it will be easier for Ma to keep clean.

I havint heard from Willard yet, it was a week ago this morning I heard. It looks like I am not going away at all.

Monday Aug. 18.—1902.

Again the postman passed without bringing me a letter from Willard, I am not impatient to leave *home* because I am tired but having been here so long and to stop the talk that is indulged in so largely at my expense, I am anxious to hear from him and get started. Two oo I want to see him and begin our new life while under Prof.s fine influence. It is going to be rather trying for me I fear and I am impatient to go and try it and get over the uncertainty.

Oh! if he would greet me and love me as he *once did,* there away from evil influences I could hold him, I would not fear the future.

Yesterday I stayed home, till evening Carrie and I went to the Baptist church to hear Dr Baker of Royce City Idaho, he delivered a fine sermon.

The singing was good too. I sat and wondered if next Sunday night Willard would be sitting by me in church? I *do want* to see him and *win him back to me again!*

Mrs Charlton took Carrie calling Sat. in a lovely surrey with two fast horses.

This aft. Carrie and I went out to Mrs Lipps and they insisted on us staying to supper, and we did so and had the nicest one, and they made us feel so welcome, I enjoy going out so much, and they seem to love to have us.

Mrs Lipp gave me one of her new photos and has refused to let any one out of her immediate family have one but me. I also have one of Maudes and Edds. It is an ideal moon light night and they walked to the car line with us.

Return

Tuesday Aug. 19th. 1902.

Have heard from Willard this morning and he says come on home, he sent me $27.00 and said let him know when I would be there.

Carrie and I went to town and I got material for a coffee jacket linen and applique, and a belt, veil, floradora comb [a barrette; popularized by dancers in the Ziegfeld Follies], lots of the little things I needed.

Thursday Aug 21st. 1902.

At last I come to the last night of my visit home, and soon I will be with my husband, the man that wooed me so long, and promised to devote his life to my happiness, yet to whom I go with misgivings!

How different this departure from home to the other one, I went without a *fear, trusting fully* to his keeping my *life!* I have been cheerful all the time, but the good nights have been said, the clock tolls mournfully eleven, and a steady rain is falling that awakens all emotions, and I face the very uncertain future.

I have determined to do my best to have the old sweet days renewed, I hope to win him fully, but if I fail, if my fate is to be that old *unhappy life,* I would rather die this night and have them lay me to rest neath the shadows of dear old Lookout, than to live to battle on in a cold heartless world!

I will leave this record of my life from the time he asked my Parents consent to our marriage up to this the beginning of a new life with him, here with Gertie, and if the old troubles come back, the old pain *fills my heart to bursting,* and they hear I am dead, I dont want them to grieve a day that I am gone, they may weep for the bitterness of the years I dreamed were to be full of brightness, but never to regret that I am beyond the power to feel such agony as only those can experience who have trodden the stony path, whose every hope has vanished, and every dream faded.

What would Prof. dear kind friend say could he see how I have given way to an awful fit of the blues, I *must not,* I will *fail sure* unless I keep up heart and appear cheerful, I must not know such a word as *fail,* I *must win in this battle!*

Mrs Lipp and Sallie and Clifton, spent the day here, and I have done an awful lot of work, waked at five, packed my trunk, made my jacket, finished rather, and so *many* odd jobs, I must retire and get some rest now, intended writing Gertie but she would advise *rest*.

I do hope that my next Journal may contain more that is pleasant to remember than this.

Pa said "I just want to say this to you, dont take any abuse, or ill treatment, this is a poor house but come to it rather than be abused, I dont want to frighten you but I have no confidence in him and I want you to remember this is home when you need it".

This I think has caused me to give way as I have, but God helping me I am going to be a better girl and *make* him better than he was.

Good night, and good bye my old confident.

[The lower half of the page is blank. Pages 298 and 299 are also blank.]

[This poem is written with the page turned upside down.]

If you could know that half of all I yearn to be to you,
    dear heart!
Each day that dawns I struggle to be strong and do my part;
Yet when at last night comes softly down, I humbly pray—
Lord, grant me still to prove my tender love just one more
    day.
Just one more day to strive to rise above small troubles,
    petty care,
That my cramped soul may break its earths forged bonds
    and dare,
To face the future and to gladly live with courage new,
Loyal and cheerful facing towards the light for truth of
    you.
And yet in spite of all the heights which I can never scale,
In spite of all the many tests in which I daily fail,
That my deep love, more deep and pure, and strong than I
    can ever show,
You some how, through my failures, doubts and fears, will
    come to know.

Return

The dreary clouds cant hide the sun for aye it glimmers
    through;
The sweet, wet violet, struggling through dead leaves still
    shows its blue,
And so I trust though oft I strike love's chord with clumsy
    hand,
You'll feel the melody I tried to play and understand.

Afterword

Margaret did indeed return to Willard, and they had a son, Benjamin Raymond, in 1905. Margaret followed Willard from Lake Mills, Wisconsin, to Douglas, Arizona—while Arizona was still a territory. Willard worked in railroading and the related field of machine tooling all of his life, and his accomplishments were noteworthy. Beginning as an apprentice, he eventually became a master machinist, and he rose from journeyman to foreman to superintendent in the railroad industry.

By the time Margaret and Willard moved to Douglas, Arizona, in the 1910s, it was the site of three copper companies and was enjoying a boomtown prosperity. Here Willard was employed as a foreman in the roundhouse for the trains that served the copper smelters. It was here, too, that Margaret's brother Clarence died in an industrial accident in 1913.

Margaret and Willard's marriage came to an end when Margaret returned to Tennessee in 1915 with her son, never to live with Willard again. Remaining in the Southwest, Willard was granted a divorce from Margaret in 1917 and a year later married again, this time to Mrs. Emily L. Harris, the landlady of the boardinghouse in which he lived. Willard eventually retired as a superintendent of the El Paso & Southwestern Railroad and died in 1949 at the age of seventy-three.

Afterword

When Margaret returned to the South, she returned to her family to live. As close as ever, the sisters shared their homes with Margaret and Raymond—Gertie in Winston-Salem and Carrie in Black Mountain, North Carolina. After her son opened a transportation company in Knoxville, Margaret joined him there. In her later years, she became a professional companion to an elderly heiress of a Knoxville furniture company.

Margaret died in the Serene Manor Convalescent Home in Knoxville on March 22, 1960. Her obituary states that she was a member of the Cross Roads Presbyterian Church and the local chapters of the United Daughters of the Confederacy and the Daughters of the American Revolution and a past president (1942–1943) of the Asheville Chapter of the U.D.C. She was buried in the Lynnhurst Cemetery in Knoxville.

One final note: Margaret's interest in writing continued throughout her lifetime, especially in poetry, a sample of which can be seen as the last entry of her day book. When she died, the tribute paid to her by the Bonny Kate Chapter of the D.A.R. reveals that Margaret frequently enclosed poems in letters and gifts to friends and that her interest in poetry culminated in the private publication of a volume of her verse, titled, ironically, *Dreaming Through the Years.*

Bibliography

And To Think It Only Cost a Nickel!: The Development of Public Transportation in the Chattanooga Area. Chattanooga: David H. Steinberg, 1975.

Anderson, Lee. *Chattanooga's Story.* Chattanooga Area Convention & Visitors Bureau, 1989.

"Application Papers: Margaret Sloan Leland." Bonny Kate Chapter. Daughters of the American Revolution. Knoxville, Tenn., 8 Feb. 1952: 1–6.

Armstrong, Zella. *The History of Hamilton County and Chattanooga, Tennessee.* Chattanooga: Lookout Publishing Co., 1940.

Bleser, Carol K., and Frederick M. Heath. "The Impact of the Civil War on a Southern Marriage: Clement and Virginia Tunstall Clay of Alabama." *Civil War History* 30 (1984): 197–220.

Cash, W. J. *The Mind of the South.* New York: Random-Vintage, 1941.

"Certificate of Death: Margaret Sloan Leland." Department of Health and Environment. State of Tennessee. 4 Apr. 1960.

Chafe, William H. *The American Woman: Her Changing Social, Economic, and Political Roles, 1920–1970.* London: Oxford University Press, 1972.

Chattanooga Area Maps. Map. Chattanooga Area Convention & Visitors Bureau, 1989.

Bibliography

Eliot, Elizabeth. *Heiresses and Coronets: The Story of Lovely Ladies and Noble Men*. New York: McDowell, Obolensky Inc., 1959.

Govan, Gilbert E., and James W. Livingood. *The Chattanooga Country: 1540–1976*. 3rd ed. Knoxville: The University of Tennessee Press, 1977.

Gragg, Walter. Personal interview with author. Taylor, Mich. 15 July 1989.

Hart, James D. *The Popular Book*. Los Angeles: University of California Press, 1963.

Hawks, Joanne V., and Sheila L. Skemp, eds. *Sex, Race, and the Role of Women in the South*. Jackson, Miss.: University Press of Mississippi, 1983.

Hayostek, Cindy. "A Short History of Douglas, Arizona, up to 1918." Douglas, Ariz., 1989.

Livingood, James W. *A History of Hamilton County Tennessee*. Memphis: Memphis State University Press, 1981.

———*Chattanooga and Hamilton County Medical Society*. Chattanooga: Chattanooga & Hamilton County Medical Society, 1983.

McGuffey, Charles D. *Standard History of Chattanooga, Tennessee*. Knoxville: Crew & Dorey, 1911.

"Obituary: Clarence R. Sloan." *Chattanooga Times* 5 Dec. 1913.

"Obituary: Dr. R. A. Sloan." *Chattanooga Daily Times* 29 May 1912.

"Obituary: Margaret Sloan Leland." *Knoxville Journal* 23 May 1960.

"Obituary: Mrs. R. E. Sloan." *Chattanooga Times* 25 Apr. 1927.

"Obituary: W. B. Gragg." *Asheville Citizen*. 9 June 1964.

Reagan, Linda Leland. Personal interview with author. Gatlinburg, Tenn. 18 Feb. 1989.

Register of Marriages. Centenary Methodist Church. Chattanooga, Tenn., 1900.

Scott, Anne Firor. *The Southern Lady: From Pedestal to Politics 1830–1930*. Chicago: The University of Chicago Press, 1970.

The Tombstone. Cochise Genealogical Society. Pirtleville, Ariz. Spring, 1989.

United States. National Archives Trust Fund Board. *Veterans Records*. "Spanish War: Willard C. Leland." Washington, D.C., 1989.

United States. Veterans Administration. *Chattanooga National Cemetery*. VA Pamphlet 40–38M. Chattanooga, Tenn., 1989.

Wheaton, William L. C., Grace Milgram, and Margy Ellin Meyerson, eds. *Urban Housing*. New York: Free Press, 1966.

226

Bibliography

Williams, Tom "An Interview with Penelope Johnson Allen." Oral History Project: Chattanooga-Hamilton County Public Library. 28 Mar. 1982.

Wilson, John. *Chattanooga's Story*. Chattanooga: Chattanooga News-Free Press, 1980.

Wiltse, Henry W. *History of Chattanooga*. 2 vols. Unpublished manuscript, 1916.

Young, Thomas Daniel, Floyd C. Watkins, Richard Croom Beatty, eds. *The Literature of the South*. Rev. ed. Glenview, Ill.: Scott, Foresman and Company, 1968.

Index

Index

Index

Index